THE
$\mathcal{C}$OTTAGE $\mathcal{G}$ARDENER'S
COMPANION

A Seasonal Guide to Plants & Plantings
❧ *for Informal Gardens* ❧

CLIVE LANE

WITH CONTRIBUTIONS BY PAT COLLISON

EDITED BY PAT TAYLOR FOR
THE COTTAGE GARDEN SOCIETY

David & Charles

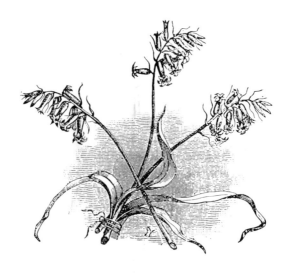

A DAVID & CHARLES BOOK

ISBN 0 7153 0020 2

Typeset in Horley Old Style by ABM Typographics Ltd, Hull
and printed in Italy by New Interlitho SpA
for David & Charles
Brunel House   Newton Abbot   Devon

CONTENTS

*F*OREWORD
by ROSEMARY VEREY

Anemone japonica – *'Queen Charlotte'*

It was a red-letter day for me when the Cottage Garden Society came into my life, but it all dates back much further. In 1960, when I was still more interested in horses than horticulture, our groom, by a chance comment, brought home to me the fact that what I had created at Barnsley was a cottage garden around a manor house. It took me several years to understand his meaning, to realise that it was a compliment, made by a perceptive countryman with earthy instincts.

Many of us have our own idea of a cottage garden, where there is a feeling of freedom and exuberance, leisure and opportunity to potter, to water, to contemplate. The cottage gardener has time to grow marigolds from seed or 'Mrs Sinkins' from cuttings – the flowers which our grandmothers loved and which personify the plants and herbs they grew for pot pourri, and others for the kitchen pot and the bedroom sill. Flowers, vegetables and fruit mingled together are the epitome of the cottage garden, where bounty may be gathered at every season. The cottage gardener makes salads, apple jelly, herbal medicine, plum and damson jam from her garden; there is something even in midwinter when parsnips and turnips, brussels sprouts and leeks come into their own.

Cottage garden style has been deeply rooted in our philosophy through many centuries; it was first written about by William Lawson in the *Country Housewife's Garden* published in 1617, banished by the eighteenth-century landscape movement, and revived by William Robinson and Gertrude Jekyll a hundred years ago. Today we are searching for simplicity of life combined with an advancing sophistication. This book is refreshing in its attitude, useful in its detail, inspiring in its knowledge – truly a cottage gardener's companion, often echoing our own thoughts.

Shakespeare, Shelley and John Clare knew it all, and Matthew Arnold expressed it:

> . . . gold-dusted snapdragon,
> Sweet-William with its homely cottage-smell,
> And stocks in fragrant blow;
> Roses that down the alleys shine afar,
> And open jasmine-muffled lattices . . .

The Cottage Garden

Fashions change in gardening, as in clothes. But one style of gardening has been around for a very long time and is increasingly popular today – the 'cottage garden' style. Why is this style still so popular, since few of us live in a cottage? Partly because of a nostalgic view of the past as idealised by Victorian painters and that many of us still cling to now – roses and hollyhocks round the door of a thatched cottage is an image hard to beat. More importantly, and on a strictly practical level, the cottage garden style can be adapted to suit many types of gardens: a small front garden in a city terrace filled with lavender and framed with honeysuckle; a border crammed with aquilegias, old-fashioned paeonies, Canterbury Bells and clove-scented pinks in the suburbs; pots brimming with herbs and roses in a small back yard – any of these features can make us feel we are in the heart of the country.

It has been said that there is no such thing as the typical cottage garden, and that is true. The cottage garden has been evolving and changing for at least the past six hundred years. There is a famous description by Chaucer of a garden (a yard as he called it, a term still used in America today) owned by a 'poor widow' with two daughters to support. It contained not only flowers which are in our gardens now – hellebore, caper spurge and centaury – but also had room for three pigs, three cows, a sheep, a cock and seven hens plus sundry medicinal herbs – a combination few of us would envisage today.

But this clearly illustrates the original purpose of a cottage garden. Primarily it provided food: flowers were an optional extra and then only if they had a practical use, for example, as 'old wives cures' or seasoning for food or to strew on the earthen floor of the house to discourage bugs.

Over the centuries the dependence on livestock dwindled but the need for food continued, and vegetables with herbs became an indispensable part of the cottage garden until the advent of the car, the supermarket and the farm shop brought reasonably cheap, labour-free food within the reach of almost everyone. And so the cottage garden, set free from the need to provide vegetables, fruit and honey, swung away from utility to pleasure – to flowers and shrubs.

To recreate a seventeenth- or eighteenth-century cottage garden, growing only plants from the period, although a pleasant pursuit, could not be completely authentic. Who would want to reintroduce the pig, still less an outside dry privy? The modern cottage garden though very different from its predecessors is in their direct descent, and a hundred years from now will not be the same as today.

So what is the cottage garden style? Like a horse, it is easier to recognise than to describe. Perhaps the chief hallmark is informality. One cannot lay down rules, and only a pedant would argue that we couldn't have a lawn just because lawns were not part of cottage gardens in the past. We do not live in a time warp. As to plants, there are of course the traditional old favourites which have been grown for hundreds of years – roses, hollyhocks, honeysuckle, hellebores, columbines, foxgloves, feverfew, lavender, thyme, mint, pinks, geraniums and many more. But we are more fortunate than our ancestors in the variety of plants from all round the world and the marvellous cornucopia of modern cultivars available to us and it would be sad to limit our choice too severely in the pursuit of 'authenticity'.

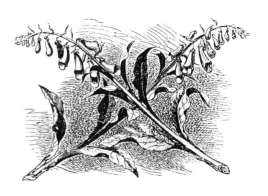

One certainty about cottage gardens is that every available square inch of ground was used. Vegetables and flowers crowded happily together and although nowadays we may prefer to keep a separate vegetable patch, the hallmark practice of dense planting is a direct legacy from the past.

The cottage garden style is essentially England's gift to gardening (historically it is absent from Ireland and much of Scotland and Wales), and emigrants have taken it around the world, especially to America, Australia and New Zealand. There is many a little piece of England across the seas.

In this book, Pat Collison, our President, garden writer and artist, creates the atmosphere of each season with its characteristic colours and scents. Her vivid descriptions of the cottage scene guide the reader towards a realisation that the cottage garden has something to offer at all times of the year.

Then, on a practical note, she leads the gardener through the tasks to be tackled at a particular period.

For each season, a detailed plant dictionary based on the knowledge gained from many years' experience in his own cottage garden has been compiled by Clive Lane, Vice-Chairman of the Society. To have described all the plants which might be at home in such a garden would have required a much longer book, and his choice is a personal one based on his own enthusiasms plus a strong desire to encourage new gardeners to search out and so conserve plants which are in danger of disappearing from our gardens. His wide knowledge of more unusual forms and cultivars of traditional plants will, I feel sure, be appreciated by more experienced gardeners while the wealth of plant associations will, we hope, give inspiration to all those seeking to create their ideal cottage garden.

As with anthologies of poetry, I have no doubt that some readers will complain that their favourite is not mentioned. But we could not include everything, and I hope that the treasures within will more than compensate for those left outside.

DOUGLAS TAYLOR
Chairman, The Cottage Garden Society

SPRING

Long before winter is ready to leave the cottage garden, spring has started to coax blossoms from the bare branches and the cold dark soil. Hazel twigs are hung with pale yellow 'lamb's tail' catkins, and the mahogany wands of pussy willow are studded with beads of silvery white. Buds are plumping along the chaenomeles' knobbly twigs, while below ground the multicoloured legions of spring bulbs are on the march upwards towards the light.

A SEASONAL PICTURE

The mood of spring is urgent and vital. Almost imperceptibly the hours of daylight extend, and the midday sun climbs higher in the sky, bringing a welcome warmth in its rays. Each day brings new signs of re-awakening growth. It is a time of 'firsts' – the first bright blue scillas like chips of sapphire, the first yellow primroses nestling amongst the dead leaves in the hedge bottom, and the first narcissus bobbing and swaying in the brisk spring breezes. On rough banks, at the foot of trees, and in shaded, cold and windswept places, the trailing green shoots of the lesser periwinkle are studded with flowers of blue or burgundy, and the yellow and orange stars of celandine glitter like fresh varnish. Later in the season honesty blooms here, along with scented Spanish bluebells in blue, clover pink and white.

As the days lengthen, buds swell along the twigs of cherry, rowan and crab, and break into tiny leaf in a multitude of tender shades of green, gold and bronze. The spreading branches of amelanchier are clad in a haze of coppery red, speckled with points of white as the blossoms expand, while in the dappled shade below, shorn of their winter cover of last year's foliage, epimediums reveal their dainty yellow, pink or white flowers. Porcelain-hued erythroniums nod above their marbled brown and green leaves as fresh ferns, clad in copper, silver or gold fur, rise from amongst the old dried fronds. Sky blue omphalodes, in bloom for many weeks, skirts the stems of a yellow-leafed dogwood and mingles with the grey-green, ferny leaves of a dicentra. New shoots of hostas, always cautiously late risers whose foliage can be badly scarred by frost, pierce the soil like sturdy spears of green and white or yellow, while around them wood anemones, ajugas and violets weave a tapestry of flowers and foliage.

At the base of a sunny wall, orange and yellow tulips rise above misty blue forget-me-nots, a perfect blend of elegant symmetry and informality. Dark red velvety wallflowers add a note of richer colour, their strong, sweet perfume as indispensable to spring as that of roses to summer. While not absent from the winter garden, fragrance, like colour, has been strictly rationed. Now spring makes amends by filling the garden with the scents of flowers and foliage. *Clematis montana* drapes walls and arbours with garlands of pink or white vanilla-scented blossom. Clouds of delicious perfume drift from the small white flowers of osmanthus and osmaria, and even the lowly Cypress Spurge, its invasive roots safely contained in a narrow pathside bed, fills the surrounding air with a powerful honey scent. Its parakeet-green flowers form an ideal setting for flame-red and white tulips, or china-blue grape hyacinths and starry white ornithogalums.

Spring showers alternate with sunshine, refreshing the perfumed lilac blossom. In the border the stately Crown Imperials are in bloom, their pendant orange bells overlooking the swelling buds of cottage paeonies and the yellow-green leaves of hemerocallis. Soon the early shrub roses will open their first flowers and spring will merge into summer.

Seasonal Tasks

FOR SPRING

Clear all dead stems, leaves and other debris from the borders. Weed, then spread a general fertiliser and lightly fork into the surface of the soil.

Position plant supports around clumps of flop-prone perennials as soon as growth starts, so that leaves and stems can grow through and disguise them.

Move, lift or divide perennials that require it, before growth is too advanced. If unavoidable, these plants can be moved at any time, provided they are moved with a good rootball and planted without delay into a well-prepared hole. They must be kept well watered until the roots have had time to re-establish their feeding capacity. Spraying twice daily with clear water and twice a week with foliar feed during the growing season is very beneficial, as is shading from sunlight.

Watch out for slug damage on young shoots of hostas, asters, delphiniums and other highly susceptible plants, and use a slug bait which will not harm birds or pets as soon as there are signs of activity.

Half-hardy annuals are sown in early spring, in warmth under glass. Alternatively, many can be sown in the open in late spring and early summer. Hardy annuals are usually sown *in situ* in mid-season. Sweet peas are generally sown under glass in autumn or early spring and set out in their growing positions in early to mid-season.

Apply a generous mulch of shredded bark or mushroom compost after weeding and feeding and when the soil is moist. This helps minimise weed growth and retain moisture. It will also gradually incorporate with the soil and improve the texture.

Lightly prune forsythia and other spring-flowering shrubs after flowering. Check all trees and shrubs for winter damage and cut back broken or frosted twigs and branches to sound wood. Hard prune *Clematis jackmanii* and *C. viticella* varieties in early spring; lightly thin *C. montana* varieties if necessary after flowering. Hard prune *Cornus alba* varieties, *Buddleia davidii* and *B. fallowiana* varieties, caryopteris, fuchsias, santolinas, artemisias and helichrysums in early to mid-season when, hopefully, the worst danger of prolonged hard frosts is over. In early spring, hard prune old deciduous hedges where necessary and feed well to encourage vigorous new growth.

 Plant new trees and shrubs and be sure to provide adequate supports.

 Clear overgrown ponds as early in the season as possible before frogs arrive to spawn, in order to avoid disturbing their breeding cycle. Plant new aquatics and oxygenators in mid- to late spring or early summer when the water has started to warm. This will minimise the risk of plants rotting before they can root, and ensures rapid growth.

 Comb lawns with a wire rake and apply a spring fertiliser. Mow when the grass begins to grow strongly, but take care not to cut it short when there is danger of hard frosts.

 Sparrows often attack silver foliage plants, primulas, especially polyanthus and some flowering shrubs. Where this is a problem, it is a good plan to spray at-risk plants with a repellant, or to cover with netting or black cotton thread.

 Prune roses in late winter to early spring during frost-free weather, cutting out dead, diseased, weak and unwanted stems, and crossed twigs and branches. Old wood with no vigorous young shoots can be cut to just above ground level.

 Watch out for signs of frost damage, but do not pull up a plant that looks dead. It may show signs of revival in early summer and in this case cut the dead wood right back to above a growing bud.

SPRING-FLOWERING
TREES

The frequency of the name 'Cherry Tree Cottage' bears witness to the popularity of the **cherry** as a cottage garden tree, either as a tall single specimen or planted against the wall as a fan. The sweet cherry is a big, fast-growing tree, not for a small garden, and it needs another cherry as a pollinator. The sharper flavoured Morello is useful because it will grow against a cool wall and is not too vigorous, while the 'May Duke Cherry' is a cross between the other two, setting a large crop.

A familiar sight in an old garden is a stately **pear** tree, its branches picturesquely contorted and its crop a mass of hard little fruits high up out of reach. Pears are very ornamental and it is worth consulting a specialist catalogue (see Sources of Plants) for its description of a wide range of these and other fruit trees.

Few people grow **damsons** any more but their pure white blossom, along with that of the **wild plum**, is the earliest to appear, delicate against black branches. However, for beauty of blossom in spring and again in autumn when the ripening fruit hangs on the boughs, nothing can beat the **apple** tree.

There are early blossoming varieties like 'George Cave' which can produce fruit as early as midsummer, and later flowering ones like 'Annie Elizabeth', the fruits of which keep for months and months. The vigorous 'Bramley's Seedling' is

exceptionally rich in vitamin C, but it is for a large garden, unlike the small and short branched 'Rev W. Wilks'.

The expert can tell which variety a tree is simply by looking at its unpruned form, such as the broad and spreading 'Blenheim Orange', but what the experts disagree on is which is the tastiest. Some swear by the fragrant, sweet-tasting eighteenth-century 'Reinette d'Orleans' while others go for the 'brisk' flavour of 'James Grieve'. The names and descriptions in the catalogues are so appealing that it is easy to get carried away, so think carefully before you decide.

Even if space is limited, it is possible to choose your favourite variety on a rootstock such as M26 which makes a sturdy tree about 2.4m (8ft) in height, or the even shorter M27 which gives a 1.2m (4ft) high tree. Then there is the latest solution for lack of space – a tree or cordon onto which several different fruits have been grafted.

Another small tree which flowers in spring and is traditional in a cottage garden is the **Flowering Thorn**, the crataegus. Legend claims that *Crataegus* 'Biflora', the Glastonbury Thorn, was brought there from the Holy Land by Joseph of Arimathaea. Its sweetly scented white flowers blossom intermittently all winter in very mild areas, but it is not quite as hardy as the common hawthorn and should be given a sheltered position. There is a double white-blossomed

long golden showers of pea-like flowers, is 'Vossii'. It doesn't set seed either, which is an advantage since every part of this tree is poisonous. *L. alpinum* has racemes which seem more in proportion to the size of the tree, and there is also a weeping form. One of the most attractive ways of growing laburnums, even in a smallish garden, is a laburnum arch, perhaps under-planted with large-headed purple alliums as at Barnsley House in Gloucestershire.

crataegus and a very pretty double shell pink one, as well as the better known 'Paul's Scarlet' which has double rose-crimson flowers. In the country the thorns make a tough, spiny hedge. The trees hold their own in polluted city areas or salt-laden seaside gardens and will grow in almost any soil or situation.

Lastly, to carry the spring-flowering season into summer, comes the **laburnum**. It, too, is scented. The most famous variety, because of its extra-

White lilac is surprisingly effective against the white walls of this cottage, with honeysuckle climbing through the hedge

SHRUBS

❧ RIBES ❧

Ribes sanguineum, the old flowering currant, is still one of the best early-flowering cottage garden shrubs, its branches densely hung with racemes of blood-red flowers 5-10cm (2-4in) long. Despite its 'tom cat' smell, *Ribes sanguineum* remains as popular today as it was when first introduced from North America by the plant hunter David Douglas in 1826.

A hardy, deciduous shrub, with currant-like leaves and growth similar to fruiting currant bushes, *Ribes sanguineum* is an extremely good-natured plant, perfectly content anywhere in the garden and not in the least fussy about soil or conditions. *Ribes* make delightful flowering hedges and are frequently seen in cottage gardens planted with the yellow spring-flowering forsythias, both allowed to develop naturally to provide a rich splash of spring colour and a useful summer screen.

Some of the ornamental currants are in fact gooseberries – the two sub-families being united under *Ribes* – and the most beautiful of the latter is the fuchsia-flowered gooseberry, *Ribes speciosum*. This makes a large, erect shrub, anything between 1.8 and 3m (6 and 10ft) in height, with spiny branches and gooseberry-like foliage. The pendulous, brilliant scarlet, fuschia-like tubular flowers are borne in clusters of two to four, each flower about 1.2cm (½in) long. It is a most attractive, somewhat showy shrub, but not altogether hardy. It should be given the protection of a wall and certainly looks best when grown in this way.

There is also an interesting variegated ribes called *Ribes americanum* 'Variegatum'. This plant has mottled pale green and cream leaves, and is a lovely old white-flowered form. The whiteness of the racemes, which are flushed with a faint stain of pink, looks delightfully fresh and spring-like with drifts of blue muscari underneath.

The *Ribes* will thrive in any garden soil, but are best planted where they will have the benefit of all the sunshine available. An over-rich diet is not advisable as it tends to encourage rank growth. Trim after flowering and again in late summer if you wish to keep a compact bush. *Ribes sanguineum* and its varieties can be easily propagated by cuttings of leafless shoots taken in late autumn and rooted in a cold frame. *Ribes speciosum* is better layered as it does not root so readily from cuttings.

○ ***Ribes sanguineum* 'Pulborough Scarlet'**
This variety was a chance seedling that appeared in a bed of yews at Cheal's Nursery at Pulborough, Sussex in 1930 and is certainly one of the finest flowering currants, with rich crimson-red flowers.

○ ***R. s.* 'Red Pimpernel'**
An aptly named variety of this popular shrub with deep red flowers on drooping racemes in early spring, followed by rich green currant leaves.

○ ***R. s.* 'Brocklebankii'**
A very popular, and perhaps the best, ribes with reddish-pink flowers in early spring and bright yellow leaves, which remain colourful throughout the summer – even in shade, although slightly less brilliant.

○ ***R. s.* 'Tydeman's White'**
A variety with bright white flowers and deep green leaves, which contrasts well with the better known pink- and red-flowered forms.

○ ***R. odoratum***
Known as the Buffalo Currant, *Ribes odoratum* has pale green, three-lobed leaves which are richly coloured in late summer and autumn. In early spring it produces bright golden-yellow, scented flowers.

❧ ROSA RUBIGINOSA ❧

Rosa rubiginosa, also known as Sweet Briar, Eglantine, or *Rosa eglanteria*, is not usually grown for its rather fleeting, single pink flowers or its scarlet oval hips in autumn, but for the strangely aromatic foliage which gives off a delicious fragrance

when touched or ruffled by the wind, scenting a garden for yards around on a warm spring day after rain.

Growing to 2.4x2.4m (8x8ft), the Sweet Briars need plenty of room, but can be fairly rigorously pruned each winter to prevent their growing into a rather untidy tangle. Although this does mean sacrificing most of their flowers and hips, it ensures that the young leaves continue to be produced right into the autumn, releasing their spicy, fruit fragrance, something akin to a basket of ripe apples, during damp summer evenings.

The Sweet Briar has been grown for centuries. In cottage gardens it was often planted near the outside 'privy' for the practical use of perfuming the air to hide unpleasant odours. The flowers and foliage, when dried, were (and still are) used for blending in pot pourris. 'The Sweet Brier,' wrote John Gerard in *The Herball, or General Historie of Plants,* 1597, 'doth oftentimes grow higher than all the kindes of Roses; the shoots of it are hard, thicke, and wooddie; the leaves are glittering, and of a beautifull greene colour, of smell most pleasant'.

There is a most appealing double-flowered form, 'Mannings Blush' which grows no more than 1.5-1.8m (5-6ft) in height with small, pretty, double pinkish-white flowers. Fortunately, this charming old cottage garden plant is still available from specialist rose nurseries today. During the late nineteenth century, Lord Penzance crossed the Sweet Briars with some of the Bourbons and the Hybrid Perpetuals to produce the Penzance Briars. Although not as robust as the Sweet Briar they are generally speaking similar in growth, although some of the natural fragrance of the leaf

has been lost in the breeding. They make a pleasant if vigorous hedge.

Sweet Briars will grow in most garden soils, but prefer a light soil enriched with garden compost before planting. Propagate by half-ripe cuttings taken from shoots that have flowered in late summer, or by layers.

○ **Rosa rubiginosa 'Amy Robsart'**
Large pink flowers, semi-double, with scarlet hips in autumn. One of the Penzance Briars, raised in 1894.
○ **R. r. 'Lord Penzance'**
Introduced in 1894, with single flowers of a fawny-yellow and growing to about 1.8m (6ft).
○ **R. r. 'Lady Penzance'**
Regarded as possibly the best of all the Penzance Briars, with single, yellowish-copper flowers in late spring and early summer.
○ **R. r. 'Meg Merilees'**
A Penzance Briar with crimson, single, scented flowers, raised in 1894 and about the same size as 'Amy Robsart', 2.4x2.4m (8x8ft).

❧ SYRINGA ❧

The pale mauves and soft purples of the fresh-scented lilacs mark the end of spring and fill a valuable role in the cottage garden. The common lilac, *Syringa vulgaris,* with its rather washed out colour, reached us via Turkey sometime in the sixteenth century. Sir Thomas Hanmer, writing in his *Garden Book* in 1659, tells us that he has got 'The LILAC with the PALE BLEW Flowers, which is very common. That with the WHITE flower, very sweet, scarce here. And that with the RED flower, scarcest of all.'

It wasn't until the 1890s that the French nurseryman, Victor Lemoine, by careful selection and crossing introduced many double-flowered varieties in a wide range of shades. Amongst them are the pure white 'Madame Lemoine', the deep rose 'Charles Joly' and later on, in 1922, the deep purple 'Katherine Havemeyer'. Many cottage gardeners still prefer the less opulent, single-flowered lilacs like the popular, wine-purple 'Souvenir de Louis Spaeth', the pink, early-flowering 'Esther Staley' and 'Primrose', a yellow lilac produced in 1940.

MORE FRAGRANT SPRING-FLOWERING TREES AND SHRUBS

Azara microphylla

6x4.5m (20x15ft). Graceful evergreen shrub with tiny, glossy dark green leaves. The miniature mimosa-like yellow flowers scent the air with their vanilla fragrance.

Coronilla glauca

90x60cm (3x2ft). Evergreen, bushy shrub for a sheltered position, with grey-green leaves and pea-like yellow flowers. Very fragrant.

Daphne cneorum 'Eximia'

15x45cm (6x20in). A prostrate evergreen shrub good for growing over a low wall. Dark green, leathery, oblong leaves and dense clusters of rose-pink flowers in late spring. Strong scent.

Magnolia stellata

2.4x2.4m (8x8ft). Tree or shrub. Deciduous, slow growing. Narrow, mid-green leaves and many rather 'tattered' starry white flowers. Delicate fragrance.

Malus coronaria 'Charlottae'

4.5x5.4m (15x18ft), possibly larger eventually. Broad-headed, deciduous tree with oval, serrated, mid-green leaves which colour well in autumn. Clusters of violet-scented, pale pink blossom in spring.

Osmanthus delavayi

1.8x2.4m (6x8ft). Evergreen with glossy, dark green leaves which are oval and serrated. Bears clusters of very fragrant, tubular flowers in abundance from an early age.

Prunus yedoensis

7.5x6m (25x20ft). One of the earliest cherries to blossom. Deciduous, with dark green foliage and clusters of pink buds which open pale pink. Sweet scent evident on a warm day.

Skimmia japonica

90cmx1.5m (3x5ft). Evergreen shrub for light shade. Leathery, light green leaves and panicles of creamy-white flowers, followed by red berries in female forms. Male plants are the most heavily scented.

Viburnum carlesii

1.2x1.5m (4x5ft). Deciduous, dull green leaves which redden in autumn. Exceptionally fragrant, waxy white flowers.

For very small gardens there is the dwarf *lilac S. palibiniana* which only reaches 90cm-1.05m (3-3½ft). The bigger lilacs, which almost all grow to about 4.5m (15ft), can be kept in check by shortening the shoots, thinning out the stems after flowering, and removing suckers with a sharp upwards tug rather than using secateurs.

Lilacs will grow in most soils and in slight shade but are best planted in a rich, deep compost in sun. Roses which are not too vigorous can use them as a prop. White Japanese anemones make an attractive contrast in autumn and, in spring, primroses, violets and muscari will spread themselves beneath the bare branches.

ℭLIMBERS

☞ CHAENOMELES ☜

Chaenomeles japonica, Japanese Quince, or simply japonica is very much a cottage garden plant. In nine cases out of ten it is to be found planted where its lovely apple blossom-like flowers on leafless shoots can be warmed by a supporting wall, and will sometimes flower as early as mid-winter during a mild spell, but it is at its best in early spring.

The flowers, which measure about 3.5cm

(1½in) across, are carried in clusters on the old wood, some with pinkish-white flowers, others red or scarlet, whilst some are double or semi-double, all providing a splash of brilliant colour in the late winter or early spring. The dark, glossy leaves are usually well advanced before the show of flowers is over. Flowering quinces enjoy a well-drained loamy soil. They are tough plants, per-fectly hardy, thriving on wall or fence at any point of the compass.

The chaenomeles, although mostly wall grown, are not natural climbers and do make excellent free-standing shrubs. Wall-grown plants should be pruned in early spring by cutting back secondary shoots to two or three buds after flowering. Container-grown plants can be planted out at any time from autumn to spring. All pro-duce big, quince-like fruits which make excellent jelly – said to be like the guava jelly made in the West Indies.

The most popular and best-known varieties are those that provide orange-scarlet flowers, al-though on a red wall the large pure white flowers of *C. speciosa* 'Nivalis' look quite charming. *C. s.* 'Moerloosii' has large, apple-blossom pink and white flowers. *C. s.* 'Falconnet Charlet' or *C.* 'Rosea Plena' has double rose-pink flowers, whilst *C. s.* 'Cardinalis' is garlanded with bright cardinal-red flowers and can easily reach 2.4m (8ft).

Chaenomeles x *superba* is a cross between *C. speciosa* and *C. japonica*, and there are some very handsome cultivars to choose from. Each flower is exquisite and the richness of the petals is enhanced by the gold of the boss of stamens.

C. x *superba* 'Knap Hill Scarlet' has mahogany-red flowers. Those of *C.* x *superba* 'Pink Lady' are of a quite outstanding, clear rose-pink on a plant of spreading habit, while *C.* x *s.* 'Texas Scarlet' has brilliant scarlet flowers.

❧ CLEMATIS ❧
(SPRING-FLOWERING)

Clematis montana or the Mountain Clematis (also known by its old name of White Virgin's Bower) and all its various forms are among the most decorative and vigorous of the early spring-flowering clematis, with long growths smothered with masses of white, anemone-like flowers, tumbling and falling over walls or showering down from trees in the cottage garden. Coming from the Himalayas, where it reaches a height of 9m (30ft) or more, *Clematis montana* is com-pletely hardy, growing well in sun or shade in any

Clematis montana, *given its head, easily reaches the chimneys of this thatched cottage*

reasonable soil. It is famed for clothing unsightly twentieth-century outbuildings and fences, and is simply magnificent seen growing up through large conifers such as the low-forking pines.

Our native *Clematis vitalba,* which Gerard named 'Travellers Joy' because it was to be found 'decking and adorning waies and hedges, where people travel', is an even stronger grower, although not spring-flowering, with long, vigorous, jungle-like vines garlanding the hedgerows and covering them with a luxuriant, almost rainforest tropical growth. It does best in a limey soil. The masses of small, slightly fragrant white flowers are a lovely sight during July and in autumn, particularly in the south of England. Yard after yard of hedgerow is covered with clouds of beautiful, fluffy seedheads – hence its other name, Old Man's Beard. These remain throughout the winter months, much sought after for flower arrangements and the making of hop garlands.

Clematis armandii, one of E. H. Wilson's discoveries in China at the beginning of the century, has large, handsome, evergreen foliage offsetting the creamy-white, deliciously scented blossoms which come in axillary clusters during early spring. Armand's Clematis, as it is sometimes called, does need a warm, sheltered position and the company of other plants for protection from sharp frosts. Its slight tenderness has, however, never been a hindrance to cottage gardeners, who can usually be relied upon to find a sheltered wall in a closely packed corner of the garden for tender plants.

When happy, this lovely clematis will easily make young shoots 1.8-2.4m (6-8ft) long, sending

them out in every direction except from the bottom where the long, bare stem will need covering up. Grown through the base of a forked shrub or tree, *Clematis armandii* can be trained and left to grow as big as it is wanted, with any essential pruning taking place after it has finished flowering.

The dozen or so varieties of *Clematis alpina* are at their best in early spring, and this is usually one of the first clematis to open. Seldom growing more than 1.8m (6ft) tall, *C. alpina,* with its small, nodding, bluish bell-shaped flowers, enjoys a cool, shady place in a fairly rich soil that doesn't dry out. It looks lovely clambering over and through small shrubs and bushes with the pretty, fresh-looking blue flowers like stars spangled against palest green foliage. The leaves of *C. alpina* are deciduous and little pruning is necessary other than thinning out old growths in the winter. Propagate by seed or cuttings placed in a frame in late summer.

Clematis macropetala, the Downy Clematis, has been known for over two hundred years, but was not introduced to Britain until the beginning of this century. It first flowered at Kew in 1920 and has since become a popular and widely grown climber. A plumper version of *C. alpina,* the flower of *C. macropetala* has a 'bunched up' look, with the centre packed with numerous, petal-like segments. There are four sepals about 5cm (2in) long and 1cm (⅓in) wide, blue or violet-blue in colour, with different parts of the plant covered with down. Several excellent varieties exist and are easily obtainable from specialist clematis nurseries.

Spring-flowering clematis, *C. montana, C. alpina, C. macropetala* and their cultivars need only be pruned where space is restricted. Cut out all or a proportion of the shoots which have flowered and trim back as necessary immediately after flowering.

○ *Clematis montana rubens*
A natural form, it has a purple tinge to the foliage, especially when young, which enhances the soft pink of the flowers. *C. m. rubens* blooms a little later than

the type, producing thousands of pink blossoms in mid-spring. Pleasantly scented.

○ **C. m. grandiflora**

C. m. grandiflora has much larger flowers, some 7.5cm (3in) across, on long stems, but unfortunately no scent. A vigorous form, but it does take two or three years for the plant to settle down and flower well.

○ **C. alpina 'Frances Rivis'**

The flowers of 'Frances Rivis' are soft blue and twice the size of other *C. alpina* varieties.

○ **C. a. 'Columbine'**

An early-flowering variety with soft lavender-blue, bell-shaped flowers 7.5cm (3in) in length with long, pointed sepals.

○ **C. macropetala 'Markham's Pink'**

Flowers are rosy-mauve, flushed purple at the base. Best in semi-shade and flowering in late spring.

○ **C. m. 'Lagoon'**

Flowering in mid-spring, 'Lagoon' has deep lavender, semi-double nodding flowers and pointed sepals.

○ **Clematis afoliata**

A most unusual species likely to appeal to the connoisseur, with yellow, star-like, powerfully scented flowers on leafless stems. A native of New Zealand, the plant requires a warm, sunny, sheltered wall and should be given the protection of other wall plants. Flowering in mid-spring, the flowers are especially scented at night.

℘ERENNIALS

❧ ALYSSUM ❧

Alyssum saxatile, the perennial alyssum known as 'Gold Dust', is the yellow plant which is seen in gardens all over the country in early spring, billowing and frothing from walls and banks, along with aubrieta and arabis. The sun-loving *Alyssum saxatile* prefers a hot, dry spot in a wall or rockery. To keep the bush tidy and compact, the flowers should be cut off as soon as they are finished.

Alyssum saxatile is perhaps too vigorous to be planted amongst choice alpines but is excellent for creating large mats of bright colour in walls and banks or wherever there is room for it to spread. Good drainage is essential as the plants tend to rot away during the winter from the effects of excessive moisture.

■ Selected forms may be increased by cuttings of firm young growth taken during the summer and inserted in sandy soil in a cold frame. Riper shoots, pulled off with a heel of older growth, will very often root quite freely outdoors in late summer or early autumn.

■ For those who find the colour of this grand old plant a little overpowering, there is a cool lemon-coloured variety *A. s.* 'Citrinum' which because of its rather poor constitution and the tendency to change colour, is perhaps best grown as a biennial.

○ **Alyssum saxatile 'Gold Ball'**

A comparatively new improved form of *A. s.* 'Compactum'. Dense heads of sweetly scented, brilliant golden-yellow flowers over neat, silvery foliage.

○ **A. s. 'Dudley Neville'**

Raised by Mr D. Neville of Burley in the 1930s with neat silver foliage and soft, golden buff flowers. There is also a variegated form, *A. s.* 'Dudley Neville Variegated'.

○ **A. s. 'Plenum'**

An extremely showy, double golden form.

○ **A. s. 'Gold Dust'**

A popular and colourful plant with grey-green leaves and masses of golden-yellow flowers in late spring and early summer.

❧ ANEMONE BLANDA ❧

Anemone blanda is an early spring-flowering anemone and one of the easiest and most colourful of all spring-flowering plants. Making large clumps and spreading through beds and borders, it turns whole areas into sheets of blue. The neat, narrow petals, perhaps twenty or more altogether, fan out in the sun like large, refined daisies some 5cm (2in) across, contrasting well with the fresh green foliage.

There are several forms of *A. blanda* available in colours ranging from soft blue to rich deep blue, white, and rose-pink, with or without a circle of white surrounding the golden bosses of stamens. Seedlings vary enormously. The blue forms seem to come true from seed whilst the pink forms tend to cross·with the blues producing wishy-washy, mauve-coloured seedlings which are not very attractive. Sometimes, though, seedlings occur with colours and shades as interesting as any of the named varieties.

The foliage of *Anemone blanda* disappears after flowering, and although plants may be growing thickly all through the beds, no one would know it until early spring when the area bursts into colour again. Primroses, which flower at the same time, make excellent companions and contrast well with the blue *Anemone blanda*.

Anemone blanda is perfectly hardy, flourishing in most soils, although perfection would be a position in light or dappled shade in a peat or leaf mould-rich soil. The rhizomes should be planted with the indented surface upwards and may need a year or two to settle before giving of their best.

■ Propagate by careful root division, or from seed which, taken from the various colour forms in summer and sown in a sheltered border outdoors, lightly covered with a sandy soil, will produce flowering plants in two or three years.

○ *Anemone blanda* **'Ingramii'**
An old variety worth searching for, with the deepest blue flowers. It is the latest blue to flower.

○ ***A. b.* 'White Splendour'**
Large, showy white flowers in early spring with a faint rose suffusion on the reverse of the petals. Raised by Van Tubergen.

○ ***A. b.* 'Radar'**
Another variety raised by Van Tubergen, with bright reddish-purple flowers with a white centre.

○ ***A. b.* var. *rosea***
Bright, attractive clear rose-coloured flowers. 'Charmer' has pure pink flowers.

Anemone blanda *seeds freely, then obligingly disappears completely after flowering until the next year*

Helleborus corsicus *with clusters of pale green flowers and evergreen, three-lobed leaves forms a dramatic backdrop to the deep red polyanthus.* Euphorbia amygdaloides *'Rubra', with yellow-green flowers and maroon-flushed dark green leaves forms a dense block of colour in the middle ground, and sets off the purity of white narcissus.* Anemone nemorosa *nods its white flowers to reveal a pale flushed pink on the reverse in contrast to the young shoots of astilbes, like dense, dark red plumes.* Epimedium rubrum, *with its old leaves bright coppery red and young leaves light green, heavily marbled in coppery red, unites the two aspects of the colour theme.*

BACK ROW *Helleborus corsicus.* Evergreen perennial. 60cm (2ft). White narcissus. 35-45cm (14-18in).
MIDDLE ROW *Euphorbia amygdaloides* 'Rubra'. Perennial. 30cm (1ft). *Epimedium rubrum.* Perennial.
30cm (12in). Astilbes. Perennial. 30cm (12in).
FRONT ROW Deep red polyanthus. 10-15cm (4-6in). *Anemone nemorosa.* 20cm (8in).

ANEMONE NEMOROSA

Anemone nemorosa, the native Wood Anemone grows wild in the woods, hedgerows and banks in many parts of the country, whilst the choice forms in various shades make carpets of colour in the garden in early spring.

The woodland anemone establishes and naturalises best in a heavy soil in semi-shade, beneath shrubs and at the margins of borders. However, the old-fashioned double white form with flowers like tiny roses is probably happier in a light, peaty soil and is certainly more at home in a rock garden than planted in the shrubbery.

There are a number of different forms of *Anemone nemorosa,* all quite delightful, some with light blue flowers, some shaded pink and others with large white flowers. A close relation, *A. ranunculoides,* the yellow woodland anemone, has small yellow flowers over bronze foliage. *A x seehmannii,* a cross between a white *A. nemorosa* and *A. ranunculoides,* has soft yellow flowers over ferny foliage.

New varieties from Denmark are making their mark, extending the choice and colours available. These are gradually becoming more widely available through alpine and specialist nurseries.

 As the foliage of the woodland anemones disappears by midsummer, it is perhaps as well to mark their territory in order to avoid dumping them unceremoniously on the compost heap when their presence is forgotten in the rush to tidy up the garden in the autumn. Propagate by division after flowering.

○ *Anemone nemorosa* **'Robinsoniana'**
A handsome old variety with large, rounded blooms of delicate lavender-blue with yellow anthers.
○ *A. n.* **'Alba Plena'**
This lovely old double form has a tight central pompom of tiny petals.
○ *A. n.* **'Danica'**
A superb, giant white form originating from the Sjaelland area of Denmark.
○ *A. n.* **'Royal Blue'**
Another superb variety, this time with rich violet-blue flowers.

ARABIS

Arabis albida (syn *caucasica*) – the cottager's Snow on the Mountain – is the common variety, best grown in walls or naturalised in bare or rocky corners where it can be permitted to spread to its heart's content, sending down great mats of foliage a foot or more in length.

The pink-flowered varieties are much better behaved and can be used effectively as a carpet for beds of spring-flowering bulbs, whilst the magnificent, fully double *A. a.* 'Flore Pleno' with its sturdy spikes of double, stock-like flowers is ideal for edging paths or framing borders.

Arabis will succeed in any well-drained soil and planting should be undertaken either in autumn or in spring after the flowers have faded. Straggling shoots should be cut right back after flowering to encourage a tufted habit of growth.

■ Double and named varieties must be propagated by root division or cuttings. Cuttings can be taken from the young shoots at any time during the summer and will root easily in a shady border. Roots of all varieties can be divided at planting time in the autumn or during the spring.

○ *Arabis caucasica* 'Snowdrop'
A compact and very profuse arabis with brilliant white, rounded flowers.

○ *A. c.* 'Rosabella'
An easy and long-lived variety with pink flowers on light green hummocks.

○ *A. c.* 'Corfe Castle'
A recent introduction and a first class spring-flowering plant with flowers best described as magenta.

○ *A. ferdinandi-coburgii* 'Variegata'
A variegated form with tight, evergreen cushions of striking, cream and green-striped leaves and white flowers.

○ *A. f-c.* 'Old Gold'
A colourful, non-invasive, creeping arabis from Macedonia, with golden-variegated leaves and sprays of white flowers in spring.

❧ AUBRIETA ☙

Aubrieta, or the purple Rock Cress, is almost invariably (but mistakenly) spelt 'aubrietia', somehow over the years acquiring an extra 'i' before the final 'a'. It is one of the most popular and valuable of garden plants although, when badly associated, one of the most gaudy.

Named in honour of the seventeenth-century French botanical artist Claude Aubriet, who is credited with discovering the garden aubrieta, the Rock Cress is unlikely to thrill the alpine purist, but to the average gardener it is certainly an excellent rock plant – a good tempered old favourite with masses of mauve, purple or plum-coloured flowers, produced with the minimum of care.

PLANT ASSOCIATIONS
A Pink and White Scheme Strengthened with Red

A classic combination in unusual colours is achieved with pink tulips and pink forget-me-nots in the foreground, while burgundy-red hyacinths contrast well with white-flowered arabis. Pulsatilla vulgaris 'Rubra' *with dusky red flowers and lovely pinkish, silky seedheads completes the underplanting, along with white-flowered muscari. The young foliage of* Cornus alba 'Elegantissima' *in pale green and white contrasts well with the dusky red young foliage of paeonies and highlights the refinement of white narcissus. Pink and white lupins will follow for early summer when the paeonies are in flower, as will white flag irises.*

BACK ROW *Cornus alba* 'Elegantissima'. Deciduous shrub. 3m (10ft).
MIDDLE ROW Paeonies. Perennial. 60cm (2ft). Lupins. Perennial. 1.2m (4ft). White flag irises. Perennial. 1.2m (4ft). Tulips. 45-60cm (18-24in).

Narcissus. 45cm (18in).
FRONT ROW Forget-me-nots, hyacinths, arabis, *Pulsatilla vulgaris* 'Rubra', muscari – none more than 23cm (9in).

Grown alone, its purple mounds can look rather unappealing, but planted tumbling over a grey stone wall with the yellow *Alyssum saxatile* it creates one of the many beautiful seasonal variations of that delightful colour scheme, mauve and yellow.

There are today many named varieties with excellent characteristics, including magnificent large flowers, deeper colours, double flowers, and a striking silver-variegated form, 'Argenteovariegata', with lavender flowers. All provide excellent, rich spring colour and are useful in bridging the gap between the late spring- and early summer-flowering plants.

 Aubrieta is happiest growing on a wall or rockery where winter moisture drains away easily.

■ Cutting or shearing aubrieta right down to the ground the moment it shows signs of getting brown or leggy will often encourage a second flowering and a tight crop of new leaves.

■ Plants are increased by division of roots in autumn or cuttings of young growth, about 5cm (2in) in length, inserted in very sandy soil in a cold frame or shady border in summer. Seed grown in a frame in early spring, or in a shady border a little later, germinates well and is a very easy way of producing mixed plants. However, it should be noted that named varieties do not breed true from seed.

○ *Aubrieta* '**Dr Mules**'
Vigorous, with bright green foliage and deep purple flowers. An old favourite.
○ *A.* '**Bob Sanders**'
A vigorous plant with large, fully double, reddish-purple flowers.
○ *A.* '**Greencourt Purple**'
Large, double flowers of a deep velvety purple-blue.
○ *A.* '**Maurice Prichard**'
Pale green foliage and light pink flowers.
○ *A.* '**Novalis Blue**'
The medium blue flowers of this first F[1] hybrid are twice the size of normal seed-raised varieties.
○ *A.* '**Red Carpet**'
Deep wine flowers. A really vigorous and free-flowering cultivar.

❧ BELLIS ❧

The Anglo-Saxon name for *Bellis perennis* was 'daeges eage' or 'day's eye' because the flowers open with the dawn. It is the common daisy that studs our lawns and from which the old cultivated varieties descend.

In the fifteenth century, bellis are described as salad herbs and Parkinson mentions them in his *Paradisi in Sole, Paradisus Terrestris,* written in 1629 and the first book to deal with plants as ornamental rather than medicinal. The double daisies have been grown for centuries and few cottage gardens today are without at least one of the old named varieties, edging paths and borders with their pink and white or scarlet buttons.

Parkinson's 'Double fruitful Daisies or Jack-an-Apes on horsebacke' or *Bellis prolifera,* is better known by its cottage garden name of Hen-and-Chickens Daisy. It is a curious form, and is one of the real old timers which you would expect to come across in old cottage gardens. Somehow it has survived the years and is now much sought after by latter-day enthusiasts.

Bellis prolifera looks exactly like any of the other double daisies except that it sends out offsets of identical miniature flowers from the central blossom, attached to the parent by thin stalks which grow to about 0.6cm (¼in). Unfortunately, there is no guarantee that this will always happen, but a rich diet will certainly help it to perform properly.

Bellium minutum, a tiny little daisy with white petals backed with red, is particularly useful for planting in cracks in paving where its roots enjoy the cool run, and it will happily work its way along

Aubrieta with alpine phlox, lily of the valley and forget-me-nots in a rocky bed

as far as it can go. The flowers of *Bellium minutum* are so tiny that it almost requires a magnifying glass to see them properly, but it is a tough little plant and not too difficult to please.

The larger double daisies are available in a delightful variety of colours. Frequently grown from seed, they can be used as biennials. There are several mixtures to choose from. *Bellis perennis* 'Goliath' has enormous 10cm (4in) flowers surrounded by a rosette of bright green leaves and *B. p.* 'Pomponette', which has smaller, fully double flowers with quilled petals in delicate shades of red, rose and white, is equally at home in the border or in the rockery and will seed itself here and there in the garden.

and planted out 15cm (6in) apart in a good sandy compost. Newly planted divisions attract the attention of birds which, unless deterred by black cotton, will remove them in the search for worms.

○ **Bellis perennis 'Dresden China'**
One of the loveliest and probably best known of all the old, named double daisies with deep rose-pink flowers which are a joy in early spring.
○ **B. p. 'The Pearl'**
The white counterpart of 'Dresden China', also called 'Robert' in some parts of the country. Difficult, and needs a rich soil and lots of attention.
○ **B. p. 'Rob Roy'**
An early Victorian quilled variety with large, bright crimson flowers suitable for a mixed border.
○ **B. p. 'Aucubifolia'**
A variegated sport of *Bellis perennis* with mottled leaves like those of the aucuba. It prefers a cool, shady border. A much improved form is 'Shrewley Gold'.

❧ BERGENIA ☙

Bergenia, commonly know as Elephant's Ears and occasionally referred to as Pig Squeak because of the noise made by the leaves when they are rubbed between the fingers, did not become popular until the end of the nineteenth century and most of the first-class hybrids which we see today in gardens are modern.

Although not perhaps the most glamorous of perennials, bergenias are certainly among the

All the double daisies are completely hardy, but resent dry conditions in summer and require frequent division otherwise too many crowns will develop and the plant will become woody. A rich, moist soil is essential to their well-being.

■ Propagation of all the double daisies is comparatively easy and should be undertaken in spring or autumn. The plants should be pulled to pieces

Bergenia is grown mainly for its bold foliage, but the flowers are a welcome bonus early in the year

most useful. The huge, leathery, shiny evergreen leaves make excellent ground cover and superb weed suppressants. Several forms have leaves which change from green to reddish-purple or plum-red in winter whilst the squarish, bell-shaped, fresh pink flowers are a welcome sight in early spring.

The bergenias are classified as saxifrages and are in fact a giant version of London Pride, very popular with flower arrangers to whom they really owe much of their present-day popularity, the large, heart-shaped leaves forming the base of many an award-winning floral arrangement, and the flowers equally attractive.

'Ballawley' not surprisingly, is the hybrid everyone wants to grow. The laurel-green leaves are softer than the norm, and the handsome heads of bright rose-red shaded flowers are borne on red stems to a height of 60cm (2ft). It had its origins over 40 years ago in Ballawley Park, Dublin. *Bergenia cordifolia,* which has been grown for more than two hundred years, is the one you would expect to find in old gardens. An excellent garden plant with its rounded leaves and heads of pinkish-mauve flowers borne on 45cm (1½ft) stems, it is also popular for growing in containers, as is its variety 'Purpurea' which takes on purplish overtones in winter.

 Bergenias will grow almost anywhere in practically any well-drained soil, but tend to flower best in full sun. They appreciate a top dressing of leaf mould in autumn or winter. Propagate by division in early spring or early autumn. The plants are best divided every third or fourth year before the quality of the flower and foliage begins to fail.

○ *Bergenia 'Abendglut'*
'Abendglut' or 'Evening Glow' has glowing rosy-red flowers and deep red winter foliage.

○ *B. 'Beethoven'*
Large clusters of white flowers fading to pink in early spring, with good bronze foliage in winter.

○ *B. 'Bressingham White'*
Outstanding for its pure colour, freedom of flower and leafy robustness. Probably the best white.

○ *B. 'Sunningdale'*
Vigorous growing, with deep reddish-pink heads and foliage changing to red-brown in winter.

○ *B. stracheyi*
The smallest bergenia only 15-20cm (6-8in) tall, with small, rounded leaves and short-stemmed pink flowers. There is a white form with light green calyces which is very attractive.

❧ CHEIRANTHUS ❧
(AND ERYSIMUM)

Cheiranthus, or the wallflower, in its ordinary form will hardly need introducing to cottage gardeners, as it is far and away the most popular spring bedding plant. With its brown, blood-red, mauve and mustard-yellow single flowers it fills the air with fragrance from early to late spring. The double-flowered forms, however, may not be as well known.

Long before the wallflower enjoyed its enormous popularity and reputation as a cottage garden plant, it was to be found growing wild, attaching itself to the ruins of old walls on desolate castles and old abbeys. Because of the tales of star-crossed love associated with it, the flower became the symbol of faithfulness in adversity.

Single forms, mostly yellow or brown-red but sometimes with the colours striped together, have been grown in gardens since Elizabethan times, with white and scarlet varieties appearing in the eighteenth and nineteenth centuries. A variety of a rich mulberry colour called 'The Negress' was very popular with the Victorians and changed hands in 1852 at five shillings a plant.

Double-flowered forms have been in existence since the sixteenth century. Gerard calls it the 'Yellow Stocke-gillofloure' and mentions only the yellow kind which he described as having 'a very sweete smell', but Parkinson describes both the yellow and a double red. The double-flowered forms became very fashionable in Georgian and Victorian gardens. The many good seed strains existing then yielded a high proportion of double-flowered plants, while choice doubles were propagated by cuttings, and named.

A variety much sought after during the early nineteenth century was one called 'Chameleon'. The petals of 'Chameleon' first appeared bright yellow, gradually became paler until nearly blanched white, and then took on a purple tint so that flowers of three different hues appeared on the plant at the same time. Another fine old variety with lilac flowers was known as 'Old Cottage'.

Several of the old, named doubles are still grown and have become much sought after by modern-day cottage gardeners. One supplier (See Sources of Plants) lists a rarely offered double-flowered seed mixture 'Early Wonder' with a surprisingly high success rate of doubles, giving today's cottage gardener the chance of raising his or her own 'Chameleon'.

 Double wallflowers enjoy a well-drained, sandy soil containing a little decayed manure in an open, sunny situation. The Erysimums, a related genus, are more suitable for the rock garden, although also at home in the border.

■ Double-flowered cheiranthus are chiefly propagated by cuttings. Remove the blooms after flowering and allow the plants to remain in their beds. They will quickly form an abundance of shoots from the base. These can be removed when they are about 7.5cm (3in) long. Remove the lower leaves of the cuttings and insert them in boxes of sandy compost where, protected from the sun, they will root in four weeks and can be potted up and grown on in a frame until early spring.

■ Seed for wallflowers to be used as bedding plants should be sown in a shady seed bed in early summer and transplanted, as soon as the seedlings have formed their third leaf, to a nursery bed until the autumn, when they may be set out in their flowering quarters about 30cm (1ft) apart each way.

○ **Cheiranthus 'Old Bloody Warrior'**
A dark, blood-red, heavily perfumed, double wallflower which has somehow survived the centuries despite its well-deserved reputation for being difficult. Margery Fish, whose books written in the 1950s have inspired many gardeners to grow old-fashioned flowers, wrote in *Cottage Garden Flowers* of her struggle to keep Old Bloody Warrior going and suggested reversing the first words of his name!

○ **C. 'Harpur Crewe'**
An outstanding bushy, sweetly scented, double, golden-yellow wallflower, possibly Elizabethan and

---

PLANT ASSOCIATIONS
A Red and Yellow 'Cottagey' Scheme

Euphorbia polychroma *with dense heads of brilliant yellow-green flowers forms clusters beneath* Dicentra 'Bacchanal' *with arching sprays of pendulous, red flowers.* Geranium maculatum 'Album' *with white flowers and downy, roundish leaves is set off by airy aquilegias in shades of red and yellow, and the young, deeply divided, mid-green foliage of variegated astrantias.*

Euphorbia polychroma. Perennial. 45cm (18in). *Dicentra* 'Bacchanal'. Perennial. 75cm (30in). *Geranium maculatum* 'Album'. Perennial. 75cm (30in).

Aquilegias. Perennial. 75cm (30in). Variegated astrantias. Perennial. 60cm (2ft).

rediscovered in the last century in a kitchen garden near Christchurch, Hants, by the Reverend Henry Harpur Crewe, Rector of Drayton Beauchamp in Buckinghamshire. The Reverend Henry Harpur Crewe's garden was said to contain one of the richest collections of hardy plants in Europe and he was certainly just the right visitor to the Hampshire garden to recognise the wallflower as 'special' and to ensure its continuation by cuttings.

Some types of wallflowers are now classed as *Erysimum.*

○ **Erysimum 'Bowles Mauve'**
A superb single-flowered variety of wallflower forming a vigorous bushlet of upright habit, with glaucous foliage and large spikes of rich mauve-purple flowers in early summer and intermittently throughout the year. Raised by the famous plantsman E. A. Bowles of Enfield.

○ **E. (Cheiranthus) 'Constant Cheer'**
Compact mounds of dark green foliage and showy heads of dusky red and purple single flowers.

○ **E. 'Moonlight'**
Pale, single, sulphur-yellow flowers over mats of dark green, crinkled foliage. Excellent for growing over walls and in rockeries.

○ **E. 'Mutabile'**
A very interesting single-flowered, spreading, perennial wallflower which comes from the Canary Isles. The flowers are a curious mixture of purple and rose madder – there is also a variegated form E. m. 'Variegatum'.

❧ CONVALLARIA ❧

Convallaria majalis, or Lily of the Valley, is an ancient plant with deliciously scented, pure white, waxy bells, ten to twenty per stem in spring, followed by red berries in the autumn. The leaves and flowers grow from a creeping rootstock, the lush foliage being deep green in colour. The plant is happiest in dappled shade in a moist, humus-laden soil.

In Victorian times, Lilies of the Valley were widely planted in walled kitchen gardens. This situation suited them particularly as they were left to flower and multiply without disturbance, which they resent. Even today they are frequently

---

(right) **Cheiranthus 'Old Bloody Warrior', a rare but much-prized old double wallflower. Here its rich red flowers are set off by a background of astrantia leaves**

PLANT ASSOCIATIONS
A Warm and Sparkling Colour Scheme

Euphorbia characias 'Lambrook Yellow' or E. wulfenii *with huge truncheons of flowers above handsome blue-green foliage forms a bold centrepiece, fronted by Siberian wallflowers with bright orange flowers, white tulips and red Greigii tulips. The flame-red bells of* Fritillaria imperialis 'Rubra' *make a striking contrast with white hyacinths.* Cytisus praecox *with showers of pale yellow blossom provides a background alongside dark red-flowered chaenomeles and* Berberis ottawensis *with bright, coppery bronze young leaves maturing to darkest mahogany-purple.*

BACK ROW Chaenomeles. Shrub. 1.8m (6ft) or more against a wall. *Cytisus praecox.* Shrub. 1.5-1.8m (5-6ft). *Berberis ottawensis.* Shrub. 2.4m (8ft). **MIDDLE ROW** *Euphorbia characias* 'Lambrook

Yellow'. Perennial. 90cm (3ft). *E wulfenii.* Perennial. 1.2m (4ft). *Fritillaria imperialis* 'Rubra'. 1.2m (4ft). **FRONT ROW** Siberian wallflowers. 45cm (18in). *Greigii* tulips. 20cm (8in). White hyacinths 20cm (8in).

seen in old cottage gardens growing under a mossy, shady wall, where they flourish on a liberal surface-dressing of well rotted manure and an abundance of moisture.

Clumps of Lily of the Valley planted near a favourite garden seat which catches the late afternoon sun will refresh the weary gardener taking a rest from his or her chores, as the warmth of the sun draws out every last drop of scent from the flowers. When picking a posy of Lily of the Valley, give the stalks a sharp upward jerk and leave at least one leaf to each plant.

There are several interesting forms available, although the 'curiosities' with striped flowers so popular in the mid-eighteenth century are now no longer grown.

 Lilies of the Valley will survive almost anywhere, consequently they are often grown in poor conditions – under hedges and in between crazy paving – and dismissed as weeds. Given a rich, loamy soil in dappled shade with some added lime for perfection, they will repay handsomely with attractive, lush foliage, each leaf pair producing a spike of richly scented, pendant waxy bells in early spring. Propagate by dividing the crowns when replanting. The small crowns, planted out in a nursery bed, will soon reach flowering size.

○ **Convallaria 'Fortin's Giant'**
With plain green leaves and large, hanging bells twice the normal size, it requires a rich soil to maintain the size differential.
○ **C. 'Rosea'**
An attractive, soft pink-flowered form which develops its best colour out of direct sunlight.
○ **C. 'Prolificans'**
A double-flowered form with deep green leaves and spikes of blooms in which each individual flower is replaced by a cluster of several fully doubled, pure white pompons.
○ **C. 'Variegata'**
A charming form with rich green leaves, lined along their length with gold stripes drawn with the precision of a draughtsman's hand. A stable form, but sometimes not giving of its best in the year after planting.

○ **C. 'Vic Pawloski's Gold'**
An outstanding new variety, still in very short supply but worth waiting for.

❧ DORONICUM ❧

Doronicum or Leopard's Bane – something like a daisy, something like a single sunflower – brings an early splash of colour just at a time when colour is most wanted: between the period when the bulb display is almost over and the early summer flowers have yet to perform.

The doronicums are simple, cheerful cottage garden plants, seldom growing more than 60cm (2ft) in height, ideal for the front of a border and excellent for cutting. The old *Doronicum plantagineum* with its oval and toothed leafy stems has been grown in gardens for centuries and still gives a very good show. There are several excellent named varieties and a double-flowered form, all suitable for the herbaceous border.

 Doronicums will grow in any reasonably well-drained soil which should remain moist during the growing season. They are tolerant of sun or semi-shade, although a sunny situation should be avoided on drier soils.

■ The masses of yellow daisies are tempered by bright green foliage and will often appear in autumn as well as in spring, providing that they are cut down before the seed ripens.

■ Doronicums need frequent splitting and replanting and this is the simplest means of propagation. Ensure that the hard centre portion of old clumps is discarded and only the younger and more vigorous outer portions are retained.

○ **Doronicum 'Miss Mason'**
The best of the dwarf, single-flowered forms with big, bright yellow flowers and heart-shaped leaves. Easy.
○ **D. 'Harpur Crewe'**
A late-flowering variety with big, golden-yellow daisy flowers larger than the type and more robust in growth. Recommended at the end of the nineteenth century as one of the best hardy plants for mixed borders.

○ *D. caucasicum magnificum*
An abundance of rayed yellow flowers in early spring with kidney-shaped leaves, deeply toothed.

○ *D. 'Spring Beauty'*
An outstanding double-flowered form of German origin, also known as 'Fruhlingspracht'.

✎ EUPHORBIA ✎

A vast family of plants with an amazing variety of forms. Some, like the poinsettia, are definitely not for the cottage garden; some are cactus look-alikes; others provide some of the finest architectural show-pieces.

Of the dozen or so British euphorbias, the Petty Spurge is a prolific weed, as common as groundsel and equally unpopular. However, two natives described below deserve a welcome in the garden, although the best are imports from southern Europe and Asia.

Garden euphorbias are unfussy about soil conditions and will thrive well in sun or part shade. Even quite poor soil does not worry them at all provided it is well drained.

▪ Self-sown seedlings, about which euphorbias are very obliging, are the easiest way to obtain new plants. Alternatively, they can be grown from seed in pans of soil-based seed compost under glass in spring, for planting out in the autumn. Alternatively, cuttings can be taken from the base shoots and placed in a 50/50 mixture of peat, or preferably a peat substitute, and sand in early summer for planting out when well rooted. Root division is also possible during the winter.

▪ One warning about euphorbias. The milky substance they exude when cut is highly irritant and can cause a very painful rash which lingers for several days. In the garden, handle with gloves and, if using them for flower arrangements, seal the stems by burning them.

○ *Euphorbia wulfenii*
A tall and stately plant growing to a height of 1.2m (4ft) with imposing cylindrical drumheads of pale lime-yellow, on stems clothed in whorls of blue-green leaves. Grown in front of a wall it looks equally splendid in a cottage garden or a castle.

○ *E. characias*
Similar to *E. wulfenii* in height and spread. The heads are not so large and each flower has a dark maroon, almost black eye.

○ *E. amygdaloides*
A native plant smaller than *E. wulfenii* reaching only 30-60cm (1-2ft) high. The variety *E. a. purpurea* (syn. *rubra*) has rosettes of dark green leaves heavily tinged purple-red and bears yellow-green flowerheads. Useful ground cover on poor soils. Another interesting form *E. a.* 'Variegata' has leaves edged with cream.

PLANT ASSOCIATIONS
A Grouping for Fragrance

The dark green foliage and fragrant, creamy white flowers of Osmanthus delavayi or O. burkwoodii form a background to Euonymus 'Emerald 'n Gold' with its bright yellow and green variegated leaves, and the lime-yellow flowers of Euphorbia polychroma. At the front, Euphorbia cyparissias mingles similar flowers with the blue or white spikes of hyacinths. These, with Cytisus praecox, a peppery, sweet-scented broom bearing cascades of creamy yellow, pea-like blossom and the late blooming, lilac-flowered Syringa palibiniana will, with narcissus and wallflowers, make a group for spring.

BACK ROW *Osmanthus delavayi*. Evergreen shrub. 1.8-2.4m (6-8ft). *O. burkwoodii* (syn. *Osmarea burkwoodii*). Evergreen shrub. 1.8-3m (6-10ft).
MIDDLE ROW *Cytisus praecox*. Deciduous shrub. 1.2-1.5m (4-5ft). *Syringa palibiniana*. Deciduous shrub. 1.5m (5ft). *Euonymus* 'Emerald 'n Gold'. Evergreen shrub. 70-90cm (2½-3ft). *Euphorbia polychroma*. Evergreen sub-shrub. 45cm (18in).
FRONT ROW *E. cyparissias*. Perennial. 30cm (12in). Hyacinths, narcissi, wallflowers – none over 45cm (18in).

○ **E. myrsinites**
A semi-prostrate spurge, excellent for the front of the border or hanging over a low wall. Its trailing stems are clothed in whorls of fleshy blue-green leaves. Flowerheads bright yellow-green.

○ **E. cyparissias (Cypress Spurge)**
A small and elegant plant, 30cm (12in) high, with bright lime-green flowers and stems covered in slender, pointed mid-green leaves. Useful as border edging or for ground cover, but can be invasive.

○ **E. polychroma (syn. epithymoides)**
A very fine rounded, clump-forming plant which adds effect to any border. Reaching 45cm tall and 60cm across (18x24in). Mid-green leaves and wide heads of bright yellow flowers.

○ **E. griffithii 'Fireglow'**
An aptly named variety because it is predominantly red, with red stems, vivid orange-red flowers, and narrow soft-green leaves, red on the underside and with a prominent, reddish pink mid-rib. Altogether a very handsome plant.

○ **E. lathyris (Caper Spurge)**
Often seen in old cottage gardens, this probably native spurge is a tall and statuesque plant, 90cm (3ft) or more in height. Few would call it beautiful but it is an eye-catching and unusual-looking plant, well worth its place in the garden. It is also reputed to act as a mole repellant.

Except for the Caper Spurge, which is an annual or biennial, all the above euphorbias are perennial.

✎ IBERIS ✎

Iberis sempervirens, the common perennial candytuft, has pure white flowers over dark, evergreen foliage. Planted with great effect to hang over dry walls and rockeries, it produces a dazzling sheet of snowy white from early spring onwards. Candytuft has been grown in gardens for hundreds of years and derives its name from the island of Crete (Candia) from where it came.

Planted as an edging to a border, the perennial candytuft will more than earn its keep even after the snowy white flowers are over, quickly spread-

---

Euphorbias are first-class plants for dry shade, and their long lasting lime-green heads fade attractively

ing to clothe bare patches during the winter months with its neat, evergreen mats of foliage.

Several named varieties are available with showier flowers, ideal for the front of the border.

 The perennial Candytuft requires good drainage but will grow in sun or shade. It is best planted in early spring. Any straggly, established plants should be trimmed back into shape immediately after flowering. Propagate by means of half-ripened shoots taken in summer, or by division of roots after flowering.

○ **Iberis sempervirens 'Snowflake'**
A firm favourite, with large snowy-white flowers, growing to about 30cm (1ft) in height.

○ **I. s. 'Little Gem'**
A small, evergreen shrublet with white flowers, growing only 15cm (6in) in height.

○ **I. gibraltarica**
Perhaps not always hardy, but a delightful, spreading perennial smothered with flowers tinged red or lilac and with flower stems often branched.

✎ LUNARIA ✎

Lunaria annua (syn. *biennis*) or Honesty, also known as satin-flower, money-flower and moon-wort, is another of those old-fashioned biennials that is rather difficult to lose once it has been introduced to a garden. It seeds itself freely but is not difficult to control as the seedlings are easily identifiable and can simply be removed or transplanted.

The plant is grown chiefly for the beauty of its moon-like seedpods (hence its Latin name) which, when dry and 'skinned', are much prized by flower arrangers. Butterflies love the plant too.

The leaves are ovate and toothed and the flowers, borne in branching sprays in early and late spring, have many colour variations, ranging from pure white through purples and reds, with the leaves of *L. a.* 'Variegata' margined creamy white. Honesty has a rather curious habit which can be puzzling to the uninitiated. Plants which start off rose-pink or mauve-purple suddenly one year will appear all white, and then by some strange trick of genetics the next year will be pink again.

L. annua makes a very pretty woodland plant and the stems of seed-pods should be left throughout the winter months so that the gardener can enjoy the sight of their ghostly silvery moons fluttering in the breeze.

Honesty will grow well in any normal garden soil providing it is given an open, sunny situation. Plants of this biennial are rarely offered for sale by nurseries or garden centres so you must grow your own from seed. Once established, however, seedlings will provide all the plants you will ever need.

○ *Lunaria annua alba*
This is the delightful, white-flowered form. The form with white flowers and variegated leaves is much sought-after.
○ *L. a.* 'Atro-coccinea'
A crimson form which is much admired.
○ *L. a.* 'Munstead Purple'
A variety with beautiful, rich purple flowers.
○ *L. rediviva*
L. rediviva is the perennial species with small, fragrant, purplish flowers in late spring and early summer, followed by elongated seedpods.

❧ MYOSOTIS ❧

Myosotis arvensis is the true wild form of the forget-me-not, probably the commonest of the ten native species, with small, bright blue flowers from early spring until autumn. It requires no further description, except to say that it is so easily grown you should only ever need to buy one packet of seed.

Forget-me-nots are a traditional feature of the cottage garden. Perfect with daffodils, they make an attractive back-cloth for the spring-flowering tulips. A traditional planting which never palls is the pink cottage tulip 'Clara Butt' rising from the forget-me-not's blue haze.

The myosotis family includes several members with pink flowers, white flowers, and a recently introduced wonderful brown-leaved forget-me-not with white flowers, *M. rakiura*, which is ideal for a rock garden or trough.

Myosotis will grow freely in most garden soils. They invariably produce a far finer display from an autumn rather than a spring planting and seed themselves everywhere.

■ To be certain of a fresh stock which you can plant where you want it, the method of propagation is simple. After the forget-me-nots are over, pull them out and lay them down in a shady place. The seeds will drop out and germinate to give hundreds if not thousands of new plants.

○ *Myosotis alpestris*
The so-called Alpine forget-me-not, which makes dense carpets of gentian-blue flowers with a yellow eye, thrives on the rock garden.

○ *M. a.* **'Ultramarine'**
The finest strain available; dwarf, compact plants and flowers a glowing, deep indigo-blue.

○ *M. a.* **'Rose'**
A particularly attractive and much sought after variety with pale rose-pink flowers.

❧ POLYGONATUM ❧

Polygonatum multiflorum, the old-fashioned Solomon's Seal, also known by its country names of David's Harp and Ladder-to-Heaven, is one of the loveliest of cottage garden plants, indispensable in light woodland and excellent for a cool, shady border.

Once established, Solomon's Seal is almost indestructible, although one has to be on guard in early summer for the sawfly caterpillars which can strip the foliage overnight. It has elegant, oblong, pale to mid-green leaves and tall, evenly arched stems, beneath which hang the drooping, tubular, greenish-white flowers about 2.5cm (1in) long, in late spring.

The seal of Solomon was a six-pointed star and there is no satisfactory explanation for how the plant got its name. Gerard describing it, mentions that 'The root of Solomons Seale stamped while it is fresh and greene, and applied, taketh away in one night, or two at the most, any bruise, blacke or blew spots gotten by falls or womens wilfulnesse, in stumbling upon their hasty husbands fists or suchlike'!

Solomon's Seal is an old garden favourite, easy to grow, delightful with primroses and lilies of the valley and, like so many other cottage garden favourites, much sought after by flower arrangers.

There are a number of interesting varieties, including a double-flowered one and several variegated forms.

All the polygonatums are plants for semi-shade or woodland conditions, and are best in a leafy soil with plenty of moisture when they are in active growth. Planted in dry shade they do not attain their full size, but can be useful where nothing else will grow. The best time for planting is in early autumn.

■ Propagate by carefully dividing the fleshy root stock, ensuring that each portion retained for planting has at least one terminal growth bud together with a reasonable amount of root. When planting, the growth buds should be just covered with soil.

○ *Polygonatum odoratum*
The scented form, with large white flowers followed by blue-black berries which have a grapey 'bloom' on the outside.

○ *P. o.* **'Variegatum'**
A rare form of great attraction with graceful, arching branches clothed in green, white-edged, somewhat pointed leaves and tubular flowers of creamy white.

○ *P. o.* **'Gilt Edge'**
Very effective for its arching, red-tinged stems carrying deep green, gold-bordered leaves.

○ *P. o.* **'Flore Pleno'**
In this cultivar the flower is fully doubled to yield a green and white crinoline, not unlike the centre of a double snowdrop, much sought after and slow to increase.

○ *P. hookeri*
A charming, small, carpeting species not more than 5cm (2in) tall which displays comparatively large, solitary, bright pink flowers. Best for a moist, peaty, open spot such as a peat garden.

❧ PRIMULA ❧

Of all the flowers in the garden the primrose, in all its many forms, must be one of the best loved, and it has been grown in cottage gardens since Tudor times.

Primula vulgaris, the lovely British native **primrose**, is the earliest to flower. It often produces a bloom or two before midwinter and opens spasmodically throughout the winter in a well-sheltered garden. As spring approaches, the flowers cheer up dull shrubberies, and stud banks and hedgerows with their simple beauty.

Coloured hybrids abound, and seed can be bought to provide an astonishing range of colours with some really intense shades. Sadly, these all too frequently lack the delicious, fresh, woodland fragrance of the common primrose.

Polyanthus run through a gamut of colours, from pale lavender to deep chocolate, rosy-pink and crimson, with *Primula vulgaris,* the wild primrose, and *P. veris,* the cowslip, in their parentage, but it is the gold and silver 'laced' polyanthus which are usually identified with old-world gardens.

From the mid-eighteenth to mid-nineteenth century the gold-laced polyanthus predominated, and the word 'polyanthus' became synonymous with these striking plants with their deep velvety red or black flowers, gold centres and gold lacing round the petals. Florists' clubs were formed which were, in effect, horticultural societies devoted to these and other popular plants, and over many years the florists improved and perfected the lacing and rounded shape of the flowers until, in 1844, a publication called *The Polyanthus* was able to list no less than ninety-six varieties all said to possess outstanding qualities.

By the end of the nineteenth century, however, fashion had changed and these florists' flowers had all but disappeared. Here and there in country cottage gardens the gold- and silver-laced polyanthus continued to be grown, and it was here that they were rediscovered and subsequently re-introduced in the early 'sixties to a wide-eyed new breed of cottage gardeners, who were eager to

The charming gold-laced polyanthus, once in vogue with nineteenth-century 'florists' clubs', is popular again after a long period of neglect

P. 'Bon Accord Purple'. This beautiful double primrose is rare but well worth searching out

rescue the old cottage garden plants which were at that time in real danger of disappearing forever.

The double primroses and curiosities – the Jack-in-the-Greens and the Hose-in-Hose primroses (see page 39) – owe their very existence to the sanctuary of the cottage garden, where plants teetering on the brink of extinction or discarded as unfashionable from larger gardens have always found a peaceful haven, enjoying the packed, damp atmosphere of a well shaded garden, thriving and glowing with health in the rich, manured soil so essential for their well-being.

Double primroses are not only delightful garden plants full of interest, but they are also excellent for cutting. The flowers should be kept in their separate colours and each little bunch must have a frill of its own leaves. This is essential, as the leaf of each variety is almost as distinct as the flower and a bunch of 'Double White' would look quite wrong with the leaves of

'Our Pat'. Closely packed altogether in a large, shallow dish they will glow like jewels and last for an amazingly long time.

Although double primroses have always had a reputation for being difficult their needs are in fact few, but what they need they insist on having, or they will give up trying and just fade away. Humus and yet more humus in the soil is the prime necessity, particularly in the top 23-25cm (9-10in) as the young roots of the double primrose grow outwards and not downwards.

The need for humus cannot be stressed enough, whether the soil is light or heavy, but it can come from a number of sources. Pig is better than farmyard manure for light soils, but if your soil happens to be heavy then use farmyard manure or stable manure if you can get it, the older the better. Spent mushroom compost and artificially composted straw are both rich in nitrogen and will make an excellent alternative in light or heavy soils if manure is unavailable.

The shade of deciduous trees or shrubs is probably the next most important requirement, although if the soil has been properly prepared this is perhaps not vital providing, of course, that a little artificial shade can be organised during a really hot spell. Double primroses look quite charming, carpeting the ground beneath flowering shrubs, with the added bonus that the shrubs shade the primrose in the summer, the leaves from the shrubs mulch the ground in winter, and the primroses help to keep the soil around the shrubs cool and, if thickly planted, smother the weeds.

Double primroses and double polyanthus went out of fashion for many years and as a result a number of the charmingly named old varieties have disappeared, many feared gone for ever. Enthusiasts dream of coming across these treasures in old forgotten cottage gardens and may very occasionally strike gold, their finds having grown undisturbed, for a century or more.

Both primroses and polyanthus will grow freely in any moderately rich garden soil where the roots will not suffer from drought. The double primroses are particularly exacting in their requirement for humus in the soil and shade from deciduous trees. Care should be taken when planting out double primroses not to let soil fall on the crown, an occurrence they abhor.

■ Before planting out primroses in the spring or autumn, the plants should be removed from their containers and immersed in water for one or two hours. When refreshed, the roots should be separated and spread out naturally in the soil without injuring them, pressing the soil firmly.

■ The stronger-growing double primroses can be increased by pulling the plants apart with the fingers, preferably in late spring or early summer during a showery spell. However, it may be necessary to take a sharp knife to the Bon Accords and the red forms, cutting a little of the main stem with each division.

■ Growing from seed can produce some interesting results. Seed should be sown in gentle heat in spring, pricking out the seedlings into boxes, and subsequently hardening them off in preparation for planting out as soon as weather conditions permit.

DOUBLE PRIMROSES

○ **Primula vulgaris 'Alba Plena'**
The old, double white primrose, or 'Gerard's Double White', is one of the easiest of the old-fashioned double primroses with beautiful, fully double, white blooms on long stems which make it ideal for picking.

○ **P. v. 'Lilacina Plena'**
Another comparatively easy double primrose. Its common name is Quaker's Bonnet or Lady's Delight. This old variety has beautifully formed, double, lilac-mauve flowers and a strong constitution.

○ **P. 'Marie Crousse'**
Large, double flowers of mauvish-red, splashed and edged with white, with a delicious, honeysuckle fragrance. Introduced from France over 150 years ago and a firm favourite ever since. There are several forms available. All are worth growing.

○ **P. 'Our Pat'**
'Our Pat' was found amongst a batch of P. juliae at the Daisy Hill Nurseries, Newry in 1935 and named after the owner's daughter. The double, sapphire-blue flowers are borne in great profusion on strong, polyanthus-like stems and it is one of the last double primroses to flower, extending the flowering season.

○ **P. 'Bon Accord Purple'**
'Bon Accord' is the motto of the city of Aberdeen in Scotland and this plant is one of a dozen double primroses raised at the turn of the century by the Cocker Brothers' Nurseries near Aberdeen. It has large, deep purple flowers shaded blue on the reverse side of the petals and borne on polyanthus stems.

A number of the other Bon Accords with their rather distinctive compact growth and erect, well-formed, double flowers are still grown today including 'Bon Accord Lavender', 'Bon Accord Lilac', 'Bon Accord Gem', 'Bon Accord Beauty' with purple-blue flowers and a very thin silver lacing at the edge of the petals, and 'Bon Accord Purity' with creamy-white flowers tinged green.

UNUSUAL AND QUAINT FORMS ———

○ **Hose-in-Hose Primroses and Polyanthus**
These are the delightful cup-and-saucer 'sports of nature' where one bloom grows out from another so there are in effect two single flowers, one slipped behind the other. They have been cottage garden 'oddities' for generations, although the old, named varieties 'Lady Lettice', 'Old Spotted Hose' and 'Old Vivid' are now no longer available – just a memory – and the plants we see today are mostly unnamed. A hose-in-hose variation of the modern *P. juliana* hybrid 'Wanda' with its glorious show of claret-crimson flowers is, however, quite widely distributed and well worth growing.

○ **Jack-in-the-Green Primroses and Polyanthus**
These have single flowers in a variety of colours with attractive little green ruffs under each flower. Apart from 'Tipperary Purple', a distinctive variety with soft purple-pink flowers, and a recently introduced, double white variety which has attracted enormous interest and which has been named 'Dawn Ansell', the 'Jacks' in the cottage garden have largely been raised from seed and are as such unnamed.

❧ PULSATILLA ❧

Pulsatilla vulgaris (syn. *Anemone pulsatilla*) or the Pasque Flower, flowering as it does at the beginning of spring, was used as early as the reign of Edward I to produce a bright green dye to colour Easter eggs.

The leaves are finely divided and the large, up-turned, bell-shaped flowers borne on silver, silken stems are usually lavender-purple with golden stamens. However, there are several different coloured forms in cultivation and varieties are available in deep violet, various shades of red, and a superb, creamy-white form which contrasts beautifully with the purples and reds.

There is or was a double form which was widely grown in the nineteenth century, but is sadly no longer seen in gardens today and probably extinct.

 An open but sheltered position in a well-drained soil with compost added are the essential ingredients for success with the pulsatillas, which are widely grown in rockeries. Propagate by division of the rhizomes after flowering, or by seed sown in a pan under glass in spring, preferably after exposure to frost.

○ *Pulsatilla vulgaris* '**Grandis**'
A magnificent variety bearing enormous, deep violet-purple flowers, the petals pleated and toothed, followed by large, silky seedheads.
○ *P. v. rubra*
Beautiful chalices of rich maroon red.
○ *P. v. alba*
Light, ferny foliage and huge, creamy-white cups. A superb form with some interesting variations.

❧ VINCA ❧

Vinca is the 'official' name for the familiar periwinkle freely used in cottage gardens for covering awkward banks, unsightly corners and stretches of sunless rockery, and grown in Britain for so long that nobody is quite sure whether it is a native or not.

There are two forms, *Vinca major,* the Greater Periwinkle and *V. minor,* the Lesser Periwinkle. Collectable varieties of both may have bigger leaves, longer-lasting flowers, double flowers or variegated foliage. All forms produce trailing, evergreen, glossy foliage which is never blemished by frosts, and bear pretty, lavender-blue, wheel-like flowers which wink open in early spring, flowering on and off throughout the summer months.

SIX OLD PERENNIAL COTTAGE GARDEN FAVOURITES FROM SPRING TO EARLY SUMMER

Pimpinella major 'Rosea'
PINK COW PARSLEY

60cm (2ft). The elegant ferny leaves make a good contrast with heavier foliage when the pale pink flowers have faded. Late spring/early summer.

Saxifraga granulata
FAIR MAIDS OF FRANCE (MEADOW SAXIFRAGE)

30cm (12in). Shiny, wavy-edged, kidney-shaped leaves. Long stems with dainty five-petalled flowers. Disappears after flowering. Moist soil best.

Cardamine pratensis 'Flore Pleno'
DOUBLE-FLOWERED LADY'S SMOCK or CUCKOO FLOWER

20cm (8in). Bunched heads of small, double flowers in lilac or white over leaves like watercress, to which family it belongs.

A damp shady spot will suit this pretty double form of our native Lady's Smock

Silene dioica 'Flore Pleno'
DOUBLE-FLOWERED RED CAMPION

45cm (18in). A clump of large, dark green, hairy leaves from which rise deep rose-coloured flowers, a little like untidy double pinks.

Ranunculus aconitifolius 'Flore Pleno'
BACHELORS BUTTONS

30cm (12in). Sometimes shares the name Fair Maids of France with the Meadow Saxifrage. A most beautiful plant with dark green buttercup leaves and petals tightly packed in white buttons. Difficult. Should be lifted every other year, the roots carefully prised apart and offsets potted up individually, then the parent plant replanted in moist, humus-rich soil.

Omphalodes verna
BLUE-EYED MARY

15cm (6in). Pointed oval leaves, mid-green, on long stalks. Bright blue, forget-me-not flowers with a white eye in early spring. Front of border or rockery.

V. major with its long, arching shoots and rampant growth is best restricted to the wild garden. Indispensable as ground cover, its vigorous growth is valuable in dry shade under trees or on banks. The many forms of the less vigorous, mat-forming *V. minor* are welcome almost anywhere in the garden and are particularly suited for planting under low-growing shrubs or for trailing over low walls and rockeries.

Periwinkles have long had a reputation as herbs, and were used in various charms and potions. One of their names was Sorcerer's Violet, and they were supposed to have power against 'wykked spiritis'.

Suitable for growing in any garden soil, in sun or shade, vincas usually flower more freely in a sunny situation. To make a close mat of ground cover, a new planting should be made with a lot of little plants in order to be effective. Use a rich compost in the planting holes to speed the growth, and pin the runners down into the moist compost: hairpins will do admirably. Keep well weeded until established.

■ *V. major* may be divided at planting time or will root easily from cuttings 10-12.5cm (4-5in) in length taken in the autumn. *V. minor* usually roots from the joints as it spreads and it is comparatively easy to detach a few rooted runners and plant them on separately.

○ **Vinca minor alba**
The white-flowered form with small leaves, marbled light and dark green in spring and early summer.

○ **V. m. 'Bowles Variety'**
A charming small plant, perhaps the best. Smothered with crop after crop of bright blue flowers.

○ **V. m. 'Alba Variegata'**
Starry, pale blue flowers and prettily marked leaves in green and white. The white-flowered, variegated form *V. m.* 'Variegata Alba' has leaves which are totally gold and look a picture grown with the orange tulip 'General de Wet'.

○ **V. m. 'Azurea Flore Pleno'**
One of the several double and semi-double vincas available today, 'Azurea Flore Pleno' has lovely, double, sky-blue flowers over a long period.

○ **V. difformis**
A charming early and late-flowering periwinkle with much the same habit as *V. major* but less invasive, although it fancies itself as a climber and will climb several feet into a tree or shrub given the opportunity. *V. difformis* will thrive in the poorest of soils but it is not entirely hardy. Slate-blue or starch-white flowers.

VIOLA

Violas, the cottager's Hearts Ease, sometimes called Tufted Pansies, are easy to distinguish

The charming little 'faces' of Viola *'Jessie East' in the shade of shrubs at the border's edge*

from the pansy itself, having a spreading habit of growth, a mass of delicate roots which enable them to be propagated with ease, and a constant show of dainty flowers as graceful as butterflies. A cottage garden flower if ever there was.

Violas are hybrids, the result of crossings between the Show Pansy and some of the native species of viola, notably *Viola lutea*. Careful selection and intercrossing over many years has produced a whole range of these charming plants which, unlike Show Pansies, which are bred for the production of large flowers and with little or no regard for the habit of the plant, are ideal border and edging plants.

Violettas, or miniature Tufted Pansies, a strain of 'rayless' violas, were raised by a Doctor Stuart of Chirnside, Berwickshire in 1872 by crossing a little blue bedding pansy and a species named *Viola cornuta*. The clear-coloured blooms of the violettas are more oval-shaped than those of pansies and violas and are borne on stiff, erect flower stems well above the foliage. They are richly scented, flowering with the first primroses and on through until the autumn and first frosts. There are a number of lovely varieties to choose from in various colours and shades. Plants should be lifted and divided every three or four years in the spring, and are excellent for the rock garden.

The exceptionally hardy and trouble-free *Viola cornuta,* a species introduced from the Pyrenees in 1776, is to be found in most cottage gardens. The pure species has pale blue or mauve flowers, but today there are many varieties in white and deeper blues. A prolific seeder, *V. cornuta* will sow itself all over the garden, the little pansy 'faces' peeping out from unexpected places, sometimes even in the depth of winter.

Another great seeder is the tiny, black, velvety *Viola* 'Bowles Black' introduced by nurseryman Amos Perry in 1901 from seed given to him by E. A. Bowles, the famous gardener. Apparently Bowles, a modest and unassuming man, much disliked the name, but preferred it to *V.* 'Black Bowles' which he spotted on a label at a Chelsea Show and quietly altered. A tiny pinch of seed produces a multitude of plants so appealing that only the strong-willed are able to weed them out.

○ *Viola cornuta alba*
The white form, with lots of chalk-white flowers over good evergreen foliage.

○ *V. c.* **'Boughton Blue'**
A good mid-blue, strong-growing variety.

○ *V.* **'Jackanapes'**
An old garden favourite, with the upper petals red-brown and the lower ones bright yellow. Said to have been named after Gertrude Jekyll's monkey.

○ *V.* **'Maggie Mott'**
'Maggie Mott', with its exquisite silvery-mauve flowers, is everyone's favourite viola. Vigorous and free-flowering, it has been grown since 1901, but many plants sold with this name today are questionable.

○ *V.* **'Irish Molly'**
Described by Margery Fish as having a dirty brownish face, 'Irish Molly' has greenish, bronzy-yellow flowers. It is somewhat difficult to keep, as it does not seed itself and has to be propagated by cuttings.

$\mathscr{B}$ULBS

FRITILLARIA
❧ IMPERIALIS ❧

Fritillaria imperialis or *Crown Imperial* is among the oldest of garden plants, having graced our borders for nearly four centuries. Yet, apart from cottage gardens, where it is usually grown in rows, this spectacular plant is not commonly grown in gardens today.

The stately Crown Imperials grow to a height of 60-90cm (2-3ft) from a mass of shiny green, pineapple-like leaves crested by dense whorls of drooping, bell-like flowers and crowned by a tuft of green foliage. In the bottom of each hanging flower there are several drops of shining liquid, described by Gerard as resembling 'fair orient pearls', which defy the law of gravity by keeping their place in the drooping bell. Few can resist the temptation of lifting the handsome heads to see

the 'drops', which will immediately reappear if shaken from the flower.

Both the red and yellow forms are right for a natural border, or among shrubs in a well-drained sunny position, probably well away from the house as they have an appalling smell – a mixture of garlic and foxes. For the connoisseur there is a very attractive, variegated form and a rare, double-flowered, orangey-red curiosity, 'Crown-upon-Crown' which has survived from the seventeenth century.

 The Crown Imperials enjoy a well-drained limey soil, with established clumps benefiting from an annual top dressing of strawy manure given just after growth begins in spring. A frequent complaint is that they are difficult to establish, and the cause can nearly always be traced to late planting. Bulbs planted in early autumn and placed on their sides with a covering of coarse sand will usually be more successful.

- Clumps doing well should be left alone, as Crown Imperials resent disturbance. Propagate by offsets taken while the plant is dormant. Plants resent movement while in growth, and premature die-back and lack of size will result.

○ *Fritillaria imperialis* 'Lutea Maxima'
A stately Crown Imperial with deep yellow hanging blooms in mid-spring. Very effective in the spring border, where it will grow to around 90-120cm (3-4ft) in height.

○ *F. i.* 'Rubra Maxima'
A very sturdy variety 90-120cm (3-4ft) high with large, red, bell-shaped flowers with the petals about 7.5cm (3in) long.

○ *F. i.* 'Aureo-Variegata'
In cultivation since 1867 and much sought after. Distinctive, gold-variegated leaves and pure orange, pendulous blooms. Shy to flower.

❧ HYACINTH ❧

The hyacinth, according to Greek mythology, was the flower that spread from the blood of young Hyacinthus, a friend of the god Apollo. One day when the two young men were engaged in a game of quoits, Apollo hurled a quoit hard; it went off course, hit Hyacinthus and killed him. Apollo had not the power to restore his companion to life, but he changed him instead into the beautiful flower that has since borne his name. Milton described the metamorphosis:

> . . . Apollo with unwitting hand,
> Whilom did slay his dearly-loved mate,
> Young Hyacinth, the pride of Spartan land;
> But then transformed him to a purple flower.

Hyacinths grown in the old-fashioned way, massed together or bedded out to fill flower beds, are certainly an impressive sight in a large garden or park, but the owner of a small garden has to be content with a few bulbs planted here and there in the border for a colourful and cheerful display in early spring.

The many varieties of the large florist's hyacinth used for spring bedding and for pot cultivation are derived from *Hyacinthus orientalis*. They have strap-like leaves, tight flower spikes with bell-shaped flowers on thick stems, and a colour range varying from white to yellow, orange, red, blue, pink and purple. Hyacinths are very strongly scented, almost overpoweringly so.

First-year bulbs are best planted in groups for support, preferably in a single colour, as the huge flower heads on newly planted hyacinths, often too heavy for the stalk, will frequently fall to the ground.

After a few years they eventually deteriorate into small flower trusses – much looser and looking more like their seventeenth- and eighteenth-century cousins, but without losing any of their rich scent. By those who dislike the enormous, stiff flower heads, this deterioration is seen as an improvement rather than a disappointment.

Hyacinths are particularly adapted for culture in bowls, pots and containers, and specially pre-cooled bulbs may be brought into bloom in mid-winter, given the right treatment and appropriate temperatures.

Narcissus with **Millium effusum** *and brunnera in a shady spring border*

Hyacinths require a well-drained soil, enriched with a dressing of decayed manure. Fresh manure tends to burn the roots. Planting should be carried out in the autumn, the bulbs covered to a depth of 10-15cm (4-6in) and about 20cm (8in) apart. A mixed display is apt to look ragged at flowering time, as there can be quite a difference in flowering periods.

○ **Hyacinthus 'City of Haarlem'**
Undoubtedly the best pale yellow hyacinth, which can be brought indoors early to flower in pots. Late flowering in the garden.
○ **H. 'L'Innocence'**
A very popular variety with large flower heads of purest white and a rich perfume.
○ **H. 'Ann Mary'**
An early-flowering variety with large, thick spikes and delicate pink flowers. Excellent for pots.
○ **H. 'Chestnut Flower'**
A choice and rare variety, first introduced in 1880. The dawn-pink flowers closely resemble those of the horse chestnut tree.
○ **H. 'Violet Pearl'**
A splendid, beautifully shaped hyacinth with bells of violet-amethyst. Definitely an eye catcher.
○ **H. 'Hollyhock'**
A good variety for forcing with deep carmine-red, double flowers so densely packed they hide the stem.

The spectacular Crown Imperial, although it looks exotic, is a traditional plant in the cottage garden

PLANT ASSOCIATIONS
A Gentle Mix of Mauve, Pink and White

Pimpinella major rosea, *with its soft, dusty-rose umbels in late spring, rises above* Cardamine pratensis flore pleno, *discretely pretty with pale pinkish-mauve, very double rosette flowers in masses lasting from early to late spring.* Erythronium *'White Beauty' or* E. dens-canis *will both continue the woodland theme with flowers in white or shades of mauve-pink, while pale lemon narcissus add a sharper hint to the colour scheme, as does an underplanting of* Ranunculus ficaria *'Primrose', a pale yellow celandine. A sprinkling of wood violets and honesty adds the finishing touch to a semi-wild, lightly shaded corner.*

BACK ROW *Pimpinella major rosea.* Perennial. 75cm (30in). *Cardamine pratensis flore pleno.* Perennial. 45cm (18in).
MIDDLE ROW Narcissus. 35-45cm (14-18in). Honesty. 75cm (30in). *Erythronium* 'White Beauty'. 20-30cm (8-12in).
FRONT ROW *E. dens-canis.* 15-25cm (6-10in). *Ranunculus ficaria* 'Primrose'. Perennial. 5cm (2in). Wood violets. 7cm (3in).

**With its ferny foliage and lacy umbels of flowers
Pimpinella major rosea, *a pink cow parsley, makes*
an attractive border plant**

❧ NARCISSUS ❧

The term narcissus is more often than not used to describe the small, sweet scented, cup-shaped varieties, while daffodil tends to be used for the larger, brassy, trumpet types, but, botanically speaking, all are members of the genus *Narcissus* regardless of size or form.

Narcissus pseudo-narcissus, our native Lent lily, and *Narcissus obvallaris,* the so-called Tenby daffodil, grow wild in the country, flowering in copses and fields during early spring. They are both miniature replicas of the large-flowered trumpet daffodils and are frequently used in gardens for naturalising in grass, although they are becoming rather scarce and expensive.

Hybridising did not become fashionable until the latter half of the nineteenth century, since when, however, something like 8,000 registered varieties in an enormous range of size, shape and colour have become available to gardeners today. Few if any of the old Victorian hybrids are still obtainable. 'Horsefieldii', a bicolour raised by John Horsefield in 1845, with white petals and a light yellow trumpet, fringed on the rim, was widely planted before being upstaged by the famous yellow trumpet daffodil 'King Alfred', and may well survive in a few old gardens.

Narcissus 'Rip Van Winkle' is a very unusual double-flowered form in which both the petals and trumpet are split into narrow segments closely resembling a small dandelion. As it grows only 15-20cm (6-8in) tall, it is perhaps best suited for a rockery, where it can be fully appreciated. The *Jonquilla* narcissi are distinguishable by their scent, which is sweet and almost overwhelming at times. They are excellent in the garden or for growing in pots and are perfect for a conservatory, where the yellow scented flowers will breathe the very essence of spring into the house.

Modern varieties abound, and bulb catalogues today can provide endless hours of pleasure, with section after section of choice bulbs listed for the spring garden.

 An early planting in late summer or at the beginning of autumn gives the bulbs a chance to establish a strong root system. Always buy the largest bulbs offered for sale as these will throw up several flower stalks, but avoid the temptation to buy cut-price bulbs offered by nurseries at the end of the season.

■ Unquestionably, daffodils are unsightly after the flowers are gone, but any attempt to tidy up the dying foliage should be avoided, as this is one of the reasons why daffodils do not always settle down in gardens and naturalise as well as they should. The old-fashioned 'double daffs' always look at home in the cottage garden, where they are planted in clumps or groups towards the back of the border, allowing the foliage of other plants to hide the unsightly withering leaves which take an age to disappear.

■ In most soils, narcissi will increase rapidly by means of offsets, which can be detached from the parent bulbs and planted out in a nursery bed until they reach flowering size. This is really the only practical means of propagation, as bulbs grown from seed rarely flower in less than seven years from the date of sowing.

TRUMPET DAFFODILS ────────

○ **'Golden Harvest'**
Extra-large but well-proportioned flowers of a deep golden yellow, which can be forced easily if required.

○ **'Mount Hood'**
Large white perianth with an impressive, pure white trumpet. Increases rapidly and flowers for a long time.

○ **'Dutch Master'**
A really beautiful, golden trumpet daffodil which is also suitable for growing in pots.

○ **'Vincent Van Gogh'**
A handsome, strong golden-yellow trumpet. Named after the colourful artist.

A Blue and White Scheme against a Gold Background

Euonymus 'Emerald 'n Gold' with bright yellow variegated leaves is a perfect acid contrast to Hyacinth 'Blue Magic' with midnight blue flowers. White, lily-flowered tulip 'White Triumphator' rises cool and refined above the foamy flowers of forget-me-nots in pale blue, while Iberis sempervirens provides a solid anchor with its white flowers. Geranium magnificum *will follow with violet-blue flowers in summer. In the meantime, its spring foliage will cover that of the bulbs as they fade.*

BACK ROW *Euonymus* 'Emerald 'n Gold'. Shrub. 60cm (2ft).
MIDDLE ROW *Geranium magnificum*. Perennial. 60cm (2ft). Tulip 'White Triumphator'. 60cm (2ft).

FRONT ROW *Hyacinth* 'Blue Magic'. 20cm (8in). Forget-me-nots. 20cm (8in). *Iberis sempervirens*. Perennial. 23cm (9in).

DOUBLE-FLOWERED NARCISSI

○ **'Dick Wilden'**
An excellent, fully double, golden-yellow daffodil. A sport of 'Carlton', it increases rapidly and has proved to be a good garden plant.

○ **'Texas'**
A large, yellow-flowered variety with vivid orange segments. Best for a sheltered spot in the garden.

○ **'White Lion'**
This narcissus produces a waxy white flower with very broad, overlapping petals. The centre is slightly shaded with soft yellow.

JONQUILLA NARCISSI

○ **'Baby Moon'**
Soft buttercup yellow. Very free-flowering with many flowers per stem. A few of these dainty flowers in a small vase will scent a large room.

○ **'Bell Song'**
A lovely new Jonquilla hybrid which only grows 30cm (12in) tall. The softly-scented flowers are very special because of their white cups.

○ **'Suzy'**
An unusual variety with dark orange cups which contrast vividly with the bright yellow perianth. Each stem bears two to four delightfully fragrant blooms. Late flowering.

NARCISSUS BULBOCODIUM

Known as the yellow 'hoop petticoat'. Small petals with vivid yellow trumpets. Suitable for naturalising in light grass, provided that the soil is moist.

POETICUS NARCISSI

Poeticus narcissi are especially recommended for the more 'wild' corners of the garden where they look at their best. Very fragrant flowers appear in late spring and they are usually the last narcissi to flower.

○ **'Actaea'**
Snow-white, somewhat formal perianth with a bright red-edged cup, and large blooms. One of the best and loveliest of the *Poeticus* varieties.

○ **'Old Pheasant's Eye'** (*Poeticus recurvus*)
An old favourite and virtually the last to flower. Smaller flowers than 'Actaea', with rather 'loose' petals. It does not increase very rapidly but will bloom year after year.

TEN MORE SPRING-FLOWERING BULBS, CORMS AND TUBERS

Chionodoxa
GLORY OF THE SNOW

10-20cm (4-8in). There are several different species which flower at different times from late winter to the end of spring. The leaves are strap-shaped. Flowers mostly different shades of blue but also pink or white, all with a distinctive white eye. Suitable for rockeries, front of border or in grass.

Erythronium dens-canis
DOGS TOOTH VIOLET

10-15cm (4-6in). Leaves mottled grey or brown. Nodding flowers, with reflexed petals in pink, purple or white. Needs a rich, moist soil and some shade.

Fritillaria meleagris
SNAKESHEAD FRITILLARY

10-15cm (4-6in). Narrow, grey-green leaves with slender stems bearing drooping chalice-shaped flower heads in shades of white, pale mauve, mahogany or purple. Some chequered with a deeper colour. Moist, humus-rich shade.

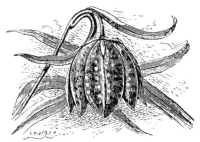

Ipheion uniflorum

15-20cm (6-8in). Narrow, pale green, grass-like leaves which have a garlic smell. Starry violet-blue flowers. For a well-drained, sheltered position.

Leucojum vernum
SNOWFLAKE

20cm (8in). Looks like a robust snowdrop, taller and with a more rounded flower and six petals all the same length, which are tipped with green. Leave undisturbed in moist soil.

Muscari 'Blue Spike'
GRAPE HYACINTH

15-20cm (6-8in). All the muscaris, which look like miniature hyacinths, are easy spring plants for any situation. This one has very fragrant, dense spikes of deep blue, almost globular flowers with a lighter blue mouth edged with white.

M. ambrosiacum

In subtle shades of pale yellow and light grey, with blue leaves and an exquisite perfume.

Ornithogalum
STAR OF BETHLEHEM

30cm (12in). Grassy leaves and heads of starry white flowers with green stripes on the outside of the petals. Hardy in any well-drained soil.

Puschkinia scilloides

10-20cm (4-8in). Very similar to scilla and chionodoxa. Mid-green leaves, and stems with four or five star-like pale blue flowers with a darker blue stripe.

Scilla siberica 'Atrocoerulea'

10-15cm (4-6in). Strap-shaped glossy leaves followed by nodding bell-shaped flowers of an intense blue. Easy.

Tulip 'Queen of Night', on its own here, but lovely against pale or cream-variegated foliage

❧ TULIP ❧

The tulip, despite being linked in our minds with Holland, actually originated in Turkey, where it was grown and nurtured in gardens during the sixteenth century. A clue to its origins lies in its name, which comes from the word for a turban – which it clearly resembles.

Bulbs were first introduced to western Europe during the mid-sixteenth century and the tulip would appear to have made its debut in England in 1577, where it was taken up with great enthusiasm. Parkinson, a generation later in his *Paradisus* of 1629, was able to describe over a hundred varieties and John Rea, in the reign of Charles II recounts over 180, which later became 300.

It was about this time in 1634 that 'Tulipomania' was reaching its peak. In Holland, the craze among all classes to possess bulbs of the striped tulip brought the everyday running of the country to a near standstill. Fortunes were invested in the purchase of collections of bulbs which were sold by weight – calculated in perits, which were less than a grain. A bulb of 'Semper Augustus' the most famous of all Dutch tulips, weighing 200 perits, was reported to have changed hands in 1635 for the staggering sum of 5,500 florins (about £370).

When the bubble eventually burst, pandemonium set in, and tulips which had been worth five and six thousand florins suddenly dropped in value to five or six hundred, with actions for breach of contract threatening to overwhelm the courts. History records that years elapsed before the country recovered from the effects of 'Tulipomania' and returned to normality, but from that time until the present the Dutch have always remained faithful in their love and admiration for tulips.

The immense popularity and success of the tulip continued in England until the middle of the eighteenth century, but then declined through neglect and apathy. It was left to a small band of enthusiasts to continue with the good work, breeding and selecting patiently over the years to perfect the characteristic Old English tulips, which by 1820 were held in greater esteem than the Dutch ones.

The only remaining link with this period is the Wakefield and North of England Tulip Society which was established in 1836, with membership still open today to anyone wishing to preserve our floral heritage. Pilgrimages are made each May to Wakefield for the annual show, where the most sumptuous and exquisite flamed tulips with names like 'Old Sam Barlow', 'Lord Frederick Cavendish' and 'Sir Joseph Paxton' are displayed in shiny, darkest brown beer bottles on purest white tablecloths – a reminder that such matchless beauty has its roots in the hands of the humble artisan growers of old.

Unassuming self-coloured tulips, which were discarded from larger gardens during the clamour for the elaborate striped tulips, came into the possession of cottagers who certainly were in no position to pay large sums for bulbs, and these rather plain, simple tulips have long been known as 'cottage' tulips and are still to be found growing in cottage gardens today.

Not everyone has access to the old bulbs and fewer still the space for a grand display. However, small groups of different types of tulips which are easily obtainable from garden centres everywhere, planted in beds and borders, can provide a striking feature. The tulip season can be extended for some months if varieties with different flowering times are chosen.

Tulips should be planted in late autumn to a depth of at least 15cm (6in). If you require a staggered display then plant the bulbs at varying depths, which will cause the flowers to open at slightly different times. Tulips appreciate a rich soil, but not a soil which is over-heavily manured. They stand relifting and replanting when the foliage is still green almost as well as snowdrops. Propagate by means of offsets removed when cleaning the bulbs in summer and grow on in a nursery bed of light soil.

SINGLE EARLY TULIPS

○ **'General de Wet'**
A beautiful tulip in a lovely shade of golden-orange which looks particularly effective when grown with *Muscari armeniacum,* blue violets or forget-me-nots. Very fragrant.

○ **'Diana'**
A pure white variety which is excellent in the garden or for pots.

○ **'Bellona'**
A first class, pure yellow, very fragrant tulip.

DOUBLE EARLY TULIPS

○ **'Schoonoord'**
Probably the best white double tulip, it looks lovely planted with *Muscari armenicum.*

○ **'Carlton'**
A fine, long-lasting variety, with deep scarlet blooms, it is ideal for bedding.

SINGLE LATE TULIPS

○ **'Queen of Night'**
Virtually black, this tulip is the darkest of all, with large blooms on particularly sturdy stems.

○ **'Bleu Aimable'**
Frequently described in catalogues as the tulip with the finest shade of lavender-mauve. The beauty of the flower increases as it develops, and it is recommended to be grown with yellow flowers.

○ **'Sweet Harmony'**
A striking combination of colours: lemon-yellow with an ivory white edge. A perfect tulip for growing with 'Bleu Aimable'.

DOUBLE LATE TULIPS

○ **'Mount Tacoma'**
An old favourite with strong, long-lasting, snow-white flowers.

○ **'Angelique'**
Fragrant, delicate pale pink flowers, becoming lighter at the edges. A strong-growing, long-lasting tulip.

○ **'Carnaval de Nice'**
Pure white flowers, striped reddish-pink, fading away to the inside, with beautifully variegated leaves.

TULIPA SPECIES

Mostly small-flowered, the *Tulipa* species and hybrids are ideal for growing in rockeries, along path edges or in pots in a cool greenhouse.

○ *Kaufmanniana* **Type**
The original 'Waterlily' tulip. The creamy white petals with golden-yellow bases are tinged purple on the outside. Very early flowering.

○ *T. bakeri* **'Lilac Wonder'**
A dainty little tulip with lilac-mauve flowers. The inside is rose-lilac with a large yellow circular base.

○ *T. pulchella violacea*
Vivid purple-violet with yellow centre. An early-flowering tulip which is ideal for the rock garden.

SUMMER

For maybe three or four weeks, spring links hands with summer in the cottage garden. The sunshine is hot but the atmosphere still has the vitality of spring. The foliage of trees and shrubs is a lively mixture of gold, bronze and blue-toned greens, and, though in near-full leaf, there is a refreshing play of sunlight and shadow beneath the canopies of apple, cherry and plum.

A Seasonal Picture

At the beginning of summer, nights are still cool, and in the mornings the lawn is glistening with dew. The risk of a late frost is a receding anxiety, though the effects at this time of the year can be devastating. Gradually, almost imperceptibly, the last narcissus to flower, sweetly scented Old Pheasant's Eye, gives way to the first roses of summer, as the ferny-leaved 'Canary Bird' almost sparkles with daffodil-yellow blooms.

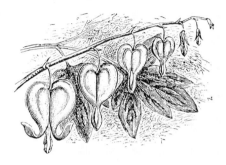

Elegant lily-flowered tulips rise above the dainty lockets of pink and white dicentras, while fantastically feathered 'parrots' flaunt their colours against a sober background of box or yew. Weigela and deutzias have twigs bowed with a profusion of red, pink and white blossom, and ceanothus, mists the cottage walls with blue. Honeysuckle fills the air from twilight to early morning with its sharp-sweet perfume to attract nocturnal moths. In front of a cornus, delicately clothed in pale green and creamy white, an old-fashioned double paeony spreads its fingered leaves, topped by crimson blooms filled to bursting with satin-textured petals. Round its feet, forget-me-nots and lily of the valley weave a tapestry of blue, white and green – but the opulence of paeonies is short lived. All too soon they bow their heads to a summer storm, strewing their thousand petals on the ground. Oriental poppies, too, blaze in brief splendour and tall bearded irises fare little better but, like paeonies and poppies, their dramatic display compensates for their brief appearance.

In the deepening shade beneath the trees, foxglove spires rise above the apple-scented foliage of *Geranium macrorrhizum* and the green lace of ferns. Martagon lilies flourish here, their turkscap blooms borne elegantly on straight stems, and, at the pathside, the neat evergreen rosettes of London Pride carry a thin mist of tiny pinkish white flowers. Hostas, their leaves edged with yellow or white, Gladwyn irises with green and striped blades, and the yellow-leaved meadowsweet contribute to a gentle colour scheme that looks both cool and refreshing on breathlessly hot summer days.

Each season in the cottage garden has its own spectrum of scents, but summer is supreme. Flower perfumes drift on the air, some, like honeysuckle, jasmine, and night-scented stock, releasing their fragrance after dusk, while others need the sun's warmth to give of their best. Lilies and philadelphus, phlox and stocks, pinks and carnations and, of course, roses, all make their contribution to the pot pourri of scents that is the signature of summer in the cottage garden.

In the sunny borders, spikes of violet-blue salvias dazzle against yellow achilleas or pale pink lavateras, and clouds of misty-mauve nepeta mingle with pink and blue geraniums, grey-leaved stachys and the lemon-yellow daisies of anthemis. Tall spires of verbascum, woolly white and studded with yellow flowers, tower above a sea of blue love-in-a-mist, and orange marigolds crowd the feet of red day lilies. But the rose is the queen of the summer garden. With blooms as full as crinoline skirts or with clusters of dainty single flowers no larger than apple blossom, the roses weave their special magic through the long summer days.

SEASONAL TASKS

FOR SUMMER

Plant out dahlias and tender bedding plants when danger of frosts has passed, in late spring to early summer. Use *Helichrysum petiolatum*, *Convolvulus sabatius*, pelargoniums and fuchsias to fill gaps in borders as well as in tubs and window boxes.

Sow hardy and half-hardy annuals where they are intended to flower and remember to keep well watered in dry, hot and sunny weather. In early summer, sow biennials such as wallflowers, foxgloves and stocks to flower the following year. Most perennials can also be sown outside in early to midsummer, though they should be sown in pots rather than directly into their flowering positions.

Prune and feed early-flowering shrubs when the flowers are over, to encourage strong new growth. Remove old, weak and twiggy stems. Take time over pruning – remember you are shaping the shrub, so cut to achieve an attractive balanced framework. Try to avoid an unnatural 'beachball' effect or an ugly square.

Watch roses of all kinds for signs of mildew, blackspot or rust and spray with the appropriate fungicide at the very first signs of trouble.

Take cuttings of shrubs and climbers. Softwood cuttings are taken in early to midsummer, semi-ripe cuttings from mid- to late summer. Most cuttings can be taken either with a heel or just below a leaf joint (nodal cuttings). An exception to the rule is the clematis family, where cuttings are taken between leaf joints (internodal). All cuttings should be inserted in a mixture of two parts sand or perlite and one part peat (or peat alternative) and kept covered with glass or plastic to maintain a moist atmosphere for several days, or until the leaves of the cuttings do not wilt when exposed to the air for a few hours. Rooting occurs in three to twelve weeks, depending on species and conditions. Some cuttings form a callus but do not develop roots until the following spring. Do not despair! Patience is often rewarded.

Deadhead roses and border perennials throughout the season to keep them looking fresh and tidy, and to encourage a continued supply of flowers. Hardy geraniums that bloom early can be cut to the ground after flowering. This will promote fresh foliage growth, forming a neat mound which will still look attractive for the rest of the season. After any cutting back of this sort – as with hard pruning of shrubs – always sprinkle some general quick-release fertiliser round the plant.

Support tall-growing or flop-prone plants. The earlier this is done the better, as it will result in the plants growing through their supports in a natural manner, but some tall flowers such as dahlias, delphiniums and lilies also need stakes for individual stems at flowering time.

Collect seeds for sowing in autumn or the following spring. Most umbellifers are best sown when fresh, and this also applies to many daisies. If kept, they are less likely to germinate. Other seeds should be dried off (away from direct sunlight) and stored in a cool, dry, dark place until they are sown in spring.

Look out for interesting seedheads to dry for winter vases indoors. Most will dry perfectly well if they are tied together in small bunches and hung upside down in a dry, airy room or shed, away from direct sunlight. If, however, you want to bleach items like teasels, foxgloves, aquilegias and grasses, then sunlight is a help, but make sure that they have dried sufficiently to keep their shape, as sunlight on freshly picked material, even seedheads, can cause them to wither slightly. Cut stems as long as possible. It is easier to shorten them to the length you want than to wire them to make them long enough.

Sprays of beech to be preserved in glycerine and water should be cut in late summer, before the leaves begin to turn. Cotoneaster, mahonia, laurel and other evergreens to be preserved by the same method can be cut whenever the foliage is mature. Eucalyptus foliage is particularly successful when treated this way.

SUMMER-FLOWERING
SHRUBS AND CLIMBERS

There are many flowering shrubs for the summer cottage garden, notably philadelphus, kolkwitzia, deutzia, weigela and viburnum, as well as numerous cistuses and hebes. Some of the most common summer-flowering shrubs for the cottage garden are described below.

SHRUBS FOR THE COTTAGE GARDEN

Cytisus x *praecox*
WARMINSTER BROOM

1.5x1.5m (5x5ft). Deciduous. Cascading sprays of fragrant, creamy white, sweet pea-like flowers on bright green stems in early summer. Good hanging over a wall. Likes a well-drained, poor soil. Yellower and white-flowered forms available.

Deutzia

1.5x1.5m (5x5ft). Deciduous. Graceful arching shrub with hawthorn-like fragrance. Many species and cultivars. 'Magicien' has lilac petals edged white and striped purple on the reverse. 'Mont Rose' has rose-coloured flowers, while those of 'Perle Rose' are paler. 'Compacta' is smaller with fragrant white flowers. Cut back flowering stems by 50 per cent immediately after flowering to keep these shrubs in shape. Sun and well-drained soil.

Kolkwitzia amabilis
BEAUTY BUSH

1.5x1.5m (5x5ft) Deciduous. Lives up to its popular name. Bell-shaped flowers in pale pink with a yellow throat, peeling bark and dark green oval leaves. Seems sprawling at first but don't despair, when taller it displays a fine arching habit. Sunny position, well-drained soil. Prune like deutzia.

Philadelphus
MOCK ORANGE

Deciduous. Wonderful choice of single or double flowers, tall or compact growth. All are very fragrant, particularly 'Belle Etoile'

2.4x2.1m (8x7ft) with creamy white single flowers splashed purple at the base. 'Manteau d'Hermine' is a small compact shrub 90cmx1.2m (3x4ft) with double, creamy white flowers. *P. coronarius* 'Aureus' has yellow young foliage. Prune as for deutzia.

Viburnum opulus 'Sterile' ('Roseum')
GUELDER ROSE OR SNOWBALL TREE

Deciduous. With lilac, a truly cottage garden shrub, probably introduced in the sixteenth century. This is a big shrub with coarse leaves and balls of sterile white flowers. To enjoy gleaming red berries as well choose *V. o.* 'Notcutt's Variety'. 'Compactum', which grows to 2.4m (8ft), is the best garden variety. Easy, but best in moisture-retentive soil.

Myrtus
MYRTLE

Evergreen. Another old favourite, dedicated to Venus, hence its use in wedding bouquets. Fragrant white flowers followed by purple berries with small glossy leaves are the characteristics of *M. communis*, the most common species. *M. luma* 'Glanleam Gold' has cream-edged leaves. All are tender and need winter protection, but grow well at the seaside.

A mixed planting of roses, phlomis, aconitums, paeonies, geraniums and campanulas

❧ ROSA ❧

Roses, christened by the Greek poetess Sappho the 'Queen of Flowers', are amongst the oldest and most highly treasured cultivated ornamental plants grown in gardens today, with more poetical fancies and legends woven around them than any other plant. As John Gerard wrote in his *Herball*:

> . . . *the Rose doth deserve the chieftest and most principal place among all floures whatsoever; beeing not only esteemed for his beautie, vertues, and his fragrant and odoriferous smell, but also because it is the honour and ornament of our English Scepter.*

History records that the idea of the rose as the emblem and national flower of England seems to have originated at the time of the Wars of the Roses during the reign of Henry VI, but it is probable that the symbolism goes much further back than this, for we find Pliny doubting whether the name 'Albion' referred to the white cliffs of England or to the white roses which were already known to grow in such abundance there.

Some roses are grown for their foliage – *Rosa glauca*, slate-grey leaved in shade or pink-flushed in the sun, *R. rubiginosa*, with apple-scented leaves, and *R. primula*, its foliage incense scented – but most are still treasured for their flowers and their fragrance, even though many bloom only for a month at midsummer. In hot and sunny tones, cool pastels and snowy white, rich crimson velvet or faded purple, there are roses to suit every colour scheme and to blend or contrast with the shrubs and perennials in the borders, or drape walls, fences and arbours with flowering garlands.

In cottage gardens, the older roses seem especially appropriate. Their blooms lack the rigid formality and sculptured elegance of modern varieties, and their habit of growth is less stiff and angular. In crimson and pink with blue geraniums or nepeta, purple sage and furry grey stachys, or in white with alchemilla forming a midsummer mist of tiny lime-yellow flowers beneath their arching twigs, they are completely at ease. Roses frame the cottage doorway with a traditional welcome, even the shabby old shed and modern concrete garage are no longer eyesores when hidden beneath a smother of fragrant rambler roses.

Old-fashioned roses need little in the way of pruning except, of course, to keep the bushes in shape and to remove dead or diseased wood and overcrowded canes after flowering. Whenever possible they should be planted where they can receive at least six hours of sunlight each day, and if there is a choice of morning or afternoon sun, choose morning. A deep, fertile, well-drained soil will pay dividends. Avoid planting too close to existing trees and shrubs which will compete for water and nutrients.

Before planting, the roots of the rose should be dipped in a bucket of water. Ensure that the planting hole is sufficiently large to take all the roots, well spread out, and that the roses are planted at a depth 2.5cm (1in) deeper than the point at which the top growth meets the root growth. Replace the soil and firm in well with the feet. Avoid planting when the soil is very wet.

GALLICA ROSES

The oldest rose in cultivation is *Rosa gallica*, the Apothecary's Rose or the red rose of the House of Lancaster, known to the Persians in 1000BC.

Rosa gallica has large, semi-double pink 'cupped' flowers 7.5-9cm (3-3.5in) wide which open to reveal golden stamens. The rich fragrance is even more pronounced when dried, and in medieval times it was widely grown for its medicinal qualities, a mainstay of a flourishing industry centred around the French town of Provins, hence its other name of the Provins Rose. It was used in syrups, preserves and powders which were believed to cure many and diverse ailments.

○ **R. g. 'Versicolor'**

Rosa gallica 'Versicolor', perhaps better known as *Rosa mundi* or Rosemonde, is a sport from *Rosa gallica officinalis* and one of the showiest of the old roses with crimson flowers splashed and striped with white, and first recorded in 1581. Said to be named after Fair Rosamund, the mistress of Henry II, *Rosa mundi* is an enchanting rose and perfect for the cottage garden. The bush is compact and upright, about 1.2x1.2m (4x4ft), and makes an excellent low hedging plant, although regrettably, it will almost certainly have to be sprayed for mildew.

ALBA ROSES

Rosa alba, the white Rose of York, is another antiquarian rose, and a great survivor even under difficult conditions. It makes an abundant display of somewhat flat, single white flowers flushed pink towards the centre.

It was not until the early nineteenth century, when rose breeding really got into its stride, that innumerable splendid new hybrids started to be raised. At that time, whole gardens were often devoted solely to roses and were called the 'rosary' or the 'rosarium'. Rose beds of every shape and form were filled with roses of types which required no pruning, and were allowed to grow naturally to great effect. Varieties with particularly floppy stems would be grown in circular beds edged with wirework, the stems pinned to the ground to create the effect of a basket of flowers.

Fortunately, despite a long period of unpopularity, many of these old-fashioned roses have survived and are once more widely grown, particularly by today's cottage gardeners who fully appreciate the delicacy of their velvety petals, their fragrance and their elegance.

○ *Rosa alba* **'Great Maiden's Blush'**

A very fragrant, very old rose with fresh blush-pink double blooms which tend to be slightly muddled in the centre. It grows to 1.8x1.5m (6x5ft) or more, and is one of the last of the Albas to flower, waiting until

PLANT ASSOCIATIONS

A Grouping for Fragrance

Roses such as, hybrid musks, rugosas or others, plus R. rubiginosa *with its apple-scented foliage, are the backbone of the summer scented border. Honeysuckle planted over a fence or up a post (especially the common honeysuckle of our hedgerows,* Lonicera periclymenum*), will perfume the garden for most of the summer. The heady smell of* Philadelphus *'Belle Etoile', whose single white flowers have a maroon blotch at the base of the petals, carries well on the night air, as does that of the two smaller Mock Oranges, 'Sybille' and 'Manteau d'Hermine', which has double white flowers and a slight pineapple fragrance. Later, among the shrubs, the heavily scented trumpets of* Lilium regale *or* L. candidum *take over and* Nepeta *'Six Hills Giant' and phlox rise above the aromatic herbs at the path's edge or round a seat, along with rosemary,* Artemisia abrotanum, *lavender, thymes and chamomile, and Eau de Cologne mint. For evening fragrance, night-scented stock and nicotiana will fill the gaps in the border, and for a warm, sheltered spot,* Lippia citriodora *(syn.* Aloysia triphylla) *the wonderfully fragrant lemon verbena, and the tender* Thymus mastichina *can be planted in a tub.*

BACK ROW *R. rubiginosa.* 2.4x2.4m (8x8ft). Bright pink single flowers in early summer, orange-scarlet hips. Hybrid musks vary in height from 1.2-1.8m (4-6ft). 'Buff Beauty', 'Cornelia', 'Penelope', 'Felicia' and 'Ballerina' are a few of the best. Rugosa roses generally reach around 1.5-2.1m (5-7ft). 'Roseraie de l'Hay' has double, deep mauve-pink flowers and 'Frau Dagmar Hartopp', soft clear pink blooms. *Lonicera periclymenum.* 4.5-6m (15-20ft). Late summer flowers, pale yellow flushed pinky-purple and red berries. *Philadelphus* 'Belle Etoile'. 1.8-2.4x2.4-3m (6-8x8-10ft).
MIDDLE ROW *Philadelphus* 'Sybille'. 1.2mx90cm (4x3ft) with single white flowers, blotched purple at

base and 'Manteau d'Hermine'. 1.2mx90cm (4x3ft). *Nepeta* 'Six Hills Giant'. 90cm-1.2m (3-4ft). *Lilium regale.* 1.2-1.8m (4-6ft). *L. candidum.* 1.5-1.8m (5-6ft). *Phlox maculata.* 90cm (3ft). Mauve and white flowers. 'Omega' is white with a violet eye. *P. paniculata.* 1.2m (4ft). Many different colours and named varieties. Nicotiana, 60cm (2ft). Night-scented stock. 45cm (18in).
AT PATH'S EDGE: Rosemary, low growing types. 15-90cm (6in-3ft). *Artemisia abrotanum.* 60-90cm (2-3ft) or less if hard pruned in the spring. Sub-shrub, grown for its feathery grey-green foliage. Lavender, see page 79 for low growing types. Eau de Cologne mint. 30-75cm (1-2½ft). Thymes. 5-23cm (2-9in). Chamomile. 15-23cm (6-9in).

fairly late in mid-season. Although not recurring, it does flower for some time.

Its long history no doubt accounts for the many names it has been given over the years: 'Maiden's Blush', 'La Séduisante', 'La Virginale', 'Incarnata', 'La Royale' and 'Cuisse de Nymphe Emue'. It is excellent for an informal hedge or as part of the shrub border.

○ *R. a.* 'Koenigen von Danemarck'
Dating from 1826 and often appearing in nursery lists under the translation of 'Queen of Denmark', this is one of the finest of the old roses. The carmine buds open to reveal large, beautifully formed, quartered flowers of a soft rose pink with a button eye. The grey-green leaves provide the perfect foil and the rose has a sweet scent.

Growing to about 1.5x1.2m (5x4ft), 'Koenigen von Danemarck' is excellent for a small garden and will grow and bloom in partial shade as well as sun.

○ **R. 'Alba Maxima'**
Commonly known as the Great Double White and as the Jacobite Rose of Bonnie Prince Charlie, this is one of the first roses to flower, and the rose most frequently found in old cottage gardens. It forms a huge 2x2.4m (7x8ft) shrub with full, slightly untidy, double creamy-white flowers with blush tints in the folds of the petals.

This tough, very fragrant rose has a good crop of oval hips in the autumn and will grow almost anywhere, including against a cool, shady wall.

MUSK ROSES

○ **R. centifolia 'Muscosa' or 'Old Pink Moss'**
The original moss rose, introduced in 1727 and better known as the 'Common Moss'. The buds and stems have the heavy mossing which is typical of the type, and the clear pink flowers, globular at first, later

Twentieth-century English roses like 'Alchemist' have the appearance of old-fashioned roses but bloom continuously throughout the summer

opening flat, have a wonderful fragrance. It grows 90cm-1.2m (3-4ft) tall, and forms a graceful and moderately vigorous bush with very thorny canes.

○ **R. c. 'Gloire des Mousseuses'**
This moss rose has exceptionally large double flowers of up to 13cm (5in) across with abundant, light green mossing. The light to medium pink flowers have a faint lavender tint and are long-lasting, although non-recurring. Leaves are a soft, dull and light green and the shrub, which grows to 1.5x90cm (5x3ft), is disease-resistant and winter hardy.

○ **R. c. 'William Lobb'**
The 'Old Velvet Moss', introduced in 1855, has dark crimson flowers which quickly fade to violet-grey. Growing to 1.8x1.8m (6x6ft), this tall robust rose is probably best at the back of the border mingling with other shrubs. Plenty of moss and a wonderful fragrance.

DAMASK ROSES

○ **R. damascena 'Madame Hardy'**
Raised by the superintendent of the Luxembourg Gardens in Paris in 1832, 'Madame Hardy' is a most beautiful white rose and has been described as 'exquisite', 'sumptuous', 'elegant', 'unsurpassable' and even 'ravishing'.

The flowers, which open cupped, become flat with the outermost petals curving backwards, and have a suggestion of lemon in the fragrance. This is a vigorous, upright bushy shrub growing to 1.8x1.5m (6x5ft) with moderately thorny canes and fresh-looking bright green leaves.

○ **R. d. 'Celsiana'**
This lovely old-fashioned rose has clusters of large semi-double flowers of freshest blush pink with golden stamens which emerge from dark buds. Depicted by the artists Van Huysum and Redouté, it was first grown in Holland and later introduced into France by a rose breeder named Cels.

'Celsiana' makes a graceful upright shrub with grey-green foliage growing to 1.5x1.2m (5x4ft) and is an excellent rose in every way.

○ **R. d. 'York and Lancaster'**
The blooms have different coloured petals of white and rose pink held in elegant sprays not, unfortunately, borne in any great profusion and not particularly showy, but worth growing for its supposed connection with the Wars of the Roses. A vigorous, upright plant 1.8x2.4m (6x8ft) which requires a good soil.

PORTLAND ROSES

The Portland roses are closely related to the Damask roses, but flower through the summer and autumn, forming a much more compact shrub with the flower held very close to the foliage.

○ **'Rose de Resht'**
A good, repeating Portland rose with small, neat, very full flowers of dark crimson-pink, later turning to lilac and mauve. A short, bushy plant 90x75cm (3x2½ft).

○ **'Comte de Chambord'**
A small shrub with plenty of foliage, producing flat, quartered flowers of bright, warm pink with a good fragrance. It grows to about 120cmx90cm (4x3ft).

❧ CLIMBING ROSES ❧

○ **Rosa 'Zéphirine Drouhin'**
Called the 'Thornless Rose', this is an old Bourbon rose over a hundred years old, one of the best and most continuous-flowering climbers. 'Zéphirine Drouhin' has large, semi-double, vivid-pink flowers of good shape and form with a wonderful perfume – and no thorns. It grows to about 3.6m (12ft) but can be pruned to provide an excellent hedge.

○ **R. 'Gloire de Dijon'**
An old cottage garden favourite introduced in 1850, 'Gloire de Dijon' has large, globular, golden-buff

The tall-growing moss rose 'William Lobb' makes a rich background for deep blue campanulas

flowers opening cupped and later flat. It flowers early and unendingly during the season, has a rich fragrance, is perfectly hardy and will reach 4.5m (15ft).

○ **R. 'Cécile Brunner – Climbing'**

A particularly good climbing sport of the miniature (polyantha pompom) 'Cécile Brunner' or 'The Sweetheart Rose' which has blush-pink flowers of exquisite Hybrid Tea formation slightly larger than a thimble. It is a profuse bloomer in midsummer, with the odd spray appearing later. The flowers are set off by its good, rather pointed, red-tinted leaves. Up to 6m (20ft) or more.

❧ LONICERA ❧

Lonicera periclymenum is the botanical name for the common honeysuckle. A deciduous native climber of our hedgerows and woodlands, its scent in midsummer is one of the joys of the English countryside: once inhaled, never forgotten.

There are a number of excellent cultivated varieties, even more decorative than the native form, including *L. p.* 'Belgica', the early Dutch honeysuckle, and *L. p.* 'Serotina', the late Dutch variety, both grown in Britain since the eighteenth century.

Linnaeus named the genus in honour of Adam Lonicer, 1528-86, a German botanist. Honeysuckle was a name much used in the Middle Ages for various plants whose flowers yielded honey or nectar, and red and white clovers were often referred to as honeysuckles – as in the description by a seventeenth-century writer of a field as being full of 'honie suckles both red and white'.

Woodbine is another old common name for honeysuckle, perhaps derived from a former name, woodbynde, referring no doubt to the twining nature of the climber as it binds itself around stems and branches. In old cottage gardens it would almost certainly have been grown from cuttings taken while the cottager was on a summer walk through country lanes and woods, and used to grow up into trees or ramble over walls, fences or archways.

 Like clematis, honeysuckles appreciate their feet in the shade and their head in the sun, and are trouble-free if given a well-drained soil. A light pruning and thinning out of old wood may be necessary to keep the plants healthy and vigorous and older specimens will benefit from an occasional top dressing of well decayed farmyard manure or some other organic equivalent. Pot-grown plants can be planted out at almost any time as long as they are kept well watered during the settling in period, but autumn and spring are probably the best.

○ *Lonicera periclymenum* **'Belgica'**

This makes a rather bushy plant. The flowers are reddish-purple, yellow on the inside of the petals and with reddish stems. It flowers in late spring and early summer, with another flush later on in the season. Flowers are followed by large berries, and often berries and flowers are seen together.

○ *L. p.* **'Serotina'**

Very similar, although a much stronger grower than 'Belgica', *L. p.* 'Serotina' has flowers of a slightly deeper shade of purple from midsummer till early autumn. It also produces large berries, often seen with the flowers.

○ *L. p.* **'Graham Thomas'**

Discovered in a Warwickshire hedgerow in the 1960s and named after the distinguished plantsman Graham Stuart Thomas, *L. p.* 'Graham Thomas' is a prolific and fragrant honeysuckle with creamy-white flowers that age to yellow, flowering through the summer into early autumn. This choice honeysuckle, once quite rare, is now more widely available.

○ *L. japonica*

A rampant evergreen or semi-evergreen honeysuckle, (depending on the severity of the winter) *L. japonica* has fragrant yellowish flowers which come in pairs in the leaf axils and are freely produced from early summer until early autumn. It was introduced from Japan in 1806 and is particularly useful for clothing unsightly outbuildings or high fences. Quickly covering a wide area it reaches up to 9m (30ft). The long shoots fall to the ground when they have nothing to twine around, rooting where they fall and sending up new stems in search of support.

○ *L. j.* **'Halliana'**

Like the species, this is a rampant climber but is probably better known in gardens. It has an abundance of smallish, sweetly scented white flowers which pale to a creamy yellow and are often still in bloom in late autumn. Because of its vigorous growth 'Halliana' should be hard pruned each spring, the shoots cut back to the previous year's growth.

○ *L. j.* **'Aureoreticulata'**

This is the pretty variegated form with brightly netted, golden-yellow variegated foliage, and the odd habit of producing oak-shaped leaves early in the season on old stems. It has small cream flowers which are produced along the stems and, although inconspicuous, they are delightfully scented. In the autumn, the foliage takes on an attractive bronze and pinkish tinge.

○ *L. sempervirens*

The so-called Trumpet Honeysuckle, *L. sempervirens,* is a handsome evergreen climber, introduced from the United States in 1656 and cultivated by the famous botanist, John Tradescant the Younger, in that year. It is, however, tender and more at home in mild, frost-free or coastal climates where, given the protection of a sheltered wall or fence, it will make a great show in the first half of the summer. The evergreen leaves are a rich bluish-green against which the vivid orange-scarlet tubular, but unscented, flowers show up superbly. In bloom from early summer, it is well worth growing if it can be found a sheltered home.

*P*ERENNIALS

❧ ALCEA ROSEA ❧

Alcea or *Althaea rosea*, the stately hollyhock, was for many years a feature of cottage gardens, as natural to the garden as thatch to the cottage, towering against whitewashed walls and almost reaching the eaves, as pretty as a picture.

Gerard wrote that the 'Hollihocke' was sown in gardens almost everywhere in his day, and called it 'the tame or garden mallow' since it was a magnificent relative of the common mallow. During the mid-nineteenth century the plant had become so popular that it rivalled the dahlia in the number of hybrids available.

One of the champions of the great age of the hollyhock was Mr W. Chater of Saffron Walden who, during the 1840s and 50s, grew a whole acre of hollyhocks in his garden. Named varieties of his exhibition strain included 'Model of Perfection', white with chocolate ground, 'Commander-in-Chief', towering some 3m (10ft), 'Attraction', elegantly veined puce and silver, 'Black Prince', sable-black, 'Pallida', lilac, 'Magnum Bonum', a rich glossy maroon, and many others. There were single and double varieties and some were striped.

Tragedy, however, overcame the plant towards the end of the nineteenth century when rust disease struck, wiping out all these hybrids and decimating whole nurseries overnight. As a result, interest in hollyhocks plummeted and almost none of the enormous number of named varieties is grown today, although seed strains from the firm of Chater can still be found, including 'Chater's Double' with double paeony-like flowers in a wide range of colours including yellows, scarlets and maroons.

Attempts were made during the last century to grow *Alcea rosea* as a commercial crop. A vast tract of 147 acres of land at Llanasa, near Flint in North Wales, was planted with hollyhocks in 1814 with, presumably, the intention of converting the fibres of the stalks into thread-like hemp or flax. The venture, however, was not a success, but what a gorgeous sight it must have been.

In the United States, children would often fashion dolls from the flowers. Their elegant 'ladies' wore skirts of the downturned silky flower heads, while the heads were made from opening buds like a turban, or from the flat seed pods, attached with a toothpick.

Hollyhocks are relatively short-lived perennials, but because rust disease is still a problem they are very often grown today as biennials or

Grown from a hedgerow cutting, a honeysuckle covers the wall of a cottage in Aldford, Cheshire

annuals. The stems, which grow to as much as 3m (10ft), are clad with 1.2-1.5m (4-5ft) of flowers throughout midsummer, forming a magnet for bees which often become intoxicated as they over-indulge in the rich nectar.

Hollyhocks require a sunny garden position and enjoy a rich soil and regular watering. Vigilance and fungicides will keep the plants free from rust disease.

Sow seeds under glass in early spring or in a shady border outside in late spring to early summer. Sow thinly, and if it is impossible to get the plants in their flowering positions before winter, it is best to pot on the seedlings and winter them in a cold frame. In the spring, cuttings of fine specimens can be taken from the young shoots which grow from the base of the flower stems, and then inserted singly in small pots.

○ *Alcea rosea 'Nigra'*
Flowers of this most unusual strain of hollyhock are a very dark shade of maroon, almost black and guaranteed to provoke some comment.
○ *A. r. 'Majorette'*
Dwarf hollyhocks with double, lacy blooms up to 10cm (4in) across, in glorious shades including crimson, lavender, pink, rose and salmon, bringing a mass of colour to the garden. 60-75cm (2-2½ft).
○ *A. rugosa*
A splendid plant with long spikes of clear lemon-yellow flowers with a darker centre, multiple stems to 1.8m (6ft) and less susceptible to rust disease.

PLANT ASSOCIATIONS
A Romantic Group for Colour and Fragrance

In front of Philadelphus 'Belle Etoile', *a group of soft pink and white roses combine with spiky nepeta and lavender and the grey and silver foliage of purple sage and* Artemisia 'Powis Castle'. *Scented* Lilium regale *rises above pink and blue aquilegias and blue geraniums, underplanted with* Campanula carpatica, Alchemilla mollis *in lime yellow with soft velvet foliage, and furry grey* Stachys lanata. *Just behind them astrantias, with pincushion flowers in pinkish-white, bloom in a mist of gypsophila.*

BACK ROW Philadelphus 'Belle Etoile'. 1.8-2.4x2.4-3m (6-8x8-10ft).
MIDDLE ROW Some pink roses: 'Fantin Latour'. 1.5m (5ft). Soft pink; 'Comte de Chambord'. 1.5m (5ft). Rose pink; 'Stanwell Perpetual'. 1.2m (4ft). Blush pink; 'Petite de Hollande'. 1.2-1.5m (4-5ft). Pale pink. Some white roses: 'Boule de Neige'. 1.8m (6ft); 'Iceberg'. 1.5m (5ft); 'White Wings'. 75cm (2½ft). Nepeta 'Six Hills Giant'. 60cm-1.2m (2-4ft). N. grandiflora. 60-75cm (2-2½ft). Lilium regale. 1.2-1.8m (4-6ft). Aquilegia vulgaris. 90cm (3ft). See text for varieties.

Geranium pratense. 60cm (2ft). Blue geranium. See text for others. Artemisia 'Powis Castle'. Sub-shrub. 90cm (3ft). Some salvias: Salvia haematodes. 60cm (2ft). Hardy, purple flowers all summer; Salvia nemorosa. 90cm (3ft). Violet-blue flowers; named varieties like 'East Friedland' and 'Lubecca' are smaller.
FRONT ROW Astrantia major. 60cm (2ft). Gypsophila paniculata. 60cm-1.2m (2-4ft). Campanula carpatica. 30cm (1ft). In colours from white to deep violet. Alchemilla mollis. 45cm (18in). Stachys lanata. 30cm (1ft).

An interesting combination of deep blue **Aquilegia alpina** *and creamy* **Aconitum 'Ivorine'** *in early summer*

❧ AQUILEGIA ❧

Aquilegias are old-fashioned, traditional cottage garden favourites, fondly known as Granny's Bonnets, or Columbines, because of a fancied resemblance of the flowers to the shape of doves. These graceful plants with dainty colourings flower from late spring to early summer. Their charming display is aptly described by John Clare:

> *The columbines, stone blue or deep night brown,*
> *Their honeycomb-like blossoms hanging down;*
> *Each cottage garden's fond adopted child,*
> *Though heaths still claim them where they yet*
> *grow wild.*

A. *vulgaris,* the common Columbine, and all its various forms, is the species most likely to be found in cottage gardens. It is one of our most beautiful native wild flowers, often depicted in medieval paintings and illuminations and figured in heraldry.

Single forms in a variety of colours, sometimes bi-coloured, and delightful double forms, were all popular by the late sixteenth century, as were the so-called 'starry columbines' in which the petals were suppressed, leaving a flat, star-shaped flower whose modern equivalent is A. *clematidiflora.* Striped forms were all the rage in the seventeenth century, remaining popular until well into the nineteenth. Rare today, they are only seen in a few enthusiasts' collections.

Following the colonisation of North America, new species arrived from the New World, and by the beginning of the nineteenth century all sorts of crosses were being made. Victorian aquilegia hybrids with their long spurs and narrow flowers still turn up in old cottage gardens.

Aquilegias will grow in almost any soil and situation but require good drainage. Not even the strongest and hardiest of the species will thrive on damp soil. Once established they may be left to their own devices, although an annual mulch of well-rotted manure will pay dividends. They are easily grown from seed sown during the spring in boxes in a cold frame or in a made-up bed of light sandy soil in a shady border. They cross with ease and interesting forms appear from time to time in the garden. These crosses, like any other special aquilegia, may be increased by division.

○ *Aquilegia vulgaris* 'Nora Barlow'

A curious old variety unlike any other columbine with stiff leafy stems carrying heads of tight, fully double flowers in which red, pink and green are charmingly blended. Possibly an ancient type of 'rose' columbine, it was grown for many years in the garden at 'Boswells', one time home of Nora Barlow, the granddaughter of Charles Darwin. Seed was given to Alan Bloom of Bressingham by a friend of Nora's with the suggestion that it be commercially marketed, but only on condition that the aquilegia was named 'Nora Barlow'.

○ **A. v. 'Adelaide Addison'**

Similar to an old medieval illustration, but with a modern name, 'Adelaide Addison' is a handsome, blue and white double-flowered aquilegia opening from creamy-green buds. It will eventually make quite a large clump growing 1m (3½ft) in height.

○ **A. v. 'Nivea' ('Munstead White')**

A vigorous, pure white form with large, beautiful flowers selected by Gertrude Jekyll from early white forms.

○ **A. v. variegata**

A variegated form with good, yellow variegated foliage. Look for the white and blue flowered forms rather than the indifferent pink one, the flowers of which are probably best cut off.

○ **A. canadensis**

An old American cottage garden plant, popular throughout the eighteenth and nineteenth centuries, with small lemon-yellow and red flowers, requiring a position in full sun and growing to 60cm (2ft). A number of columbines are known by this name, but it is well worth looking for the pure species.

○ **A. viridiflora**

A. viridiflora from western China is one of the smaller columbines. Early flowering, it has burnished chocolate-brown flowers with yellow stamens and finely cut foliage, and grows to about 40cm (15in). Intensely fragrant it is popular with flower arrangers.

❧ ASTRANTIA ❧

Astrantias have a quaint, old-world charm with their umbels of tiny florets crowded together, dome-like, within a circular toothed bract, just like pins in a pincushion – hence their old country name, Hattie's Pin Cushion. They come in various pastel shades of soft pink and greenish-white while selected forms have deeper reddish colours.

This curious plant has long been grown in cottage gardens but has only recently come to be valued by other gardeners. Its rise in popularity owes much to the flower arrangers who, discovering how well the beautiful and unusual flowers of astrantia last in water, have created a demand for it which nurseries have found hard to satisfy.

Depending on variety and culture, astrantias grow to 60cm (2ft) or more and produce attractive clumps of lobed leaves. The best known and most widely grown of the species is *Astrantia major*. Because it seeds prolifically, plants can vary enormously; some have bracts three times as long as normal, whilst the pale green and white flowers of others can be flushed with varying degrees of pink.

A. carniolica, a smaller version of *A. major*, has white flowers with a green centre and white bracts giving it a rather colourless appearance, something which cannot be said of *A. carniolica rubra*, a form with deep, rich crimson flowers which, like the variegated forms of *A. major*, is much in demand by enthusiasts.

A. maxima was formerly called *A. helleborifolia*, a name which suited it better, as the leaves of this astrantia are three-lobed and look remarkably like the leaves of a young hellebore, albeit in a much lighter, brighter green. The flowers are a lovely pink, making it the pinkest of the astrantias, and it has a slightly deeper pink bract, green on the reverse. Again, forms vary and there is a beautiful, though rare, white one, *A. maxima alba*.

With their pleasant divided foliage, handsome growth and quiet beauty, astrantias are reliable old plants, flowering from early summer until the autumn, excellent for informal borders and useful as a foil for the old roses or for toning down any gaudy bedfellows.

Astrantias are undemanding plants, but do need a moist soil, thriving in sun or partial shade. Light soil should be improved with organic matter. They are easily grown from seed, although selected forms should always be propagated by division in autumn.

○ **Astrantia major 'Shaggy'**
A much sought-after form named by Margery Fish, with pale green and white flowers and enormous bracts. There are several forms masquerading under this name and it is worth searching for the real thing.

○ **A. m. 'Ruby Wedding'**
This was recently exhibited at one of the RHS Shows in Vincent Square and caused something of a sensation with, as you would expect, flowers of a rich ruby red. As it is a new plant and very rare, gardeners will have to be patient.

○ **A. m. 'Sunningdale Variegated'**
This plant makes a focal point in the spring, when the leaves emerge a bright creamy-yellow. The pink and pale green flowers last well into the autumn.

○ **A. m. rosea**
A neat-growing plant with pink to rose seedling variations, from early to late summer.

❦ CAMPANULA ❦

Campanulas, or bellflowers as they are known, form a very large family of hardy perennials or biennials, whose members differ enormously. Important garden plants, they are a must for the cottage garden.

Campanula medium, the biennial Canterbury Bell, with flowers in mauve, blue, pink and white, has been grown in English gardens since medieval times, although the *Calycanthema* or 'Cup and Saucer' types are Victorian novelties. Both are very cottagey plants. They grow to 90cm (3ft) and require little attention, apart from picking off the dead flowers as soon as they have faded to keep a good show going throughout the summer.

Canterbury Bells, it is said, were named after the bells carried by those who followed the route to Canterbury known as the Pilgrims Way. Gerard noted that they grew plentifully about Canterbury but also gave them the name of 'Throatewort' because of their supposed medicinal qualities in curing sore throats. Blue and white striped varieties were popular in the eighteenth century but, alas, have long since disappeared from our gardens.

Campanula persicifolia, the Peach-leaved Campanula, possesses a timeless appeal with its graceful, single blue or white bells hanging down from slender, 90cm (3ft) stems which bend at the lightest touch. Along with the Canterbury Bell, it has been grown since the sixteenth century. Flowering in early summer, *C. persicifolia* can usually be relied on to produce scattered flowers throughout the rest of the season. It is a great seeder and very often the blue-flowered plants will produce white-flowered offspring.

Double-flowered forms of this plant were all the rage by the late 1700s, and were grown in variety until well into the nineteenth century. Then they became rarer, either as a result of changing fashions or perhaps because, like double primroses, they resent neglect and do not flower well without a good soil and division every few years. More recently they have enjoyed a welcome comeback, with several varieties widely grown and available from specialist nurseries. The very pretty cup-and-saucer types of *C. persicifolia* are of fairly recent origins but, unlike the double flowered forms, seem able to thrive on neglect.

C. pyramidalis, the Chimney or Steeple Bellflower, is another old favourite and certainly the largest of the border campanulas. It has leafy spikes of countless pale blue or white saucer-shaped flowers, 2.5cm (1in) or more across, in towering spires 1.8-2.4m (6-8ft) high. Usually

*Astrantia major **has a quiet, understated beauty and its foliage makes an attractive foil for other perennials***

treated as a biennial, and easily grown from seed, *C. pyramidalis* flowers over a long period during mid- to late summer, although individual flowers will only last a day or two once pollinated. Indoors, cottagers would often train the spikes around a hoop to form a complete circle, or would grow them fanwise to serve as a blind to the window or as a screen to the fireplace in the parlour.

Campanula latiloba is one of the showiest of the bellflowers with its wide, starry, violet, blue or white blooms on stiff 90cm (3ft) stems, a fine sight in midsummer as the flowers all open at the same time along almost the entire length of the stem. *C. latiloba* is an excellent plant for difficult places, flowering happily in the driest of soils and making evergreen carpets in sun or shade in awkward corners.

C. glomerata, the Clustered Bellflower, whose country name is Peal of Bells, is a British native

campanula with closely packed, deep violet-blue heads of funnel-shaped flowers on stout 30cm (1ft) stems in early summer. Thriving in deep shade, it is a striking plant, but can easily become a nuisance, spreading everywhere – although, like Snow-in-Summer, it is perhaps more easily contained in the closely packed cottage garden. Several lovely, white-flowered forms are available including 'Crown of Snow' and 'White Barn', guaranteed to light up any shady border.

There are campanulas, tall and short, for every situation. Some thrive in the wild garden with colonies of verbascums, comfreys and columbines while others tumble from rockeries and walls. Most are invaluable in the cottage garden.

With the exception of the double-flowered forms of *C. persicifolia* which need a deeply dug, well-manured soil, the larger herbaceous campanulas are easy plants to grow in any ordinary garden soil and have no particular fads or fancies. Plants may be planted out in early autumn or spring. Campanulas are easily grown from seed sown outdoors from early summer to flower the following year. Choice varieties may be increased by careful division at planting time.

○ *Campanula persicifolia* **'Fleur de Neige'**
An old favourite with fully double, pure white, cupped flowers on wiry stems above evergreen basal rosettes. There are several forms in circulation and all are worth growing.

○ ***C. p.* 'Pride of Exmouth'**
A delightful semi-double variety with powder-blue flowers on slender stems.

○ ***C. p.* 'Hampstead White'**
The lovely cup-and-saucer type with bowl-shaped flowers surrounded by one layer of flattened petals.

PLANT ASSOCIATIONS
A Group to Give Sparkle in Light Shade

Philadelphus coronarius 'Aureus' has yellow foliage and fragrant creamy white flowers. With the evergreen, gold-mottled leaves of Aucuba 'Crotonifolia', it forms a bright background to the soft cream plumes of Aruncus sylvester, *the white bells of* Campanula persicifolia, *and the yellow spikes of* Digitalis grandiflora. Filipendula ulmaria *'Aurea', a yellow-leaved form of meadowsweet, which gives the best foliage colour if the flower stems are removed, fits in here as well, and in front of them all* Alchemilla mollis *with acid green-yellow sprays mingles with* Lamium 'White Nancy', *a white-flowered silver-leaved nettle, dainty white violas and aquilegias, yellow* Meconopsis cambrica, *and hostas with striking yellow and white variegated foliage (such as* Hosta fortunei 'Aureo-marginata' *and H. 'Thomas Hogg').*

BACK ROW *Philadelphus coronarius* 'Aureus', 2.4-3x2.4m (8-10x8ft). Deciduous shrub. *Aucuba* 'Crotonifolia'. 2.1m (7ft).
MIDDLE ROW *Aruncus sylvestris.* 1.2-1.8m (4-6ft). *Campanula persicifolia.* 90cm (3ft). *Digitalis grandiflora.* 60cm (2ft). Perennial foxglove.

Filipendula ulmaria 'Aurea'. 45cm (1½ft). Non-flowering.
FRONT ROW *Alchemilla mollis.* 45cm (1½ft). *Lamium* 'White Nancy'. 23cm (9in). Violas. 10-15cm (4-6in). Aquilegias. 90cm (3ft). *Meconopsis cambrica,* (Welsh poppy). 45cm (18in). Hostas 60cm (2ft).

Campanula persicifolia *grows through and is supported by the thicker, spreading foliage of* Astrantia maxima

○ **C. latiloba 'Percy Piper'**
A recently introduced hybrid of real merit with large, deep blue saucers on 90cm (3ft) stems.

○ **C. l. 'Alba'**
Pure white saucers on 90cm (3ft) stems for many weeks in summer.

○ **C. glomerata 'Superba'**
A magnificent form with clusters of violet-blue flowers growing to 45cm (1½ft).

○ **C. g. 'Nana Alba'**
Stiff 30cm (1ft) spikes of large, white flowers for many weeks.

⊶ CERASTIUM ⊷

The names Snow-in-Summer and the Snow Plant, are no doubt derived from the fact that, when in flower, the blooms of cerastium make a carpet of white, the snowy effect being heightened by the silvery tint of the leaves.

Cerastium tomentosum, although a highly prized cottage plant, can easily become a nuisance in the wrong place. It is usually found growing on rockeries, smothering old garden walls or as an edging to a path or border. The flowers which appear in early summer are white with grey-green lines down the insides of the petals, and have a slight mossy scent.

With its invaluable evergreen, greyish foliage it is quite a hardy plant and will grow almost anywhere, in any soil, but is rampant if not checked, and certainly best kept away from choice treasures. Propagate by division in the spring or by cuttings taken in early summer and inserted in sandy soil, where they will root in eight weeks or so.

⊶ DIANTHUS ⊷

To the cottage gardener there are few more endearing flowers than dianthus – commonly known as cottage pinks, a term, rightly or wrongly, covering all those 'swete and goodly Gelyfloures' which have filled gardens with fragrance and colour for centuries.

Dianthus caryophyllus is said to have reached England from Normandy with the Norman invasion, attached to stones imported from northern France by the Conqueror for the erection of castles and churches. This is the theory of Canon Ellacombe, the Victorian authority on the genus, and certainly to this day *D. caryophyllus* can be seen growing on the walls of the castles of Dover and Rochester, both of which were built by the Normans, and also at Fountains Abbey in Yorkshire, where it blooms early in July.

Gillyflowers, as they were known, were found growing in tavern and monastery gardens everywhere during Chaucer's time and the petals were used in as many ways as rose petals. Mulled wine was flavoured with them and a lovely double white variety, fringed pink with an almost black centre and appropriately named 'Sops-in-Wine', still survives from this period. Petals were candied, made into conserves and pickled; they were served as a sauce with mutton, and old books refer to recipes for Clove Gillyflower syrups and wine, and to gillyflower vinegar made with the leaves of the flower.

In Tudor times there were two distinct groups, those with single flowers, known as pinks and descended chiefly from *Dianthus plumarius,* and those bearing double or semi-double flowers which were the offspring of *D. caryophyllus,* the chief flower used in the making of garlands and coronets – hence its early English name of 'coronation' from which the name carnation is a derivative.

Pinks and carnations had become amongst the most popular of garden plants by Shakespeare's time and were widely regarded as the king of flowers with the exception, perhaps, of the rose. Although natives of south and eastern Europe, pinks had acclimatised to English gardens and their popularity was possibly due to their extreme hardiness and their suitability for the small knot beds which were popular at that time.

During the early eighteenth century, a deliberate cross between a carnation and a Sweet William produced the sterile Mule Pink. Mule Pinks have the Sweet William green foliage but lack the scent of the old pinks. Several named varieties still exist, including the oldest, 'Napoleon III', which has bright crimson flowers, but unfortunately the tiresome habit of flowering itself to death. 'Emile Paré' has salmon-pink flowers and a slightly stronger constitution. However, cuttings of both should be taken regularly, to ensure their survival.

As a relaxation from their tedious and repetitive work, and as an escape from the grim realities of the industrial revolution at the beginning of the nineteenth century, the weavers of Paisley, in the south-west of Scotland, devoted their leisure hours to raising and perfecting the Laced Pink. 'Lacing' consisted of alternate stripes of white and colour starting with an edging of white at the outer edge of the petals, then a lacing of colour of the same width, followed by another stripe of white. Intensive culture of the flowers to achieve perfection led to friendly rivalry and many new varieties were raised. These flowers were, like the primulas, called 'florists' flowers' and were exhibited in the same way, but the discipline and standards at the shows were so strict that the plants eventually lost vitality and most of the named varieties have entirely disappeared. Perhaps a dozen or so varieties of Laced Pinks are listed today, several descending from the old Paisley laced varieties, but when one recalls that McIntosh in *The Flower Garden* (1839) listed over 190 varieties, and Thomas Hogg, the nurseryman of Paddington Green, 121 varieties of 'exceptional' quality, the extent of the loss of so many charmingly named varieties can be fully appreciated.

If the familiar 'Mrs Sinkins' cannot claim ancient lineage, she has a history that goes back to Victorian days and, in spite of misshapen flowers, is loved by all who grow her and has probably the strongest clove scent of any of the old pinks grown today. It is interesting to discover that the plant was named after Catherine, wife of John Thomas Sinkins, the Master of Slough Workhouse from 1867 to 1900, who raised this old favourite. It was introduced to commerce by the Slough nurseryman, Charles Turner, a great florist of the time who was also responsible for the introduction of the Cox's Orange Pippin apple. Mrs Sinkins died in 1917 and the flower named after her is incorporated in the arms of the borough of Slough.

Shortly after the First World War, the border

PLANT ASSOCIATIONS

A Low-growing Group for Sun and Good Drainage

Dictamnus albus 'Purpureus' with lilac-pink flowers and spicy lemon-scented stems, makes a strong contrast with the spiny-collared thimble flowers of Eryngium giganteum which turn silver as they age. At their feet are clumps of Erodium pelargoniflorum with pink and white flowers for months, sweet-scented dianthus, and the pink and white pincushions of armeria which offset the pink-flowered Geranium cinereum, white gypsophila and dwarf bearded irises.

TALL PLANTS *Dictamnus albus* 'Purpureus'. 60cm (2ft). *Eryngium giganteum.* 60-90cm (2-3ft). Biennial. *Gypsophila paniculata.* 90cm (3ft).

LOW-GROWING PLANTS *Erodium pelargoniflorum.* 15-30cm (6-12in). *Dianthus alpinus, deltoides* and *pavonius,* form ground-hugging tufts from 10-23cm (4-9in). For taller pinks see text. *Armeria maritima.* 15-30cm (6-12in). *Geranium cinereum.* 10-15cm (4-6in). Dwarf bearded irises. 7.5-25cm (3-10in).

One of the many old Cottage Pinks, which flower generously in early summer and make good path 'edgers'

carnation was successfully bred into pinks when Montagu Allwood succeeded in fertilising the Elizabethan 'Old Fringed' pink with the pollen of a perpetual carnation, resulting in the first *Allwoodii* pink. This new race of pinks, quite as hardy as any of the other pinks, took on the long flowering season of its larger relative whilst retaining the compact form of growth of the old pinks and, by further crossing and selection, a large number of attractive and free-flowering varieties were raised.

'Dusky', the name given to the first *Allwoodii* pink, is double, fringed, and a delightful shade of dusky pink. Other varieties include 'Thomas', double red with a bold maroon eye; 'Alice', white serrated flowers with a crimson eye; and 'Faith', semi-double rose-coloured blooms with a deep maroon eye and red lacing. *Allwoodii* blood was introduced into the London group of pinks – a group of mostly laced pinks with the prefix London, including 'London Poppet', 'London Glow', 'London Lady' and 'London Girl', raised by F. R. McQuown and easily obtainable today.

The demand for hardy, long-flowering plants has produced a flood of new modern varieties, but somehow they lack the charm of the old-fashioned pinks with their tremendous show of bloom in early summer. Certainly there is nothing to compare with the scent of the old favourites and it is no surprise to learn of the renewed interest in these lovely old plants, with the search for seemingly lost cultivars continuing anew. The old varieties we list are still grown today and are available from specialist nurseries.

Dianthus are all lime lovers. They will thrive in light rather than sandy soils and enjoy a sunny position. Able to stand intense cold but intolerant of excessive moisture, dianthus should be planted out in spring or autumn, with the beds cleaned of weeds in late autumn and given a light dressing of lime rubble. Propagation of pinks is by cuttings or slips, which are side

shoots removed with a heel, taken any time from the beginning of summer until early autumn and inserted in a very sandy soil in a cold frame. Over-wintered in the cold frame, they should be ready for planting outdoors in early spring.

○ **Dianthus 'Queen of Sheba'**
Sixteenth-century pink of the 'Painted Lady' type (a type popular in Elizabethan times, with white flowers brushed on the underside of the petals with red or pink). It bears single flowers 2.5cm (1in) across with serrated petals laced with magenta-purple on white.

Foxglove spikes provide vertical interest among the low-growing armeria and alchemilla at the edge of a cottage path

○ **D. 'Unique'**
A truly stunning pink of the same age as 'Queen of Sheba' with single red flowers which are covered all over with flashes of black and pink.

○ **D. 'Bat's Double Red'**
A pink which has been growing in the Botanic Gardens at Oxford since the end of the seventeenth century, and is thought to have been raised by a Thomas Bat

in London. Flowers are rich ruby red and have the advantage of long flowering.

○ *D.* **'Old Green Eye'**
Also known as 'Charles Musgrave' or 'Musgrave's Pink', it was named by George Allwood after the owner of the cottage where it was re-discovered and is said to be identical to the plants which have been growing in the palace gardens at Wells since the end of the seventeenth century. Single blooms 3.5cm (1½in) in diameter and of the purest white, with slightly fringed petals and a conspicuous green eye.

○ *D.* **'Gloriosa'**
An old Scottish pink from the eighteenth century possibly having a carnation for one parent. Fully double, pale pink in colour, with a crimson eye.

○ *D.* **'Beauty of Healey'**
Late nineteenth-century pink raised at Whitworth near Rochdale and named after a local village. Semi-double flowers, white ground with a very correct lacing of pale and deep purple. May also have been known as 'Beauty of Rochdale'.

○ *D.* **'Sam Barlow'**
Old cottage garden favourite resembling 'Mrs Sinkins' in form. Double white, deeply fringed petals with chocolate-purple eye.

○ *D.* **'Paddington'**
Raised on the present site of Paddington station by Thomas Hogg the nurseryman in 1820. Dwarf habit, double fringed pink with dark maroon centre.

⊷ DIGITALIS ⊶

Digitalis purpurea, the beautiful biennial native foxglove of the woods and hedgerows, is one of those well-known plants which scarcely need an introduction. Its tall handsome spikes of purple tubular flowers, darkly spotted inside, are a familiar sight in early summer and sow them-selves generously all over the garden.

The much sought after white-flowered form of the common foxglove, *D. p. alba*, has been greatly admired in borders since the end of the sixteenth century and a planting of it enhances many a corner in today's cottage gardens. Self-sown seedlings of the white digitalis may be purple-flowered, and young plants whose leaves have midribs which are brownish or pale purple should be rooted out to keep the white strain going.

Although biennial, foxgloves very often develop a strong constitution which enables them to keep flowering for several years. Cultivated varieties, groomed for stardom, have improved the wild, native plant out of all recognition. They have taller spikes, often towering 1.8-2.1m (6-7ft) tall and strong enough to stand without staking, more varied colours, which include cream, pink, primrose and apricot, and larger flowers, borne all the way round the stem and held horizontally to display the throat markings to better advantage. However, the true wild plant will always be grown for its intense rich purple-red colour, not found in the more sophisticated forms.

It is not generally appreciated that all parts of the foxglove are poisonous, so care should be taken in gardens used by children and animals, but it can also cure, as the drug digitalin used in the treatment of heart disease is extracted from the leaves.

Several interesting perennial foxgloves are now more widely grown and are gradually appearing in cottage gardens.

Foxgloves will establish themselves easily in almost any soil in either sun or shade, but are commonly found at the edge of woods in moist places. After several years, self-sown seedlings of the cultivated varieties deterior-ate and it is advisable to grub them out every four or five years and start again with fresh stock.

■ Seed can either be sown where the plants are to grow, or young plants can be raised in a nursery bed. In either case, sowings should be made in spring and the plantlets planted out in autumn to flower the following year. Perennial foxgloves may be divided in the autumn or spring.

○ *Digitalis purpurea* **Excelsior hybrids**
Possibly the best mixed strain of foxgloves, with
dense spikes of flowers in a wide range of colours,
including cream, pink, primrose and maroon. An
excellent border plant growing to 1.8m (6ft) and
excellent for cutting.

○ **D. p. Foxy hybrids**
A comparatively recent introduction from America,
dwarfer than the ordinary types, in mixed pastel
shades. Treated as half-hardy annuals and sown
early, they can be in flower in five months.

○ **D. x *mertonensis***
A particularly fine hybrid dating from 1926 which
comes true from seed. It has large, attractive flowers
the colour of crushed strawberries from early summer
until early autumn, and rarely grows more than 90cm
(3ft) tall. Perennial, and easily grown from seed.

○ **D. ambigua (syn. grandiflora)**
Known as the Large Yellow Foxglove, *D. ambigua* is
an uncommon plant from the open woodland and
clearings of the Alps and Pyrenees, with largish open
gloves which have a slightly pointed lower lip. Of an
intriguing greenish yellow, the flowers hang quite
thickly upon the spikes, which grow to 90cm (3ft)
tall.

○ **D. ferruginea**
The so-called 'Rusty Foxglove' from south-eastern
Europe and Turkey with lovely, reddish-yellow almost
globular flowers on leafy spikes up to 1.8m (6ft) tall.
An eye-catching plant and much admired. Biennial.

○ **D. parviflora**
A most interesting species from southern Europe
with dense, cylindrical, leafy spikes of small, brownish-
purple flowers. Perhaps not the most colourful of
foxgloves, but one that will nevertheless stop viewers
in their tracks to ask its identity. Perennial.

○ **D. lutea**
The Small Yellow Foxglove grown since the sixteenth
century, with glossy green leaves and pretty, pale
yellow flowers crowded down one side of a rather
thin spike. Up to 60cm (2ft) tall. Perennial, tending
to seed itself around.

❧ HARDY GERANIUMS ❧

Geraniums or cranesbills are a rich and varied
genus of well over a hundred species of perennial
herbaceous plants, not to be confused with pelargoniums, the bedding or fancy geraniums that
decorate windowsills and parks during the summer.

The true hardy geraniums are invaluable garden plants with interesting and varied leaf shapes
and textures. Known as cranesbills because of
their long, beak-shaped fruits which split and
catapult out the large seeds, they are completely
hardy, easy to grow and, because of the simplicity
of their flowers, perfect for the cottage garden.

Several are native or naturalised in Britain,
and these plants from the hedgerows and the
meadows invariably made their way into the
cottage garden. One of them is *Geranium sanguineum*
with low, tangled mats of stems and finely cut
leaves. It was called Bloody Cranesbill not
apparently because of its flowers, which are a
rather startling deep pink, but because of its use as
a supposed wound herb.

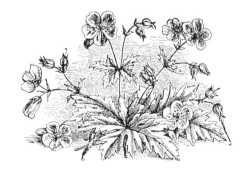

Geranium pratense, the *Meadow Cranesbill* is
another native with tall stems bearing heads of
large violet-blue 'saucers' and deeply-cut foliage.
It is without doubt one of our loveliest wild
flowers and worthy of a place in any border. It was

The strong pink of **Geranium** psilostemon *is sometimes hard to place, but looks well here with rose* '**Honorine de Brabant**', *ox-eye daisy and alchemilla*

sometimes called Blue Basins and another attractive country name for it was Loving Andrews. The double-flowered forms of *G. pratense* with their endearing little 'rosette' flowers, looking just as if they have come from a Victorian posy, should be grown in every cottage garden. *G. p.* 'Plenum Caeruleum' flowers for several weeks in early summer and has loosely formed, lavender-blue rosettes tinged with pinkish lilac. *G. p.* 'Plenum Violaceum', however, flowers slightly later, with perfectly formed deep violet rosettes, purple-tinged at the centre. The loosely formed flowers of the double white *G. p.* 'Plenum Album' are somewhat off-white in colour. Nevertheless, it is an interesting form and well worth the extra care and attention needed to keep it happy.

G. macrorrhizum is a beautiful species originating from southern Europe but cultivated as long ago as 1658 in the Oxford Botanic Garden. It has semi-evergreen, five-lobed, aromatic sticky leaves from which oil of geranium is extracted, with the magenta flowers just held above the foliage. The macrorrhizums make excellent ground cover for difficult areas. They grow more or less anywhere, even surviving and thriving in the dry and sparse conditions that exist under oak trees, and are a godsend for clothing difficult and unsightly banks.

There are several named varieties including *G. m.* 'Bevan's Variety', the most intensely coloured variety with deep magenta flowers, and *G. m.* 'Ingwersen's Variety' with shell-pink flowers. *G. m.* 'Album' has white flowers, whilst the variegated form, *G. m.* 'Variegatum' has leaves boldly splashed with white and cream. The variegated form is rather more difficult to please and should be grown in full sun and a good soil. In autumn, the leaves of *G. macrorrhizum* are tinged bronze and scarlet.

Apart from occasional slug or snail damage, the hardy geraniums are tough plants, generally ignored by pests and not prone to disease either. With pretty flowers, decorative foliage that can be as attractive when old as when young, and a long flowering season, it is hardly surprising that today's gardeners find these old cottage garden favourites irresistible, fitting conveniently the modern concept of ground covers.

Geraniums grow easily in sun or part shade. They require little attention and make excellent ground cover in any garden soil, requiring no special composts. Plants purchased from a garden centre should be planted out in the spring. All hardy geraniums divide easily and several species will come true from seed. Others hybridise, often with some exciting results.

○ *Geranium endressii* 'A. T. Johnson'
A form of 'French cranesbill' with cool green foliage and an unending succession of silvery-pink flowers all summer, *G. endressii* makes good ground cover in shade. It was much favoured by Margery Fish, who would advise people to plant it 'when in doubt'.

○ *G. phaeum*
Also known as the Dusky Cranesbill or Mourning Widow. Elegant flights of deep purple-black, somewhat sombre, dart-like flowers throughout the summer make this a quietly graceful and charming plant for a shady corner.

○ *G. psilostemon*
A handsome, cottage garden favourite with magenta-red flowers each with a black centre. The elegant foliage is often brilliantly coloured in autumn.

○ *G. cinereum* 'Ballerina'
With cushions of grey-green foliage, the flowers lilac with dark red veining and eye, this is a vigorous and free-flowering species, ideal for rockeries.

○ *G. c.* 'Lawrence Flatman'
'Lawrence Flatman' has large pink flowers, heavily blotched and lined crimson. It is vigorous, free-flowering and very colourful.

○ *G. dalmaticum*
G. dalmaticum has hummocks of small shining leaves, bronze-tinted, with pink flowers for weeks in summer. *G. d.* 'Album' is the choice white-flowered form.

○ *G. nodosum*
The so-called Knotted Cranesbill with shining green, lobed leaves and lilac-pink flowers produced perpetually throughout the summer. Another excellent ground cover plant in shade.

❧ HESPERIS ❧

Hesperis matronalis, known by the countryman as Dame's Violet, or Sweet Rocket, is a charming, informal old plant for the mixed border, amongst shrubs, or in the wilder parts of the garden. With its dark green leaves and 60-90cm (2-3ft) tall stems topped with single, white or lavender, scented flowers, it is a pretty sight for several months from early summer.

Easily naturalised, Sweet Rocket will pop up everywhere once seed has been introduced into the garden, but, in spite of its wandering ways, few can resist its charm and the delicious clove fragrance given off by the stock-like flowers, especially noticeable in the evening. Without doubt, however, it is the double form, *Hesperis matronalis flore pleno* – the Double Sweet Rocket – that everyone wants to grow. Until quite recently

The double Sweet Rocket, a rare and much treasured cottage garden favourite

it was almost impossible to obtain anywhere, although before the Second World War it was used extensively as a bedding plant both at Kew and in the London parks.

Double forms have been grown and were popular in gardens since Elizabethan times. In fact, during the nineteenth century, this traditional cottage garden plant was widely grown in variety, though it must be said that several forms were always connoisseurs' plants and already in decline. Indeed, as a result of an accumulation of virus diseases of the kind that affects other Cruciferae, including brassicas and wallflowers, the Double Sweet Rocket had been deteriorating for generations and this, combined with a lack of knowledge of its needs and changing garden fashions, brought this beautiful plant to the verge of extinction.

It is thanks to plants from a small garden in Ireland that we are able once again to enjoy the Double Sweet Rocket in our gardens, and the search is on for the double variegated form with purple and white blotched and striped flowers, which was grown at the beginning of this century.

A healthy, virus-free, pale lilac form, *Hesperis matronalis* 'Lilacina Flore Pleno', has recently been re-introduced and it is hoped that it will retain its original vigour and once again grace our gardens with its beauty and scent, and perhaps even regain its popularity as a commercial cut flower.

The Double Sweet Rocket must have a good rich soil and, like the old double primroses, only survives if constantly divided and moved to new ground. Whilst it enjoys a rich diet, it is important to avoid root contact with fresh manure. Plants will grow happily even in poorly drained, acid clay soil, provided leaf mould is incorporated to produce a loose and open soil structure, and a dressing of lime is given. What they will not endure is a light sandy soil. Moreover, they are less tolerant of severe weather conditions than is generally believed. Once a plant is established, it is comparatively easy to propagate by division in the spring, but propagation by cuttings is tricky and rather hit and miss.

❧ LAVENDER ❧

Lavandula spica (syn. *angustifolia*) the traditional 'Olde English Lavender', is as old as history, grown in every cottage garden for centuries and one of the most familiar of all garden shrubs.

Culpeper, the herbalist, was fond of introducing everyday plants with the words 'these are so wel known that they need no Discription' and lavender, the quintessential herb of English gardens, would certainly have come into that category. A number of lavender species and varieties, however, are less well known and cottage gardeners may need to be introduced to the pink- and white-flowered forms, dwarf and semi-dwarf forms, and the unusual but less hardy lavender species.

All parts of the shrub are strongly aromatic, with both flowers and leaves giving off the same clean, fresh, unmistakable lavender scent. In Tudor times a laundress was called a 'lavendre' and the dried flowers are still used today to freshen linen by placing them in chests of drawers to perfume the contents. For this purpose it is best to harvest the flowers in the morning when the scent is strongest. Whilst no soil is too hot and dry for the sun-loving lavenders, and the warm sun brings out the oil content, too great a heat and drought does cause the aromatic oil to evaporate more quickly.

Lavender soap has been popular for generations since William Yardley of Surrey first added the essence of lavender to his soap in the late seventeenth century, starting a long tradition that continues today. A whiff of lavender perfume, so refreshing, so typically English, conjures up visions of cottage gardens and an era when life was lived at a much slower pace.

Lavender is delightful planted anywhere in the garden. It is particularly effective when grown with roses or used as a low fragrant hedge, flanking paths or lawns or edging the herb garden.

 The best time for planting is in early spring. Lavenders need a warm and sunny position and a light, well-drained soil. The bushes should be trimmed over just below the base of the flower stalks as soon as the flowers fade and overgrown bushes that need severe cutting back should be dealt with in early spring.

■ If flowers are to be gathered for drying, they should be cut with long stalks just as some flowers are fully open all up the spike but before fading has occurred. Tied up in small bundles and hung head-downwards in an airy shed to dry, the flowers can later be removed from the stems and placed in bags or sachets.

■ Small new shoots about 5-13cm (2-5in) long, taken as cuttings in the spring and inserted firmly in sandy soil in a frame or in pans, will root within six to eight weeks. Hard cuttings can be taken at other times.

TALL VARIETIES

○ _Lavandula_ 'Giant Grappenhall'
A large-flowered, vigorous form with fine spikes of purple-blue flowers, making a dense bush 90cm-1.2m (3-4ft) in height.

○ _L._ 'Seal Lavender'
An excellent free-flowering form with pale green foliage and spikes of a deep, rich colour on flower stems some 30-45cm (12-18in) long, borne in such profusion that those around the side of the bush sweep fanwise. Good for drying.

○ _L. alba_
Growing 50-60cm (1½-2ft) tall, the white lavender is not as hardy as the coloured forms and is liable to die out in a cold winter. Best against a sunny, sheltered wall or in a really sheltered position in a light sandy soil. Leaves are grey-green and the flower stems some 30cm (12in) long. Flowers are fragrant.

DWARF VARIETIES

○ _Lavandula_ 'Dwarf Munstead'
Excellent for hedges or edging beds, 'Dwarf Munstead' has dull grey foliage and deep purplish-violet flowers

with a hint of reddish-purple when the flowers are fully mature. Several forms are sold under this name and plants are best purchased from a reliable source.

○ _L. nana alba_
A miniature white-flowered lavender growing some 15-20cm (6-8in) high, ideal for the rockery or sink garden. Although moderately hardy, the plant should be sheltered from the elements. The 'pocket-size' white flowers come out in midsummer.

○ _L. nana rosea_
This unusual form has 2.5-4cm (1-1½in) long, pale flesh-pink flowers. It grows some 50cm (20in) tall and has grey-green foliage. Reasonably hardy.

SEMI-DWARF VARIETIES

○ _Lavandula_ 'Hidcote Purple'
The bushes of this lovely lavender grow some 60-75cm (2-2½ft) high and 60cm (2ft) across after five or six years, with generously massed purple-violet flowers on 4cm (1½in) spikes. The flowers of 'Hidcote Purple' keep their rich colour when dried and are valuable for making patterns in pot-pourri arrangements.

○ _L._ 'Twickel Purple'
This distinctive variety has the best scent of all dwarf and semi-dwarf lavenders, with deep mauve flowers on long, graceful flower spikes. Makes an excellent hedge growing 60cm (2ft) or more with a spread of 60-75cms (2-2½ft).

LAVENDER SPECIES

○ _Lavandula stoechas_
The so-called French lavender makes a stiff, spiky little bush about 45cm (18in) high with curious, knobbly, squarish flower heads of a very dark purplish-blue, topped by a perky tuft that stands up like plumes. Very pretty, slightly tender, it has been used as a pot plant for centuries, although it will survive most winters in the open garden.

○ _L. dentata_
A distinct and scarce species with toothed grey-green leaves smelling of lemon, spice and lavender combined. The foliage will keep its scent on drying and may be added to pot pourri. _L. dentata_ will grow some 90cm (3ft) high, but can only be grown outside in a very sheltered position and is probably best as a greenhouse plant.

○ _L. viridis_
This unusual green-flowered lavender with pale greenish-yellow flowers resembles _L. stoechas_ and is a native of the Pyrenees. It is becoming more widely available and much sought after.

❧ LILIUM ❧

Within the garden's peaceful scene
Appeared two lovely foes,
Aspiring to the rank of Queen –
The Lily and the Rose

COWPER

Lilium, the rose's rival for the title of queen of flowers, is less frequently seen than it should be in modern gardens, branded, it seems, by today's gardeners as difficult. It is believed to be prone to disease, and needing all kinds of special treatment – some species preferring an acid soil, others chalk, some requiring deep planting, others shallow, and so on. This is a great pity as few other flowers have fuelled the imaginations of artists and gardeners alike for so many centuries as the lily.

Lilium candidum, the Madonna Lily, has been cultivated for thousands of years and may well be the oldest of garden flowers. It is without doubt one of the loveliest of lilies with a delicious scent, more fragrant at twilight than it is by day, and generally recognised as doing much better in a small garden than a grand one, preferring the close confines of hedges or fences and the company of other plants to shade the roots from the heat of the midday sun. Stately rows of Madonna Lilies were at one time a feature of the cottage garden, the pride and joy of their owners with dazzling white trumpets on tall, healthy plants, kept virus free, some say, by the habit of tossing pails of soapy water into the garden.

The White Lily, as it was called before the nineteenth century, was grown in every English

Chrysanthemum leucanthemum
OX-EYE DAISY

A tall very attractive giant daisy with pure white flowers and a yellow centre. Can be found almost anywhere from late spring to late summer in grassland and on roadsides. Has no particular soil preference.

Trollius europaeus
GLOBE FLOWER

Looks like a large, tall buttercup, with the sepals and petals rolled inwards forming a round, globe-like head. A plant for a damp position, ideally at the edge of a garden pond. Flowers from midsummer. Perennial. Found in damp places, particularly in northern England and Scotland.

Polemonium caeruleum
JACOBS LADDER

Every cottage garden should have this plant. Nowadays it is more easily found in garden centres than in the wild, where it is quite rare and confined mainly to the north of England. It grows up to 60cm (2ft) tall, with a head of rich blue flowers (sometimes white) and delicate ladder-like leaflets. It flowers in early summer and self-seeds prolifically.

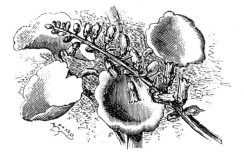

Umbilicus rupestris
PENNYWORT

A curious little plant with a 15cm (6in) spike of small, yellowish-green flowers like bells hanging on a miniature steeple. It likes to grow in the crevices of old walls, not in the ground. Quite readily found wild in western counties and Wales.

WILD FLOWERS FOR THE SUMMER COTTAGE GARDEN

Verbascum thapsus
GREAT MULLEIN OR AARON'S ROD

A stately, indeed statuesque plant, well worth a place in the border. It has single spikes up to 1.8m (6ft) tall, densely packed with bright yellow flowers. The leaves are clothed in soft, whitish, woolly hairs. A biennial, it self-seeds freely. Commonly found in waste places and on sunny banks.

Centaurea cyanus
CORNFLOWER

Sometimes known as Bluebottle. A very pretty annual with a roundish head of bright blue flowers like a many-pointed star, borne on stalks about 60cm (2ft) high. Formerly a beautiful 'pest' in cornfields but not so common now. It flowers all summer.

Valerian grows wild in many areas and is invasive in the garden, but can grow unrestricted outside the garden fence

Lychnis dioica syn. *Silene dioica*
RED CAMPION

Grows abundantly in shady places in woods and hedgebanks. The flowers are rose-red and distantly resemble a dianthus, to which they are related. Very attractive grown in clumps in the border. Height up to 75cm (2½ft). Flowers all summer.

Polygonum bistorta
BISTORT

A plant with erect stems up to 60cm (2ft) tall, topped with a cylindrical flower spike resembling a pink poker. Grows wild mainly in Scotland and the north of England. Prefers a moist situation. Flowers from early summer.

Lysimachia vulgaris
YELLOW LOOSESTRIFE

A handsome perennial up to 90cm (3ft) high with bright yellow flowers. It can be found along river banks and in marshy places and does best in a moist position in the garden. Flowers mid- to late summer.

Malva moschata
MUSK MALLOW

Has elegant finely-cut leaves and large saucer-shaped, rose-pink flowers. Very occasionally the flowers are white. It can be found in hedgebanks and on roadsides in mid- to late summer. Up to 60cm (2ft) tall. Considered to be amongst the prettiest of our wild flowers.

monastery garden, where it was used to treat cuts and sores as well as to decorate the chapel. It became Mary's emblem in paintings, the white petals said to symbolise the virgin's purity and the golden anthers her heavenly soul. During the eighteenth and nineteenth centuries a pink-striped variety and a double flowered one were very popular, both, unfortunately, now lost to cultivation. Madonna Lilies should be planted in late summer rather than autumn, with less than 2.5cm (1in) of soil covering the bulbs. Bulbs should not be left lying out of the ground for long and should be planted in a rich, moist soil in full sun where they will grow to a height of 1.2m (4ft) or more. Left undisturbed, *Lilium candidum* will multiply with ease, flowering from early to midsummer.

The martagon lily is often called the Turk's Cap Lily, since the word martagon derives from the Turkish word *martagan,* a kind of turban. It has been grown for centuries and may even be a true native of the British Isles.

No-one could call this lily sweet-scented. It is grown for its tall spikes of nodding Turk's caps in various shades of mauve, pink and purple, all spotted with dark red, and because it is easy-going, free-flowering and perfectly hardy. A plant for the most 'impossible' garden it can be grown in poor soil, flowering well in partial shade during high summer. There is a beautiful white form which bears more than forty waxy-white flowers to a stem – *L. martagon* var. *album.* Bulbs planted in early autumn should flower the following year. Any delay in planting and you will miss a year. Unlike those of the Madonna Lily, the bulbs should be planted 15cm (6in) deep.

Another lily which will grow almost anywhere but has not been in cultivation for so long is *L. regale.* One of the most popular of lilies, it was discovered as recently as 1903 in China and has been found wild nowhere else since. A magnificent white trumpet lily with a golden throat and the outsides of the petals shaded with deep maroon, it will grow 1.2-1.5m (4-5ft) tall. Its deep heady scent, acceptable outdoors, becomes cloying in the confines of a room.

L. regale is particularly easy to raise from seed, flowering the second year from sowing, and is re-commended for those who have little or no experience of growing lilies. Although hardy, early growth is frequently cut back by late frosts unless it is protected by other plants and shrubs.

Modern garden lilies, usually imported from Holland, are available in ever increasing numbers in a wide range of colours. Grown in pots they make good patio plants, or they can be sunk in the soil to fill gaps in the summer border.

The majority of lilies appreciate sharp, free drainage and will not tolerate stagnant moisture around the bulbs. As a rule, lilies should not be disturbed once they are established.

■ Offsets provide the simplest means of propagating most lilies, and the stem-rooting species also produce small bulbs on the underground portion of the stem above the bulb itself. Offsets detached in the autumn should be planted in a nursery bed of light sandy soil. Lilies come easily from seed sown in pans or boxes in a cold frame in either spring or autumn. In some cases germination is very slow, as much as twelve months.

○ *Lilium regale album*
A fine and vigorous trumpet lily similar in habit to its parent, *L. regale,* but producing on each spike up to nine pure white flowers with a yellow throat and yellow-orange anthers. Beautifully scented and easy to grow. 90cm-1.5m (3-5ft).

○ *L. chalcedonicum*
Long cultivated although still rarely seen, this native of Greece has sumptuous flowers of bright sealing-wax red in early summer. The stem itself is decorative, being covered in narrow silver-edged leaves which form a perfect foil for the flowers. Enjoys a warm lime soil with plenty of leaf mould worked in.

○ *L. x testaceum* (**Nankeen Lily**)
This is probably the oldest recorded lily hybrid, (*L. candidum* x *L. chalcedonicum*). One of the choicest of lilies with six to twelve handsome, fragrant, recurved apricot petals of waxy texture. The large anthers are covered with a rich orange pollen. Requires a good, loamy soil and is becoming scarce.

○ *L. tigrinum* '**Splendens**'
The so-called Tiger Lily produces masses of vivid orange flowers, spotted purple-black, in racemes, during midsummer. Needs a lime-free soil and will grow to 1.2m (4ft).

❧ LUPINUS ❧

Lupins, with their tall flower spikes in a wide range of colours – white to yellow, orange, flame, bronze, pink and intermediate shades as well as lavender-blue and purple – provide a magnificent if somewhat short-lived display, heralding high summer in the cottage garden, their warm peppery smell pure nostalgia – a journey back to childhood.

Lupinus polyphyllum with typical blue-purple lupin flowers, from which the first hybrids were made by James Kelway of Langport, arrived from the west coast of America in 1826. The hybrids in various shades of blue and a rather dingy yellow were themselves crossed to produce seedlings with rose-pink flowers, but it was the Russell lupins raised by George Russell that caused such a sensation when first exhibited at the Royal Horticultural Society's June Show in 1935. Nothing quite like them had ever been seen before. The tall upstanding plants with their tremendous range of rich, clear, bright colours were an immediate success and quickly appeared in gardens everywhere. Fortunately, several superb named varieties from this period are still grown today.

▪ Whilst the lupin display is rather fleeting, barely lasting a fortnight, it is possible to produce a few more side-spikes by dead-heading and, by cutting the plants to the ground after flowering, a second flowering can be induced. This process, however, will eventually weaken the plants, which may well then become susceptible to mildew.

▪ With the exception of the old named varieties, which must be propagated by division or cuttings, lupins are most often grown today as biennials, the seed sown in spring and planted out in autumn to flower the following year. The plants are then discarded after flowering, clearing the way for an annual display which, in turn, is replaced in the autumn with a fresh batch of spring-sown lupins.

▪ Growing 1.2m (4ft) tall at flowering time, lupins may need support in an exposed garden where strong winds or heavy rain can easily spoil the display, knocking the plants all over the place just as they are about to flower.

There is another type of lupin well worth growing, the so-called tree lupin – *Lupinus arboreus*. This shrub is particularly useful for growing in a dry, poor soil and will cover itself with spikes of white and yellow lupin flowers which are strongly honey-scented over a long period of time. Although not long-lived, *L. arboreus* can easily be raised from seed and once established will give plenty of self-sown seedlings which can be transplanted to where they are wanted or potted up for garden visitors.

Some of the old named hybrid lupins are still available today. 'Lady Gaye' (clear primrose flowers), 'City of York' (rich wine-red flowers) and 'Blue Jacket' (pale blue and white flowers), are the rarest but are worth searching for. Others, like those we list here, are easier to find.

 Lupins enjoy an average soil with an occasional bonemeal dressing and should not be planted in over-heavily manured soil, which encourages the production of fleshy roots liable to succumb to excessive wet and frosts.

▪ All named varieties and particular favourites must only be propagated by division or cuttings. Examination of the stools after flowering will show a set of crowns just bursting into growth at the base of each flower stem. These can easily be cut away with a sharp knife and replanted in a nursery bed, where they can be shaded from strong sunshine until rooted. Cuttings of young shoots taken in spring will also root readily in a sandy compost in a cold frame kept shaded for two or three weeks.

▪ Unlike the seedlings of *Lupinus arboreus* (see above), self-sown seedlings should be rooted out immediately they are spotted in the garden as they invariably 'revert', producing poor colouring similar to the wild blue type-plant of their ancestors.

○ *Lupinus* **'The Chatelaine'**
Luminous pale pink and white bicolour flowers.

○ *L.* **'The Governor'**
A strong growing lupin with marine-blue and white flowers.

○ *L.* **'Chandelier'**
'Chandelier' is another strong grower with yellow flowers.

SCENTED-LEAVED GERANIUMS

PELARGONIUMS

Pelargonium species, the so-called scented geraniums, were introduced from the Cape of Good Hope during the seventeenth century by English travellers and explorers. They are half-hardy, suffruticose (semi-shrubby) plants with deeply cut, almost ferny leaves and small, comparatively insignificant flowers. This description does nothing, however, to prepare the uninitiated for the sheer delight of entering a greenhouse filled with a varied assortment of scented geraniums, the fragrance of roses, oranges, lemons, nutmegs and peppermint on the air, the aromatic sweetness everywhere.

Pelargonium graveolens, the Rose Geranium has been grown in England since 1690, a popular windowsill plant in old, low-ceilinged cottages, where the fragrance – a combination of lemon, rose and balsam – would help to relieve damp and musty smells. In Victorian times scented geraniums were widely grown in greenhouses and conservatories, with dozens of different species, hybrids and sports widely available, often trained into fan-shaped plants or standards. They later became unfashionable and remained so until quite recently.

During the summer months scented geraniums can be planted out in the open, preferably near garden gates or at the edge of paths where they can be brushed against to release their pleasant scent, or plunged in beds or borders in their pots, which can be completely covered with soil to give a natural effect. This has the advantage that when the pots are lifted for the winter the roots, confined in the pots, have not spread so much that an enormous pot has to be found to accommodate them, as sometimes happens when they are put potless into the ground.

Scented geraniums have their practical uses as well for pot pourri and flavouring. Scented geranium cake is still a delicacy. When making a sponge cake, line the bottom of the tin with baking parchment and then butter it and sprinkle the buttered surface with sugar, before laying fresh leaves of *P. graveolens* (not *P. quercifolium,* as the gummy flavour of the latter species would definitely not be appropriate, although orange or lemon scented leaves would do as well) 'face' down in a pattern on top of the sugared surface before pouring in the mixture. The sponge cake, permeated with a pleasant aroma and flavour, makes a special tea-time treat.

Scented pelargoniums flower during the early spring and summer and sporadically throughout the year. If growth becomes long and woody, it is worth repotting the plant to provide fresh food material for a new start and then, after allowing a week or so for it to settle down, the stems may be cut back to a growing bud.

■ Propagation is by green or semi-ripe cuttings. Soft green cuttings will generally root within six weeks if taken in early spring, but up to three months if taken later on. Most cuttings root satisfactorily with or without 'heels' apart from *P. graveolens,* which is best propagated by 15cm (6in) cuttings, cut under a joint. A rooting powder will help, and the cuttings should be inserted in pans filled with a sandy mixture. The best position is round the edge of the pan where cuttings usually root first, having the best combination of aeration and moisture. Repot in a soil-based potting compost and avoid over-watering, which can cause stem-rot.

○ *Pelargonium tomentosum*
Large, downy, *crème-de-menthe* coloured foliage described by Gertrude Jekyll as being 'thick as a fairy's blanket' and with a pungent peppermint smell. The flowers are small, white and insignificant, but the striking foliage, covered with silver hair, is particularly useful and probably seen at its best hanging downwards over the rim of a large pot.

PLANT ASSOCIATIONS

A Lively Scheme for a Sunny Well-drained Border

Orange and yellow roses make a lively background here, along with shrubby potentillas and the free-flowering Hypericum *'Hidcote' with large yellow flowers. Spiky yellow and white irises contrast with the hypericum's shrubby foliage and mix with flamboyant oriental poppies, while* Oenothera missouriensis *with wide yellow flowers and trailing habit makes a foreground for aromatic silver mounds of santolinas and* Helichrysum angustifolium *(Curry Plant), the pale lemon-yellow daisies of* Coreopsis verticillata *'Moonlight',* Geum *'Borisii' with burning orange flowers in early summer and the cool* Anthemis cupaniana *with white daisies over ferny silver leaves for a long period. Helianthemums also do well and can supply bright red and orange shades to sprawl over the path edge.*

BACK ROW Some orange roses: 'Geraldine'. 75cm (2½ft); 'Southampton'. 90cm (3ft). Some yellow roses: *Rosa primula,* (the incense rose). 1.8m (6ft). Flowers late spring to early summer, slightly tender; 'Golden Wings'. 1.8m (6ft); 'Graham Thomas'. 1.2m (4ft). *Potentilla fruticosa.* 1.2m (4ft). Deciduous shrub, many named varieties. *Hypericum* 'Hidcote'. 1.2-1.8m (4-6ft). Evergreen to semi-evergreen shrub.

MIDDLE ROW Yellow and white tall and inter-mediate bearded irises. 45cm-1.2m (1½-4ft). Choose your own from the many varieties at garden centres. *Papaver orientale* 'May Queen'. 90cm (3ft). Bright orange. *P. o.* 'Goliath'. 90cm (3ft). Bright red.

FRONT ROW Santolinas. 45-60cm (1½-2ft). Shrubby evergreens with bright yellow button heads. *Oenothera missouriensis.* 23cm (9in). Prostrate stems. *Helichrysum angustifolium.* 45cm (18in). *Coreopsis verticillata* 'Moonlight'. 45-60cm (1½-2ft). *Geum* 'Borisii'. 30-45cm (1-1½ft). *Anthemis cupaniana.* 30cm (1ft). Helianthemums. 23-30cm (9-12in).

··Bright red poppies, Dog Daisies, Anthemis cupaniana *and feverfew, and the simple fencing create a 'cottage garden' effect*

○ **P. fragrans**

The Nutmeg Geranium has sage-green foliage with small white or cream flowers with red veins on the upper petals, and a scent in which nutmeg and pine blend – an aftershave aroma. The leaves are used in the more pungent and spicy pot-pourri recipes.

○ **P. 'Lady Plymouth'**

Silver-edged, cream-tinged foliage shaped like the leaves of *P. graveolens,* and with a peppermint and cinnamon scent. The flowers are pale pink. Is useful for planting outdoors in the summer.

○ **P. crispum**

P. crispum has small curled leaves, crimped at the edges, on rigid 60cm (2ft) stems and has a strong scent of lemon rind. The flowers are comparatively large and mauve-pink. The foliage may be dried and used in pot pourri and to give a lemon flavour in cooking. *P. crispum* 'Variegatum' is the variegated form and the most decorative, its leaves, edged with silver and cream, possessing the same refreshing pungency. Excellent for planting out during the summer.

○ **P. 'Clorinda'**

'Clorinda' has very large, bright cerise flowers. Its soft, hairy foliage is scented with rose and eucalyptus. The flowers are the equal of the show pelargoniums and it is an excellent plant for a vase on a terrace.

○ **P. 'Attar of Roses'**

Probably the best of all the scented pelargoniums, with a most delightful true rose perfume. The leaves are slightly lobed and the small pink flowers open during the summer. The leaves may be dried for pot pourri and the plant is always a pleasure to pass in the greenhouse.

○ **P. 'Mabel Grey'**

A comparatively recent introduction from Kenya. The foliage is bold in outline, palmately divided, and has a truly lovely lemon verbena scent.

OLD-FASHIONED COTTAGE GARDEN
*A*NNUALS AND *B*IENNIALS

Few cottage gardens are without a patch or two of annuals. Some appear uninvited, others are planted to fill gaps in the border and odd little corners. All bloom profusely throughout the summer, buzzing with bees and other insects. Many old-fashioned annuals and biennials are deliciously scented and have been grown in cottage gardens for generations.

Matthiola is the proper name of the stock family, but more often than not, the plant we call matthiola is the **Night-scented Stock** – *Matthiola bicornis.* From the point of view of colour and show, with its thin, pale lavender and white single flowers, this is the most humble of the stock family but it is, however, the most important when it comes to scent. By day, the Night-scented Stock is a miserable-looking, limp, rather lanky plant with the small, somewhat colourless, four-petalled flowers all folded up and hanging dejectedly on the stems like tiny bits of paper. Unfurling at dusk, however, it comes into its own, releasing its delicious scent in the warm evening air. It is a good idea to mix the seed of *Matthiola bicornis* with that of *Malcolmia maritima,* the *Virginia Stock,* so as to combine the latter's daytime colour with the other's nocturnal fragrance. Both are best sown where they are to grow.

Matthiola incana or **Stock** was a familiar flower of English gardens as long ago as the seventeenth century and was nearly always grown as a biennial. Sown during a full moon in spring, the seedlings were transplanted during three successive full moons and were set in the garden at Michaelmas for blooming the following year. Today, stocks are popular for bedding and for providing cut flowers, but above all for the wonderful clove-like scent. The double, pale lavender flowers come into flower about ten weeks from the date of sowing, and if spikes are cut off as the flowers fade they will produce a continuous show – and scent – well into the autumn.

The famous biennial **Brompton Stock** dates back to 1724, when the flowers were highly cultivated by the nursery of London and Wise in the neighbourhood of Brompton. The so-called **Ten-week Stock,** an annual strain, was bred by weavers in northern France, where it was said that each village strove to grow only one colour or variety, of which they were justly proud.

Lathyrus odoratus or the **Sweet Pea** is, as its name suggests, strongly scented. Climbing by

means of tendrils, it was one of the most prized of all cottage garden annuals. A native of southern Europe, it was unknown in British gardens until the first year of the eighteenth century, when it blossomed in the garden of Dr Uvedale, an Essex schoolmaster, who had received the seed a year earlier from Father Cupani, a Sicilian monk.

The original sweet pea was a rather weedy-looking plant bearing tiny maroon flowers with a deep purple standard but Dr Uvedale, a keen gardener, was captivated by the scent, and seeds were quickly shared amongst gardening friends. At the beginning of the nineteenth century there

were five colours. There was no comparison, however, with the brilliance and size of sweet peas grown today, but all still possessed the same strong, sweet fragrance which so enthralled Dr Uvedale – a scent so overpowering that ladies were cautioned against admitting the flowers into their chambers lest they should be overcome by it.

From these original plants, the late nineteenth century enthusiast, Henry Eckford, bred larger flowers and increased the colour range dramatically. His sweet peas became known as the 'Grandifloras' and by the turn of the century there were hundreds of named varieties. They were soon, however, to be eclipsed by the Spencer varieties with their unusual waved petals, introduced in 1901. These became so popular that, by 1914, the 'Grandifloras' had almost disappeared and but for the work of one or two dedicated enthusiasts would probably have become extinct.

Today, thanks to these enthusiasts, approximately twenty named varieties survive, and, although the flowers are smaller than those of the modern varieties, the colours are more intense and glowing and the flowers, with their strong, heady scent are borne in great profusion. Once flowering starts, they can be picked every day until mid-autumn providing, of course, they are not allowed to go to seed.

'Painted Lady' is the oldest sweet pea in existence, having been grown in English gardens since the early eighteenth century. It is an outstanding variety with highly scented reddish-pink and white bi-coloured flowers. Several of the Henry Eckford introductions of the 1890s and early 1900s are still available including 'Lord Nelson', violet, self-coloured, and 'King Edward VII', carmine-red, self-coloured.

Old-fashioned sweet peas need an open, sunny position and will not tolerate any degree of shade. They can be grown against a trellis or fence or on rough tripods of bean sticks in a mixed border. They do not require deep trenching, are relatively easy to grow, and are traditionally sown outdoors in England on 10 October, one of the few firm dates in the gardener's calendar.

Oenothera biennis, the true biennial **Evening Primrose** and the one most familiar to cottage

Instead of climbing, this perennial sweet pea is grown to tumble over an old sandstone wall

gardeners, has lovely clear primrose-yellow blooms some 7.5cm (3in) across, which sleep by day and open at dusk to emit a delicious sweet perfume, particularly attractive to moths. Introduced from North America in the mid-seventeenth century, it was named the 'tree primrose' by Parkinson, and its propensity to become a troublesome weed when allowed to seed itself all over the garden was noted by Miller in the eighteenth century.

Evening Primrose has one of the longest flowering seasons of all plants, the uppermost flowers appearing in early summer, and the stalk continually advancing in height with a constant succession of flowers until well into autumn. The plant was once cultivated in France as a salsify-like vegetable with the roots harvested at the end of the first season. Oil of Evening Primrose has recently found favour with both orthodox and alternative medicine.

Seed germinates very easily and may be scattered thinly outdoors where the plants are to flower in late spring. It may be necessary to thin out the seedlings so as to prevent eventual overcrowding of the plants which, when mature, have a spread of about 45cm (18in).

Reseda odorata or **Mignonette,** the sweet-scented 'fragrant weed of Egypt' was introduced to Britain from Egypt via France in the mid-eighteenth century. It appeared first in London florists' windows and quickly found a niche in the window boxes of London balconies, where the inconspicuous brownish-yellow flowers would release their distinctive fragrance on warm sunny days. The poet, Cowper, who came of age in the year when the flower first reached these shores, gave it a name which stuck at the time – 'Frenchman's Darling', hence Mignonette.

Of upright growth at first, Mignonette tends to develop a spreading habit, with leafy stems and

PLANT ASSOCIATIONS
Groups of Flowers for Drying

A BLUE AND YELLOW GROUP FOR A SUNNY SPOT

Achillea *'Gold Plate' (the best, though most dry well), backs the group with its tall stems topped with flat 'plates' of bright yellow flowers.* Lavandula *'Hidcote', with flowers of a good deep violet-blue follows and* Echinops *'Taplow Blue' (the best colour, but pick before flowers open in order to dry without dropping) adds deeper tones, while* Polemonium caeruleum *has seedheads following the blue flowers that dry well to pale ivory.* Larkspur, *with both flowers and seedheads that dry well,* Limonium latifolium, *so useful for its mist of tiny mauve flowers on branching stems and* Craspedia globoides, *with bright yellow globe flowers that dry well, make up the front of the group.*

BACK ROW *Achillea* 'Gold Plate'. 1.2-1.5m (4-5ft). *Lavandula* 'Hidcote'. 45cm (1½ft). *Echinops* 'Taplow Blue'. 1.5-1.8m (5-6ft). *Polemonium caeruleum.* 60-90cm (2-3ft).

FRONT ROW Larkspur, annual. 90cm (3ft). *Limonium latifolium.* 45-60cm (1½-2ft). *Craspedia globoides,* half-hardy. 20-30cm (8-12in).

A MAUVE AND PINK GROUP

At the front of the group, Agastache anethiodora *with clover pink spire flowers provides a contrast in form to the wide, starry globe flowers of* Allium albopilosum *and, behind,* A. rosenbachianum *or* A. giganteum *with tightly packed globes in shades of mauve. Tall* Teasels *at the back of the group are best dried when the flowers have dropped (hung in sunlight they bleach to pale biscuit), while in front pretty* larkspurs *in pink and blue have flowers and seedheads that dry really well. More contrasts of form and flower are provided by* Acroclinium roseum *with pink 'everlasting' flowers, and* Achillea *'Cerise Queen' which does not retain its colour so well after drying as the yellow forms, but turns a dull grey-violet to crimson. Next to these,* Papaver somniferum *has delicate pale mauve, dark-eyed flowers which fall quickly but the glaucous seed cases dry well.*

BACK ROW *A. giganteum.* 1.2-1.5m (4-5ft). Teasels. 1.2-1.8m (4-6ft). *A. rosenbachianum.* 1.2m (4ft). **FRONT ROW** *Agastache anethiodora.* 90cm (3ft). *Allium albopilosum.* 60cm (2ft). Larkspur, annual. 90cm (3ft). *Acroclinium roseum,* (syn. *Helipterum roseum).* 30cm (12in). *Achillea* 'Cerise Queen'. 60cm (2ft). *Papaver somniferum.* 75cm (2½ft).

A MAINLY YELLOW GROUP WITH SOME ORANGE-RED SHADES

Phlomis samia, *the tallest plant in the group, has yellow balls of flower carried up square stems, and dries well when the flowers fall. All varieties of* Santolina, *if allowed to flower will dry well in a range of yellow shades, while* Achillea *'Moonshine' has sulphur-yellow flowers which dry to greyish yellow.* Helichrysum annuum, *the annual 'everlasting', produces flowers in shades of yellow, orange, and rust, and is a well-known component of dried-flower arrangements; grasses are less common, but* Briza maxima, *an annual grass with delightful 'lockets' carried on wiry stems dries very well, and* Pennisetum orientale, *a perennial grass, is well worth growing for its furry caterpillar seedheads (and flowers).*

Phlomis samia. 90cm (3ft). Santolina. 75cm (2½ft). *Achillea* 'Moonshine'. 60cm (2ft). *Helichrysum annuum.* 45cm (1½ft). *Briza maxima.* 50cm (1ft 8in). *Pennisetum orientale.* 45cm (1½ft).

many small brownish-yellow flowers which are excellent for cutting. Sprays cut in late autumn, placed in water and kept indoors in a cool room will retain their delicate and pronounced fragrance well into winter. 'Tree' Mignonettes grown in pots became popular house plants in Edwardian times and were sometimes put out in the fragrant garden during the summer, their pots buried in the ground. Seeds would be sown in the pot, with the strongest plant retained and supported with a stick. Side shoots would be pinched out at the second joint, and a tall stem carefully cultivated with a standard head on top.

There are a number of modern forms available today with red and yellow, sulphur, and golden-yellow and orange flowers, as well as several named varieties including 'Machet' with pale red flowers, 'Red Monarch' with dark red flowers and 'Goliath' with double red flowers. Sadly, none of these varieties have the same strong distinctive fragrance of the unimproved Mignonette.

Although treated as an annual, Mignonette is actually a half-hardy perennial and should not be casually sown as an easy-to-grow annual. Seed should be scattered thinly in a well-prepared, well-limed position in a sunny spot in spring where the plants are to bloom, and the seedlings thinned out 10-15cm (4-6in) apart. Mignonette may also be sown in the autumn and protected by cloches. These plants will flower earlier than those sown in the spring.

Nicotiana, usually called the **Tobacco Plant**, is right at the top of the list of scented cottage garden annuals, its fragrance equal in strength to that of the stocks, particularly powerful at dusk. It

was named after Jean Nicot, the sixteenth-century French ambassador to Portugal who, it is said, obtained seeds from a Dutch merchant returning from a West Indies venture, and subsequently introduced them to France.

Nicotiana alata (syn. *affine*), known as the **Jasmine Tobacco**, is the traditional white tobacco plant which grows 90cm-1.2m (3-4ft) in height. It has tubular white flowers which, although rather lifeless during the day, flare into an enormous five-pointed star shape at dusk, emitting a strong sweet fragrance. The plants benefit from some pruning in late summer, but it is a mistake to cut them all back at the same time as several weeks of sweet-scented evenings will thus be lost.

N. alata should be grown as a half-hardy annual and planted out as soon as the risk of frost is over, preferably towards the back of a border, in a rich soil where the handsome, typical tobacco-like leaves act as a background to more colourful plants during the daytime. There are a number of popular dwarf bedding varieties available but if scent is a priority, the coloured varieties should be avoided as they hardly smell at all.

Among the most stately of the tobacco plants is *N. sylvestris*, the **Woodland Tobacco**, which holds its candelabra spikes of deliciously scented, drooping, creamy-white, tubular flowers high above huge, paddle-shaped leaves. Since it will easily reach a height of 1.8-2.4m (6-8ft) in a season, it is unsuitable for the smaller garden. A beautiful plant, it is best grown in a partially shaded position among shrubs, where it will flower from late summer onwards. The flowers, which cascade from a dense central head, are attractive throughout the day and release their exquisite scent during the early evening.

N. tabacum is the true smoking tobacco, a fine plant with attractive soft pink, funnel-shaped flowers held in small clusters, growing 1.8m (6ft) high with gigantic, pale green leaves. Again for the larger garden, this magnificent ornamental plant is particularly useful for filling large empty spaces and associates well with purple foliage and other pink flowers.

All nicotianas need a good rich soil and must be watered freely during dry weather.

Sweet Williams belong to the same family as the pinks and are botanically known as *Dianthus barbatus*. They are trouble-free, typical cottage garden plants and grow to a height of 45cm (18in), bearing flat heads of closely packed clusters of flowers, some self-coloured, others edged, eyed or spotted.

Common in gardens for centuries, Sweet Williams have always been regarded as old-fashioned. They were used extensively when Henry VIII had a new garden planted at Hampton Court in 1533, and were purchased in bulk at the going rate of 3d per bushel. There are several schools of thought as to the origin of the name Sweet William. Some traditionalists believe it was named after William the Conqueror, others that it was named by Gerard in honour of William Shakespeare, whilst Alice Coats in her book *Flowers and their Histories* suggests that it is much more likely that it was originally called Sweet Saint William after St William of Aquitaine.

During the seventeenth century, double-flowered varieties were extremely popular and cultivated everywhere, but today double varieties are a rarity, although it is sometimes possible to buy double-flowered seed strains from specialist seed merchants. 'King Willie', its full name *D. barbatus magnificus*, a low-growing, dark crimson, double-flowered Sweet William, no more than 15cm (6in) tall, does still survive from this period, although it is difficult to find and just as difficult to keep. Cuttings should be taken every year, as small plants of 'King Willie' seem to do better than bigger ones, which tend to rot off at ground level. The bronze foliage contrasts well with the dark crimson, sweet-scented flowers, the stems spreading sideways and the flowers positively glowing in the sunlight.

As one would expect from members of the Dianthus family, Sweet Williams carry a spicy clove fragrance and are excellent for cutting. Although a true perennial, *D. barbatus* is usually treated as a biennial, the seed being sown in late spring to flower the following year. Once Sweet Williams are introduced to the garden, however, and left to themselves, they will seed everywhere. Any garden soil suits them and they have no peculiar fads or fancies other than a deeply dug and well-prepared position with a dressing of lime, for, like all dianthus, they appreciate a fairly chalky soil.

Alyssum maritimum (syn. *Lobularia maritima*), popularly known as **Sweet Alyssum**, is a little half-hardy annual edging plant forming a neat mound of white flowers that go on and on throughout the summer. Its foliage is minute and almost entirely hidden by the freely produced white flowers, and it owes its popular name of Sweet Alyssum to the heady hawthorn-like perfume of the flowers which, on a warm day, fills the air, attracting bees and insects which will work on it until dusk.

Sweet Alyssum is useful and beautiful if used with discretion, but all too often it is planted in a long straight line of white between lobelia and African marigolds in bedding-out displays. However, once it has been grown in a garden, it will soon become naturalised and the seedlings can be encouraged to develop to maturity in places where they look attractive, and weeded out elsewhere.

There are many different varieties but only the whites are worth growing. The pinks tend to be a rather dirty puce and more curious than beautiful, with neither the strong fragrance of the white alyssums or their valuable spreading habit.

Sweet Alyssum prefers a light and not over-rich soil and a position in full sun. In a rich top soil it tends to lose its dwarf habit and produce a super-abundance of leaves. Sow seeds under glass in late winter and plant out where they are to flower after risk of frosts has passed.

PLANT ASSOCIATIONS
Groups for Town Courtyard Settings

Most town courtyards are paved or bricked over, with no actual soil borders, so plants have to be grown in a variety of pots, tubs and troughs. Where there are borders, these are best used to grow the taller plants such as shrubs, climbers and so forth, making sure that shade-tolerant plants are chosen for shady walls and only borders that catch a little sunlight are planted with plants that need some sun to thrive. Most clematis will take the shade of a sheltered wall; C. montana is excellent and will cover large areas, while for something smaller, C. alpina and C. macropetala should do well. Cotoneaster horizontalis will grow up a wall, showering small crimson leaves and red berries in autumn.

Euonymus 'Emerald 'n Gold' and 'Emerald Gaiety' will do well on any aspect. 'Emerald Gaiety' looks especially well with the cotoneaster, while 'Emerald 'n Gold' assorts well with the blue flowers of clematis or ceanothus. Winter jasmine, Jasminum nudiflorum, thrives with little sunlight, as do ivies. Underplant wall shrubs with a mixture of flowering and foliage plants such as Alchemilla mollis, Corydalis lutea, Campanula persicifolia and C. poscharskyana, Tellima grandiflora, violas, aquilegias, astrantias, geraniums, ajuga, mints for fragrance, spring-flowering bulbs and forget-me-nots. Fill pots and tubs with fuchsias, impatiens, Helichrysum petiolatum (this looks lovely round brightly flowered pelargoniums), lobelias and petunias. Many lilies thrive in pots, and can be moved out of the way when flowering is over. Small-leaved ivies are useful grown round the edges of tubs and large pots to trail over the sides. Roses, especially the 'patio' roses, are lovely when grown in pots and, for spring, primulas and polyanthus and most bulbs will thrive.

WALL Clematis montana. Up to 12m (40ft). C. alpina and C. macropetala. Up to 1.8m (6ft). Winter jasmine. Up to 3m (10ft). Ceanothus thyrsiflorus. 3m (10ft). Cotoneaster horizontalis. 60cm-2.4m (2-8ft). Euonymus 'Emerald 'n Gold' and E. 'Emerald Gaiety'. 75-90cm (2½-3ft) and up to 2.7m (9ft) or more if grown up a wall.
UNDERPLANTING Alchemilla mollis. 45cm (1½ft). Corydalis lutea. 20cm (8in). Campanula persicifolia. 90cm (3ft). C. poscharskyana. 30cm (12in). Tellima grandiflora. 45-60cm (1½-2ft). Violas. 23cm (9in). Aquilegias. 90cm (3ft). Astrantias. 60-75cm (2-2½ft). Geraniums. 15-75cm (6in-2½ft). Ajuga. 15cm (6in). Mints. 60cm (2ft). Spring-flowering bulbs. 15-75cm (6in-2½ft).

Lilies and alliums in a packed cottage garden border

Double feverfew in a tub of annuals gives a city patio a country air

A COURTYARD GARDEN

At Chelsea in 1990, the quiet charm of cottage-garden flowers, thickly planted around the edges of a tiny, brick-paved courtyard and enclosed by split wattle hurdles, won a silver gilt medal for the Cottage Garden Society.

Many people would like to create the same feeling of an intimate, country garden in the city but are put off by lack of space and difficult conditions such as dry shade. This garden, which measures only 4.3x3.4m (14x11ft), shows how it can be done.

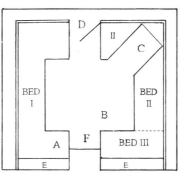

KEY

A Pump & trough

B Birdbath surrounded by Camomile

C Seating area

D Gates & posts

E Low retaining walls

F Single step

(Planting starts from the pump and moves round in clockwise fashion.)

BED I: a shady bed. The soil is damp near the trough and gradually becomes drier towards the gate.

Hosta 'Thomas Hogg'
Pratia pedunculata (now Lobelia pedunculata)
Ajuga reptans 'Alba'
Viola labradorica purpurea
Iris pallida 'Variegata'
Dicentra 'Stuart Boothman'
Corydalis lutea
Adiantum venustum
Phyllitis scolopendrium
Mimulus moschatus
Dryopteris filix-mas
Trollius 'Orange Princess'
Polystichum setiferum divisilobum
Lamium 'Aureum'
Athyrium filix-femina
Ajuga reptans 'Atropurpurea'
Aquilegia vulgaris seedling – maroon and white
Viola 'Mollie Sanderson'
Euphorbia robbiae
Saxifraga umbrosa
Dicentra spectabilis
Rumex sanguineus sanguineus
Aquilegia vulgaris seedlings – shades of pink
Ilex aquifolium
Aquilegia 'Adelaide Addison'
Viola 'Eastgrove Blue'
Dicentra 'Langtrees'
Milium effusum aureum

Hedera helix 'William Kennedy'
Lamium galeobdolon
Buxus sempervirens

CLIMBERS:
Clematis 'Twilight'
Hedera helix
Hedera helix 'Goldheart'
Clematis 'Barbara Jackman'

BED II: a sunny bed, dry and well-drained, with scented plants around the seat.

Buxus sempervirens
Artemisia ludoviciana latiloba
Artemisia pedemontana
Aquilegia seedlings – various colours
Iris germanica hybrid – mauve/lilac
Senecio monroi
Convolvulus althaeoides
Geranium asphodeloides
Geranium phaeum lividum
Hesperis matronalis alba
Solanum dulcamara 'Variegatum'
Euphorbia lathyrus
Anthemis cupaniana
Iris germanica hybrid – blue
Lychnis coronaria alba
Nepeta 'Six Hills Giant'
Helianthemum 'Wisley Pink'
Gillenia trifoliata
Rosa 'Rosamundi'
Stachys lanata
Symphytum officinale
Thymus 'Silver Posy'
Foeniculum vulgare purpureum

Viola 'Johnny-jump-up'
Sedum rhodiola
Annual chrysanthemum
Viola 'Bowles Black'

CLIMBERS:
Clematis 'Kathleen Dunford'
Lonicera henryii
Rosa 'Seagull' (in corner)
Rosa 'Buff Beauty'
Lonicera japonica 'Aureo-reticulata'
Humulus lupulus aureus
Clematis 'Proteus'
Rosa 'Great Maidens Blush'

BED III: a hot and sunny bed containing true herbs and related plants.

Laurus nobilis
Parsley
Fragaria x virginiana
Fragaria vesca semperflorens
Fragaria vesca 'Plymouth Strawberry'
Duchesnia indica
Annual chrysanthemum
Narrow-leaved golden marjoram
Creeping savory
Thymus serpyllum
Rosemary
Salvia officinalis pupurea
Thymus 'Cosmos'
Asperula odorata
Ruta graveolens 'Jackmans Blue'
Curled mint
Melissa officinalis 'Aurea'
Viola 'Bowles Black'

SMALL TROUGH:
Sedum 'Capa Blanca'
Sempervivum arachnoides
Auricula 'Dusty Miller' – red
Antennaria dioica
Erodium chamaedrioides rosea
Narcissus juncifolius
Geranium pylzowianum
Sisyrinchium bellum
Campanula cochleariifolia alba
Thalictrum kiusianum

LARGE TROUGH:
Juniperus communis 'Compressa Nana'
Saxifraga cochlearis minor
Dianthus 'Boothmans Variety'
Sedum hybrid
Sempervivum hybrid

HERB POT:
Geranium macrorrhizum 'Variegatum'
Mentha gentilis variegata
Melissa officinalis variegata
Golden marjoram
Thymus citriodorus variegatus

PLANTS IN PAVING:
Thymus 'Pink Chintz'
Erigeron mucronatus
Chamaemelum nobile
Sempervivum hybrid

GARDEN DESIGN:
C & D Hampton
D Penrose

DESIGN CONSULTANT:
Stephen Crisp

HERBS IN THE BORDER

The word 'herb' brings to mind a plant primarily used for culinary or medicinal purposes, although to our ancestors all plants were herbs, and herbalists included all known flowers in their herbals, usually finding some use for all of them.

Generally speaking, few of the culinary herbs are colourful enough for the border, and nowadays are usually consigned to a herb garden near the kitchen. As you would expect, though, there are bound to be exceptions to the rule. *Angelica archangelica* is better known for its candied stalks and other culinary uses than for its healing properties, and few cottage gardeners would consider banishing it from the border. A magnificent plant with 1.2-1.8m (4-6ft) high, hollow stalks, **angelica** bears large, showy umbels of greenish-white flowers in early summer and sculptured, lush, bright green leaves throughout the year.

The life of the plant, which is biennial, may be prolonged by cutting off the flower heads before they develop fully, but most cottage gardeners would prefer to enjoy its natural cycle, leaving the plant to self-sow and die off naturally after flowering. The flowers of angelica are alluring to queen wasps owing, no doubt, to the nectar on the open discs of the flowers. Plants may be grown in tubs where space is at a premium, and look most effective in shady corners of paved yards. They produce the tenderest leaf stalks in a light, but reasonably rich and damp soil which also encourages quick growth.

Apart from candying, the stems of angelica may be stewed with rhubarb to reduce the tartness, and a leaf or two may be chopped up and enjoyed with a salad. Angelica jam has an unusual and aromatic taste.

Artemisia abrotanum, or **southernwood**, is a member of a huge family of mostly aromatic plants. Southernwood has been known and grown in cottage gardens for centuries and has a number of common names including Lad's Love, Old Man, Boy's Love, Apple Ringie and, in France,

Garde-Robe. The whole plant is highly aromatic and the slightest leaf disturbance will bring out the strong aroma, described by some as sweet, warm and fruity but by others as strange, reminding them of the smell of damp linen in airing cupboards.

Southernwood will make a 90cm (3ft) bush of soft grey-green leaves, with spikes of small, brownish-green flowers in a good summer. It may be clipped and rounded to give a touch of formality to a border, or cut back to 15cm (6in) in early spring to make a delightful low hedge 45-60cm (18-24in) tall.

A native of southern Europe, it is mentioned in a ninth-century book called *Little Garden*. St Francis de Sales refers to sprigs of this herb being included in bouquets given by lovers to their lasses as a symbol of sweet fidelity, even in bitter circumstances. A decoction made from Southernwood was said to cure baldness, hence its common name Old Man. Leaves dried and rubbed off their stems can be used in pot pourri and against moths.

Southernwood flourishes in a light to medium soil, is perfectly hardy and, whilst it will put up with light shade, prefers a position in full sun. Propagate by softwood cuttings taken in early summer or hardwood ones in the autumn.

Borago officinalis or **borage** is one of the most decorative and oldest of the annual herbs. Equally at home in the border or herb garden, although

seeding too freely for the owners of more sophisticated gardens, borage grows 45-75cm (1½-2½ft) tall, with both leaves and stems covered with purplish-grey bristly hairs that glisten in the sun. The flowers, which open from pink buds, are an intense sky-blue with five pointed petals arranged like a star. It is an excellent bee-plant, supplying large quantities of nectar secreted at the base of the ovary.

The flowers and leaves have long been found to bring a cooling taste to drinks, no doubt due to the presence of potassium nitrate, and borage often appears as a constituent of the crown of fruits and herbs which invariably garnish a glass of Pimms No 1 or a gin sling. Flowers frozen in ice cubes give added interest and flavour to a long, cool, summer drink and are frequently floated on a claret cup. The peeled stems of borage have a cucumber-like flavour and may be used in salads, with the flowers added for decoration.

There is a white-flowered form and a rare, pink form for connoisseurs.

Seeds may be sown in a seed box in late winter under glass, or outside in mid-spring. Like most herbs, borage prefers a sunny position but will grow and flower in partial shade.

Foeniculum vulgare or **fennel** is another of the culinary herbs indispensable in the border. As a foliage plant, it has few equals, especially the elegant variety *F. v.* 'Purpureum'. Its purple, young foliage, which later turns bronze, looks most attractive planted at the back of a border either as a foil for more colourful perennials or as a feature plant to draw the eye to another corner of the garden.

The leaves of fennel are finely cut and feathery. Tall and bushy, growing 1.2-1.8m (4-6ft) in height, with its shiny stems and yellow umbels of flowers followed by aromatic seeds, fennel is distinctly cottagey but the strong aniseed-like scent of the leaves, which is quite pronounced if they are disturbed, is not to everyone's liking.

Roman gladiators were said to mix fennel with their food as a stimulant, and successful gladiators were crowned with a garland of the stems at the close of the contests.

The foliage is used, fresh or dried, as a flavour-ing with salmon, mackerel and other fish and may be chopped up as flavouring for a sauce in the same way as parsley. The swollen stems of *Foeniculum dulce*, the **Florence fennel**, have a delicate flavour when cooked as a vegetable and are also good sliced raw in a salad. Both the green and bronze fennels are decorative for indoor flower arrangements, but stems should be plunged into water for some hours before use.

Fennel enjoys a well-drained soil and sunny position. Seed should be sown in a sunny seed bed in the open in early spring. Once the plant is established, self-sown seedlings will appear and should be transplanted to their permanent positions when small, before the tap roots go down too far.

Ruta graveolens or **rue**, Shakespeare's 'Sour Herb of Grace', is an attractive, small evergreen shrub with finely-cut, lacy, glaucous foliage and sprays of tiny, mustard-yellow flowers in late summer. It is of no use in the kitchen and handling the plant can cause severe allergic reactions, so beware. The pungent scent of rue was described by Gerard as 'A very strong and ranke smell'. In times of plague, rue was used as a strewing herb, the odour believed to ward off contagion. It was widely used in prisons and law courts as protection against gaol fever, and it is still traditional for it to be carried by judges at the Assizes today.

A common cottage garden plant, rue is a hardy perennial growing some 45cm (18in) tall. Useful for ground cover and a good mixer in the border, it makes a striking blue-green mound but rapidly grows out of shape and should be replaced every few years. *R. g.* 'Jackman's Rue', an outstanding variety with neat grey-green leaves which are covered with a glaucous sheen, was found by Mr Rowland Jackman in a cottage garden at Addlestone in Surrey. There is an unusual variegated form, *R. g.* 'Variegata', with creamy plumes of young foliage breaking into yellow flowers, which is particularly decorative in foliage arrangements, and actually comes true from seed.

Rue enjoys an open, sunny position and a light to medium soil. Seed can be sown in a seed-pan or outside in early spring. It can also be propagated by cuttings of the new shoots taken during the summer and rooted in a frame or greenhouse. An

PLANT ASSOCIATIONS
Groups of Herbs for Kitchen and Pot Pourri
A GREEN AND YELLOW GROUP FOR THE KITCHEN

Rosemary forms an elegant, evergreen background with misty-blue flowers in spring. Salvia icterina, or sage, with dusty-yellow leaves contrasts well with green fennel, with its filmy foliage and yellow flowers. Creeping savory has green, very pungent leaves and white flowers from late summer into early winter while parsley and yellow thyme provide attractive foliage.

BACK ROW Rosemary (*Rosmarinus officinalis*). Evergreen shrub. 1.2-1.8m (4-6ft). Fennel (*Foeniculum vulgare*). 1.5-2.4m (5-8ft).

FRONT ROW Salvia icterina. 60cm (2ft). Savory (*Satureja repanda*). 15-23cm (6-9in). Parsley. 23cm (9in). Thyme. 2.5-7.5cm (1-3in).

HERBS FOR SCENT AND POT POURRI

Choose from Rosa moschata, *rosemary*, Artemisia abrotanum, *lavender, eau-de-Cologne mint,* Mentha pulegium *(peppermint scented and mat-forming) and* Thymus mastichina, *deliciously scented of a combination of eucalyptus, thyme, rosemary and 'floral bouquet'! Use rue for its historical associations and lovely blue leaves,* Viola odorata, *hyssop, and the pot marigold, or calendula, for its colourful petals in dried herb and flower combinations. Lemon verbena has an incomparable lemon fragrance, and should be grown in a pot and brought indoors in frosty weather. The tender* Thymus mastichina *needs the same treatment.*

Rosa moschata. 3-3.6m (10-12ft). Rosemary. 90cm-1.8m (3-6ft). *Artemisia abrotanum.* 60-90cm (2-3ft). Lavender (*L. angustifolia*). 90cm-1.2m (3-4ft). Eau-de-Cologne mint. 45-90cm (1½-3ft). *Mentha pulegium.* 7.5-20cm (3-8in). *Thymus mastichina.* 15-30cm (6-12in). Rue (*Ruta graveolens*). 60cm (2ft). *Viola odorata.* 10-15cm (4-6in). Hyssop. 30-45cm (1-1½ft). Calendula. 60cm (2ft). Lemon verbena. 1.5m (5ft).

A PINK AND SILVERY GROUP FOR KITCHEN AND PERFUME

Create a soft, delicate effect by combining shrubby plants, like the unusual pink rosemary, (Rosmarinus roseus), with santolina, probably best if its yellow flowers are removed, and lacy-foliaged artemisia. Contrast with more solid leaf shapes, such as those of sage, basil and clary, then add delicate touches with chives, thyme and the prostrate savory.

Rosmarinus roseus. 1.8m (6ft). *Salvia officinalis* 'Purpurea'. 45cm-1.2m (1½-4ft). *Thymus* 'Silver Posie'. 25cm (10in). T. 'Pink Chintz'. 5cm (2in). *Santolina neapolitana.* 60cm (2ft). Purple basil. Half-hardy annual. 30cm (1ft). Pink and white clary. 75cm (2½ft). *Artemisia* 'Lambrook Silver'. 90cm-1.2m (3-4ft). Chives. 15-25cm (6-10in). Creeping savory. 30cm (12in).

KITCHEN GROUP OF GREEN AND YELLOW WITH TOUCHES OF MAUVE-PINK

Golden marjoram, yellow-leaved and strongly flavoured, provides brilliant foliage colour. Narrow-leaved sage seldom flowers and so remains neater and less leggy than broad-leafed sage. Apple mint, particularly the white-variegated form, is delicious and pretty. Chives, parsley, tarragon, lemon thyme, basil and rosemary are all useful additions. If purple basil is grown, this adds a strong dark beetroot colour to the group.

BACK ROW Rosemary, such as *Rosmarinus* 'Severn Sea'. 90cm (3ft). Or R. 'Prostratus'. 15cm (6in). Both are lower growing, evergreen and slightly tender. Sage, (*Salvia officinalis*). 45cm (1½ft). French tarragon (*Artemisia dracunculus*). 45-60cm (1½-2ft). Apple mint (*Mentha rotundifolia*). 45cm (1½ft). **FRONT ROW** Chives, basil, parsley, marjoram, and lemon thyme: none growing more than 25cm (10in).

old superstition which could well start cottagers on the slippery slope is that for rue to thrive it must first be stolen.

Tanacetum vulgare or **tansy** is a much admired hardy perennial herb with feathery, aromatic leaves which are a joy to bruise, and vivid yellow button flowers in late summer. Tansy is frequently confused with the shrub santolina (Cotton Lavender), no doubt because both have yellow button flowers, but the foliage of santolina is quite different. Grey and encrusted like coral it is only 90cm (3ft) tall, whilst tansy has green leaves and will grow 1.2-1.5m (4-5ft) high.

Of luxuriant growth, tansy is happy in most garden soils but is very invasive, and is best planted in an old bucket or large pot to restrict root growth. The plant can be used to great effect in the border, and will enhance many an autumn flower arrangement. Tansy, dried and powdered, was formerly used as a flavouring herb, and bitter tansy cakes or 'tansies' as they were called were eaten on Easter Day to purge the body of 'bad humours' after the restricted diet of Lent. Tansy tea was used medicinally against fevers and nervous disorders.

There is a particularly good form, *Tanacetum vulgare crispum*, with sweetly scented, finely-cut leaves resembling a Prince of Wales feather. It is excellent for cutting and grows 1m (3½ft) high.

Chrysanthemum parthenium, now known as *Tanacetum parthenium* but better known as **feverfew**, is a 60cm (2ft) high, hardy, biennial to perennial plant with bright green foliage and white daisy flowers with yellow centres, and a pungent, fresh smell. Frequently found in the wild, it is the golden-leaved and double forms that are so popu-

lar today and, although short-lived perennials, they will seed themselves true to type.

In Victorian times the golden-leaved feverfew, *T. parthenium* 'Aureum' with hummocks of soft golden-yellow foliage and sprays of white flowers, was much used in bedding schemes, and double-flowered forms have been grown since the late sixteenth century. *T. p.* 'Golden Ball' is an excellent cultivated strain of compact growth producing a quantity of small, fully double, chrome-yellow flowers which will brighten any border, while *T. p.* 'Snow Ball' is a white-flowered version of 'Golden Ball' with tiny, snowball-like flowers.

As a medicine, feverfew was traditionally used in a cold infusion as a general tonic and today the leaves are recommended for migraine. The plant is also reputed to deter ants. Feverfew will grow in any well-drained soil in sun or light shade and is propagated by seed or division.

Day lilies and veronicas in a summer border with self-seeded feverfew underneath

CURIOSITIES OLD AND NEW

Traditionally, 'curiosities' and 'oddities' have always found a haven in the cottage garden, a chance find in woods or fields – perhaps retrieved by a sharp-eyed cottager and tucked away in an odd corner of the garden – surviving there undisturbed by changing fashion for centuries. Conservation-minded cottage gardeners today enjoy, and continue, the long tradition of growing and sharing these antique curiosities, at the same time collecting today's eccentrics and, incidentally, adding enormously to the garden's conversational value!

Plantago major 'Rosularis', the **Rose Plantain**, is an old plant, although it is not certain when this variant was first collected and grown in gardens. Parkinson says, 'The Rose Plantain hath been long in England' and Gerard illustrates it in 1597.

Basically, it is an ordinary lawn plantain but the usual thin, rat-tail-like spikes of seed are replaced by large, round heads, rose-like in appearance, on 23cm (9in) stems with large, strong, smooth leaves. Being completely green it tends to get lost in the garden, but when it is pointed out to visitors they are usually intrigued.

Occasionally, plants will appear with elongated heads, and sometimes with both types on one plant, making it a flower arranger's dream. Like the ordinary plantain, the rose plantain seeds freely but its seedlings can be distinguished from those of the common one by the signs of a frill about the tiny flower spikes.

Rosa chinensis viridiflora, or the **Green Rose**, is an oddity dating back to 1855. It is sometimes less kindly known as 'Rosa monstrosa' – a reflection of the opinion some people have had of it in the past. It makes a light, open bush, about 1.2mx90cm (4x3ft), with double green flowers which seem to be made up of serrated green leaves tinged with bronze. In bloom from early spring and often still flowering strongly in midwinter, its season is longer than that of any other rose. However, like the rose plantain it is not a plant which makes its presence felt, and could well be missed if you did not know where it was in the garden, for the small flowers merge in with the rather pointed leaves.

Calendula officinalis 'Prolifera', sometimes known as the **Hen and Chickens Marigold**, is a most unusual form in which the double marigold flower is surrounded by the secondary flowers arranged 'sun and planet' style, with their stalks springing from just beneath the petals of the 'parent' bloom.

Grown in gardens since the late sixteenth century, it was mentioned by Gerard: 'This fruitfull or much-bearing Marigold is likewise called of the vulgar sort of women Jacke-an-apes on horsebacke ... for this plant doth bring forth at the top of the stalke one floure like the other Marigolds, from the which start forth sundry other smal floures, yellow likewise, and of the same fashion as the first, which if I be not deceived, commeth to passe *per accidens* or by chance'.

Apart from its obvious curiosity value, the Hen and Chickens Marigold is a most attractive flower in its own right, coming true from seed which, fortunately, can still be obtained from specialist suppliers.

Introduced from France in 1773, *Fragaria vesca monophylla*, the **One-leaved Strawberry**, is one of several eccentric forms of the wild strawberry, said to be one of E. A. Bowles' 'lunatic asylum' plants which he kept in a special bed, and it is sometimes referred to as 'Mr Bowles' rare one-leaved strawberry'.

The green-flowered strawberry, *F. v.* 'Plymouth Strawberry' was found by John Tradescant in a garden in Plymouth, another oddity guaranteed to stop visitors in their tracks. Parkinson called it the 'prickly Strawberry' because the narrow fruits were covered with green hairs, and described it as 'plesant to behold, and fit for a gentle woman to wear on her arme, etc., as a raritie in stead of a flower'. A pretty, double-flowered form, *F. v.* 'Flore Pleno', has small semi-double cream flowers and vigorous runners, whilst *F. v.* 'Variegata' has good, green and cream variegated foliage and white flowers.

Fragaria indica, now renamed *Duchesnia indica,* the yellow-flowered strawberry, was first introduced from India in 1804. This rampant alpine strawberry with yellow flowers and large, non-edible, lush red berries occurring rather attractively together, was much used in hanging baskets in Victorian times, and makes excellent ground cover. A pink-flowered strawberry, *Fragaria* 'Pink Panda', introduced by Bressingham Nurseries in 1989, is not a chance find but a deliberate cross between *Potentilla palustris*, the **Marsh Cinquefoil** and *Fragaria grandiflora,* the common garden strawberry, by Dr Jack Ellis the expert plant-breeder. Easy to grow, 'Pink Panda' has bright semi-evergreen leaves and is excellent in pots, window boxes, hanging baskets or as ground cover, flowering continuously from early spring until late autumn, and occasionally producing attractive, edible fruit.

Campanula persicifolia 'Cup and Saucer' carries its wide, cup-shaped flowers surrounded with one layer of flattened petals, just like a cup and saucer, on graceful, wiry stems over a long period. An exceptionally pretty cottage garden plant, it is of fairly recent introduction.

Hemerocallis fulva 'Flore Pleno' is the curious double-flowered **Day Lily**, crowded with petals in several shades of orange. It flowers for a number of weeks and needs little attention. The rare, variegated, double-flowered form, *H. f.* 'Kwanzo Flore Pleno Variegata', with striking white-variegated leaves, was introduced from Japan in 1864.

At the Cottage Garden Society's first annual plant sale at Betley, Cheshire in 1988, three plants of *Anthriscus sylvestris* 'Ravenswing', a beautiful, **Black-leaved Cow Parsley** were kindly donated for sale by a Derbyshire member. The plant had been discovered in a hedgerow near Reading by Dr John Richards and this was the first public appearance for 'Ravenswing'. It was immediately spotted as a rare find and snapped up for the society's plant bank. About 50 percent of seeds sown come true (the green seedlings must be rogued out and only the blackest seedlings retained), and 'Ravenswing' was distributed to members of the society fairly quickly. Plants appeared in gardens all over the country and a new 'curiositie' was established.

More recently at the society's 1992 plant sale at Taunton in Somerset, a white-flowered form of the wild flower *Centaurea scabiosa*, with finely-cut, lacy, chalky-white flowers with a reddish-purple centre, was introduced. This plant, too, was found in a hedgerow (actually in a lay-by) but this time in Dorset, by a Dorset member, Mrs Janet Johnson, who named it *Centaurea scabiosa alba* 'Cottage Garden'. No doubt as *C. s. a.* 'Cottage Garden' is distributed from the CGS Plant Bank, this white form of the **Greater Knapweed** will become as popular as 'Ravenswing' and add another 'curiositie' to the cottage garden.

AUTUMN

Summer merges gently into autumn, the changes almost imperceptible from day to day. The annual cycle of growth and renewal is gradually winding down. The sun is lower in the sky, casting long shadows, and the afternoon light is golden, spread like honey over walls, roofs and hedges. Dusk now brings a damp chill to the air, forming mist in the hollows, and early morning finds the garden drenched with dew, sparkling on grass and twigs and spiders' webs.

A SEASONAL PICTURE

As the nights grow colder so the colours grow stronger, richer, in the foliage of trees and shrubs. Rowan and cherry, dogwood and crab glow with autumn fire, yet summer seems reluctant to depart, wrapping the garden in its lingering warmth and teasing into bloom a stem of blue campanulas here, a cluster of pink roses there. Butterflies and bees still throng the last flowers of buddleia and sedum, and a late dragonfly glides and darts above the sunlit borders.

Many of the summer flowers – dahlias, fuchsias, pelargoniums and all the bright half-hardy annuals – will continue to provide colour until finally discouraged by the winter frosts. Late kniphofias, elegant white Japanese anemones and rugosa roses are joined by clouds of Michaelmas daisies in shades of lilac and purple, and chrysanthemums in their tapestry tones of bronze and burgundy, ochre and rose. The sunny rudbeckias, too, will soldier on for a few more weeks, leaving behind, when their colours fade, seedheads like big black thimbles and fluffy brown plumes which will last into the winter.

One of the great surprises of the season is the appearance, as if by magic, of colchicum flowers. By the pathside, at the foot of a tangle of honeysuckle or a summer-fragrant phila-delphus, there they are, where the previous day there was nothing. Or at least nothing that caught the eye. In fact they had been expanding their white, mushroom-like buds for a few days, but the transformation from bud to spectacular flower is quite rapid. Their shining colour is something to be lingered over in admiration every autumn, but their large, all-smothering and slowly fading foliage must be endured as payment due each spring. Autumn crocuses are much more obliging, leafing up at the same time as their spring-flowering sisters and, with similar grassy foliage, easily accommodated in front of shrubs and perennials. And how lovely the crocus flowers look rising above a red and yellow mosaic of fallen autumn leaves.

Rambler roses that garlanded arch or trellis with their fragrant flowers in summer are hung now with bright hips of scarlet and orange. Berries blaze on pyracantha, cotoneaster and rowan, and the branches of crab apples are heavily laden with their small red or yellow fruits.

At the foot of a hedge or by a shady pathside, the hardy *Cyclamen hederifolium* opens its dainty flowers and marbled leaves above a carpet of wood violets and purple ajuga. Here the shade-loving epimediums and ferns take on autumnal tones of russet-red and golden-brown, and the berried spikes of *Arum italicum pictum* change from bright green to even brighter orange amidst their unfolding leaves.

Against a sunny wall, sugar-pink nerines open flowers like bunches of ribbons. A few late clematis blooms glow among their fading greenery, and the foliage of Virginia creeper blazes with every fiery shade imaginable.

The autumn days drift by. Soon the trees will be bare, and cold driving rain will clog the fluffy seedheads of echinops and aster and turn the bright carpet of fallen leaves to dull and sodden brown. Darkness will bring frosts to blacken the dahlias, and it will be time for autumn to leave the stage and winter to make its entrance.

Seasonal Tasks
FOR AUTUMN

Plant out spring-flowering bulbs such as crocus, narcissus, tulips, hyacinths and muscari, as well as some early summer-flowering types such as alliums.

Collect seeds of hardy cyclamen. These are usually ready just before the current year's flowers open and are best sown immediately.

Take cuttings of shrubs, using half-ripe wood in early autumn, hard wood in late autumn. For suitable shrubs, see plant descriptions.

Move plants when necessary. Both shrubs and perennials establish better while soil still retains some warmth. In areas of heavy rainfall it is generally considered best to wait until spring, and some plants prefer to be moved in spring regardless of area. Check plant descriptions.

Most perennials can be lifted and divided in autumn to increase stocks or, where necessary, to maintain young, vigorous growth and eliminate old woody portions. A few should only be divided in spring. Check plant description for details.

It is often a good idea to half-prune shrubs such as buddleia and lavatera which may be susceptible to damage from winter gales. This is best done in late autumn or early winter. Roses, too, can be pruned from late autumn onwards, cutting back as little or as much as necessary, though where hard pruning is required this is best left until early spring.

Clear dead leaves from around herbaceous plants to minimise damage by slugs to dormant shoots of susceptible plants, such as hostas, asters, and euphorbias.

Gather fallen leaves from paths, lawns and borders and store in wire mesh enclosures to rot down and form leaf mould. Do not add other materials, such as kitchen waste or lawn mowings, which are better kept for the compost heap. It takes up to two years to rot thoroughly, but the result is well worth waiting for.

As light levels fall and daylight hours grow shorter, re-move shading from greenhouse and frames. Gradually cut down on watering, but continue to ventilate well to deter pests and diseases.

Continue to cut interesting seedheads for drying for in-door decoration. Early autumn is the best time, too, to cut beech leaves for preserving by the glycerine method. Many evergreens are also suitable for this method of preserving, in-cluding mahonia, laurel and variegated privet.

Continue to collect seeds and store them in dry, airtight containers, remembering to label clearly with name of plant and date of collection. You may *think* you will recognise 'the tiny brown oval ones' next year, but you won't.

Plant specially-prepared hyacinth, narcissus and tulip bulbs in bowls for flowering indoors at Christmas, using bulb fibre or seed and cutting compost. Bulbs must not touch each other or the side of the bowl, and the tops of the bulbs should come just above the surface of the compost. Stand the bowls in a cool, shady part of the garden and cover them with about 10cm (4in) of peat, or place them in black polythene bags and store in a cool garage or shed for 6-10 weeks, checking occasionally to see that the compost does not dry out.

If you have a garden shredder, use it to convert spent perennial stems and any shrubbery prunings into useful material resembling chopped straw or chaff. This can be left in the open to rot down, or stored in plastic sacks and used in alter-nate layers with kitchen waste in the compost bin. The result is superb compost or mulch.

Mowers, secateurs and shears should be cleaned, oiled and put away for the winter.

TREES FOR FRUIT AND AUTUMN COLOUR

Autumn colour is not usually the cottage gardener's first consideration in choosing trees. A small garden may have room for only one or two, and traditionalists will take the opportunity to grow an **apple** tree for its fruit, of course, but also because it gives the right character to the garden.

Crab apples are an alternative. Even while young they produce fruit for jelly, and their leaves colour well before they fall. It is still difficult to beat the old favourite 'John Downie' with its egg-shaped, sharp-flavoured fruit and its spreading, slightly drooping branches. It will eventually grow to between 4.5 and 6m (15 and 20ft). Its disadvantage is that the fruit falls quickly, while the weeping 'Red Jade' will hold its clusters of bright red 'apples' well into the winter. For yellow fruit, 'Golden Hornet' is the one, but for brilliant autumn colour, *Malus tschonoskii* is the best. Its habit is more upright and formal, its head more compact and it looks good planted in pairs at either side of a straight path. If all of these are too familiar, a more unusual crab is *Malus transitoria*, a fine, shapely small tree with masses of blossom in spring, and 'apples' like amber beads which cling to the branches right on into winter.

In a Scottish or Welsh cottage garden the **Rowan** or sorbus looks at home. *Sorbus* 'Joseph Rock' has warm yellow berries with bronze-purple autumn foliage. If you like a challenge, the more ferny-leaved *S. vilmorinii* has creamy-pink berries and is one of the most beautiful of small trees. Slow and difficult to grow, it is also quite difficult to find.

The **Stags Horn Sumach** (*Rhus typhina*) is another small tree, out of fashion now, which was often seen in cottage gardens. It has striking pinnate leaves which turn a brilliant red in autumn and, as it tolerates atmospheric pollution, it will grow well in industrial areas. Beware, however, of its tendency to sucker.

Finally, one of the most brilliant autumn displays comes from the amelanchier, commonly known as the **Juneberry** or **Serviceberry**, which is halfway between a tree and a shrub. It is described in the Spring section but must be mentioned here, for it turns a bright crimson in mid-autumn – then, its firework display over, in a moment its leaves drop.

SHRUBS

❧ BUDDLEIA ❧

Hardy, deciduous, honey-scented shrubs, buddleias have been cottage garden favourites for a long time and are ideal for a mixed border or as a delightful, informal screen. They bear panicles of purple, mauve or white flowers at the ends of their young shoots from midsummer onwards and, because they grow so quickly, are one of the best shrubs for furnishing a new garden. In the late summer sunshine the buddleia is besieged by clouds of butterflies which quickly cover the flowers hence its other name, the Butterfly Bush.

The purple-flowered species of buddleia, *Buddleia davidii*, was first discovered by Père David in the 1860s and named after him. However, the best form of this plant was grown from seed sent to France in 1893 by Père Soulié, another priest-botanist. His fate was a dreadful one, for in 1905 he was captured by Tibetan monks who tortured him for two weeks, then shot

MORE SHRUBS AND SMALL TREES FOR AUTUMN FOLIAGE

Acer

Many acers give splendid autumn leaf colour and can be grown as shrubs or trees. *A. griseum* is a winner, with brilliant red and orange colour and peeling orange bark. It is a slow grower but may eventually reach 6x3.6m (20x12ft).

Berberis thunbergii (and cultivars)

1.2x1.8m (4x6ft). Deciduous, spiny shrub with palish green leaves which turn brilliant red in autumn. Small yellow flowers in spring. Small ovoid scarlet berries in autumn.

Cotoneaster

Many, from dwarf varieties to trees, including *C. adpressus*, 30x45cm (1x1½ft). *C. bullatus*, 2.4x3m (8x10ft). *C. divaricatus*, 1.8x2.4m (6x8ft) and *C. horizontalis* with its herringbone pattern of branches bearing tiny leaves which turn pinky red. Can be grown as prostrate, but when trained against a wall will reach 1.8m (6ft) or more. Bees love its blossoms. All have long-lasting red berries.

Crataegus prunifolia

Small tree 4.5x6m (15x20ft). Broad, compact head. Thorny. Glossy dark green leaves, white blossom in spring, fiery autumn foliage and large red haws lasting into winter.

Euonymus europaeus
SPINDLE TREE

Deciduous, 3x3m (10x10ft). Slender, pointed oval leaves. Small, greeny white flowers in spring and rose-red capsules in autumn, which open to reveal orange seeds.

Prunus

Many, including *P.* 'Hillieri Spire', 4.5x3m (15x10ft), and *P. incisa*, 3x4.5m (10x15ft), have good autumn colour, but blossom colour and shape, and spring foliage, are more likely to be the deciding factors in choosing them.

Rosa glauca (syn. rubrifolia)

2.4x1.2m (8x4ft). Red-tinged, arching stems, purple young foliage turning grey-green in summer and shades of bronze and ochre in autumn, with small, purple-pink, gold-stamened flowers followed by bright red hips. One of the loveliest shrubs.

Hips and autumn-tinted foliage after the flowers have gone, make Rosa glauca *a valuable shrub in the cottage garden*

and killed him. He was not by any means the only plant hunter who faced suffering and even death to furnish our gardens with the flowers we enjoy.

 Buddleias are strong growers and most types, including those we list, need to be cut back hard in the spring to within a few buds of the old wood to produce the best flowers and avoid the plant becoming leggy and losing its shape. All buddleias enjoy a deep, rich, loamy soil and a sunny position. They may be planted at any time during the winter and early spring and propagated by hardwood cuttings taken in autumn.

○ *Buddleia davidii* **'Black Knight'**
The darkest of all the buddleias, with elegant panicles of deepest violet-purple flowers with an orange eye and a strong scent.
○ *B. d.* **'White Profusion'**
Massive heads of white flowers and abundant side flower spikes. Should be deadheaded immediately as, once the flowers are past their best, they quickly fade to a dirty brown.
○ *B. d.* **'Pink Delight'**
A recent introduction from Holland with strongly scented flowers of a true deep pink.
○ *B. fallowiana*
A slender shrub with grey-green foliage and pale lavender-blue flowers in large panicles. Richly scented. The white form, *B. f.* 'Alba', has white flowers with an orange eye and greyer, almost silvered, foliage.
○ *B. crispa*
With its heavily felted grey leaves and its clusters of lilac-pink, orange-throated flowers, this rather tender deciduous plant is best grown against a sunny, sheltered wall. It is in bloom from late summer and looks well with the striped sword-like leaves of *Sisyrinchium* 'Aunt May'.

❧ CARYOPTERIS ❧

A most attractive small shrub about 60cm (2ft) tall, making a neatly rounded bush very suitable for a sunny mixed border. From late summer to the end of autumn, the caryopteris, sometimes called the Blue Spiraea, gives a continuous show of long flower spikes covered with plumbago-blue blossoms over narrow, greeny-grey foliage which releases a strong, aromatic fragrance when bruised.

The bush is hardy except in very exposed gardens but a sheltered position is best, as its brittle stems are easily damaged by strong winds and then its whole appearance is spoilt.

Caryopteris should be grown in a rich, loamy soil and never allowed to dry out at the roots during the summer, although on no account should it be planted in a place that is likely to be waterlogged in winter. It is not a long-lived shrub but is easily increased by half-ripened cuttings 7.5 to 10cm (3 to 4in) in length, taken in summer and rooted in pure sand in a frame with gentle heat. Autumn and spring are the most suitable times for planting.

○ *Caryopteris x clandonensis*
This is the best-known variety and was named after a garden at Clandon in Surrey where it was found growing in 1930 as a self-sown seedling, the result of a chance cross between two other species introduced in the mid-nineteenth century. It proved such an improvement on the other two that only one of them, *C. incana,* seems to be available any more. It gives the effect of a brilliant lavender in bloom.
○ *C. x c.* **'Heavenly Blue'**
A good form of this graceful shrub, with mid-blue flowers and scented blue-grey foliage.
○ *C. x c.* **'Kew Blue'**
A smaller shrublet with dark violet-blue flowers.

❧ CERATOSTIGMA ❧

The flowers of the ceratostigma are very like those of the plumbago and the two plants were once grouped together by botanists. Technically shrubs, although they behave like perennials, ceratostigmas die back at the slightest suggestion of a frost. It is quite late in the spring before the wiry stems show signs of life again, and the heads of pure cobalt blue flowers appear from early summer till the start of winter weather. The leaves, a fresh green to start with, turn red before they fall.

Ceratostigmas may be planted in the border or rock garden, but the best place for them is the base of a sunny wall with tulips or other spring-flowering bulbs planted in front of them to hide their bare stems until the leaves appear again. Humming-bird hawk-moths haunt the flowers during warm days in early autumn, their long tongues fashioned to reach the nectar in the tiny, tubular throats of the flowers.

Ceratostigmas thrive in almost any soil, but should be given a hot, dry, sunny position. Propagate by taking softwood cuttings rooted under glass in early spring or half-ripe cuttings taken in summer, again under glass. When rooted they should be potted up singly in a light open compost.

○ *Ceratostigma willmottianum*
This species is named after Miss Ellen Willmott who, amongst others, received seed sent from China in 1908 by the plant hunter E. H. Wilson. She alone (or perhaps one of her 104 gardeners!) managed to germinate any and raised two plants, the ancestors of today's shrubs. This good form grows to about 60cm (2ft) with a mass of sky-blue flowers over a long period.

○ *C. plumbaginoides*
This plant was originally christened Lady Lampert's Plumbago since it, also, owes its existence to a skilled plantswoman who propagated it from one plucked from the walls of Shanghai in 1844. It is a vigorous, creeping, dwarf form and a useful ground coverer, with flowers of a brilliant blue and leaves which turn scarlet in mid-autumn to sumptuous effect.

❧ FUCHSIAS ❧

The hardy fuchsia is often used for flowering hedges and windbreaks near the sea coast in Cornwall, the West Country and Ireland. It will grow in any soil and there are so many different varieties that there is one for any kind of border, sunny or shady, with the large-flowered types ideal for tubs and ornamental pots. With their pendant blooms in pink and white, purple and pink, and pink and red, fuchsias are graceful plants which will give colour in the cottage garden right through the summer and they seem to take on a new lease of life at the onset of autumn, obviously enjoying the cooler, damp air and flowering more and more profusely.

These shrubs are excellent with hydrangeas, while the dwarf varieties make good edging plants and are useful for late colour in the rock garden.

The most vigorous of the hardy fuchsias can easily make 1.5-1.8m (5-6ft) in a season, but need to be cut back to within a few centimetres of the ground after bad winters. Young pot-grown plants should be planted out in late spring about 10cm (4in) below soil level. The crowns should be covered with about 15cm (6in) of dried leaves, weathered ash or some other mulch, immediately after the first frosts in autumn.

○ *Fuchsia* 'Ricartonii'
Undoubtedly the hardiest and probably the best known of the hardy fuchsias, with a constant show of red flowers with purple sepals from midsummer till the autumn. A vigorous grower, 'Ricartonii' is particularly useful for hedges and is grown extensively for this purpose in Cornwall.

○ *F.* 'Mrs Popple'
One of the larger-flowered old favourites with showy scarlet and deep violet flowers on stiff stems. A good, hardy variety.

○ *F.* 'Tom Thumb'
A dwarf variety ideal for the rock garden or a low hedge, with large flowers in comparison to the size of the plant.

○ *F. magellanica* 'Versicolor'
A superb, variegated form with red flowers and grey-green foliage which produces a constantly changing pattern of pink, crimson and cream, the colours being more intense in the spring and autumn. Like so many variegated plants, however, this fuchsia tends to revert to plain green and offending shoots should be removed as they appear in late spring.

PLANT ASSOCIATIONS
A Group for a Sunny, Sheltered Wall

Clematis viticella 'Minuet', with creamy-white flowers tipped with reddish-purple in late summer and autumn, combines beautifully with Vitis vinifera 'Purpurea' with dusky purple leaves throughout the growing season. Underplant with pink-flowered Nerine bowdenii, Convolvulus sabateus which has spode-blue flowers throughout summer and autumn, and various hebes and cistus for foliage colour throughout the year, including winter.

CLIMBERS *Clematis viticella* 'Minuet'. 3-4m (10-12ft). *Vitis vinifera* 'Purpurea'. Up to 7m (23ft).

IN FRONT *Nerine bowdenii.* 45-60cm (1½-2ft). *Convolvulus sabateus.* 15-20cm (6-8in). Hebes. Cistus.

The deepening red of vine leaves announce autumn

⊷ HYDRANGEA ⊷

Hydrangeas are one of the most familiar flowering shrubs in our gardens. They are often seen growing in great banks in coastal areas, especially in southern and western counties of Britain, but are equally at home in cottage gardens, spilling and bulging from their beds and providing a magnificent display from early summer until the frosts.

Not all hydrangeas are to everyone's taste and perhaps some are more at home in the formal garden or conservatory than in the cottage garden, but it is difficult to take exception to the elegant lacecaps which have flattened flower heads with tiny, fertile flowers in the centre and an outer ring

Hydrangea preziosa. *The flower heads of this small hydrangea turn bright scarlet in autumn*

of sterile florets. Equally attractive are the varied species, which include the summer-flowering, climbing hydrangea, *Hydrangea petiolaris*.

Named after Hortense, daughter of an eighteenth-century botanist, the Prince de Nassau, the hortensias or 'mophead' hydrangeas are, to many people, the typical hydrangea and certainly the most popular and widely grown. Some care should be taken in colour selection, as they can overwhelm the autumn border with a rather vulgar show of brashly coloured blooms. Hortensias with pink or blue flowers are pink on alkaline soils unless treated with a proprietary bluing agent, and blue on acid soils.

A good selection of the best varieties of the hortensias and lacecaps is easily available from reliable nurseries, although some of the species may be more difficult to track down – but well worth the effort.

Although hardy in most districts, the young, early growth of hydrangeas is very often damaged by late spring frosts, and the removal of the old flower heads, attractive in themselves, should be left as long as possible to protect the new growth from late frosts. Hydrangeas will grow happily in full sun, but will also flower just as well in partial shade. They are ideal for beds or borders and look particularly effective when planted on a slightly raised bank. All hydrangeas are thirsty, hungry plants, and during hot spells and droughts should be watered every day, and sometimes more than once a day if you are to avoid a wilting, rather pathetic-looking plant gasping for water.

■ Plants can be increased by means of cuttings taken either in the spring or during late summer. Cuttings taken in the spring should be selected from lateral shoots, but the late summer ones should be made from half-ripened growths, preferably those which have failed to flower during the summer.

○ *Hydrangea arborescens* 'Grandiflora'
A fully hardy variety with large, rounded, bun-shaped heads of creamy-white flowers from late summer and a bright yellow autumn leaf colour.

○ *H. serrata* 'Greyswood'
A good shrub for a small garden, this is a lacecap with blue central florets. The outer infertile ones turn from white to rose-red to crimson.

○ *H.* 'Preziosa'
A small, hortensia type with heads which change from pink to a deeper, blotched crimson as the season progresses. It has distinctive, rather pointed leaves.

✧ PYRACANTHA ✧

Pyracanthas or Firethorns are easy, fast-growing, thorny evergreens. Their sheets of tiny, creamy-

---

PLANT ASSOCIATIONS

A Mainly Silver and Yellow Scheme with Orange Accents

Pyracantha 'Orange Glow', evergreen with bright orange berries, forms a background for Senecio laxifolius 'Sunshine' with grey foliage, white stems on young shoots and brassy yellow daisies in summer. Alongside it, plant Hypericum inodorum 'Elstead', with yellow flowers throughout summer followed by red fruits, and Rudbeckia 'Goldsturm', single yellow daisies with dramatic black centre cones. The bright green, grassy foliage of Crocosmia 'Emily McKenzie', with orange and red flowers, contrasts well with the grey-leaved Anaphalis triplinervis, with white 'everlasting' flowers in late summer and autumn.

BACK ROW Pyracantha 'Orange Glow'. 3x4.5m (10x15ft). Senecio laxifolius 'Sunshine'. 1.2x1.5m (4x5ft). Hypericum inodorum 'Elstead'. 1.2x1.2m (4x4ft). Rudbeckia 'Goldsturm'. 60cm (2ft). **FRONT ROW** Crocosmia 'Emily McKenzie'. 60cm (2ft). Anaphalis triplinervis. 60cm (2ft).

white, hawthorn-like flowers, produced in late spring, hum with insects and are followed in the autumn by a crop of red, yellow or orange berries which, birds permitting, last well into the winter.

Although the Firethorns are regarded today essentially as wall shrubs, they make excellent hedging or screening bushes, and it was as trees, shrubs and hedges that they were grown until the eighteenth century. Specimens can easily grow to 4.5m (15ft) tall and as much across in the open garden, where they flower and berry well.

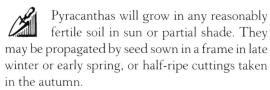 Pyracanthas will grow in any reasonably fertile soil in sun or partial shade. They may be propagated by seed sown in a frame in late winter or early spring, or half-ripe cuttings taken in the autumn.

■ A beautiful flowering and foliage hedge can be had by planting young, pot-grown plants about 45-60cm (1½-2ft) apart during the autumn or in spring, in any garden soil. Staking is advisable for the first year until the roots are established.

■ Until the hedge is at its desired height, only the side growths should be trimmed in spring and, if necessary, again in the summer. Once the hedge is at the desired height, probably about 1.8m (6ft), the top growth should be pruned at the same time. Where space is limited, severe pruning may be necessary. This will inevitably result in some sacrifice of flower and berry, but will keep the hedge compact and prevent it from becoming lanky.

○ *Pyracantha coccinea* 'Lalandei'
One of the most popular and strongest growing of the Firethorns, with orange-red fruits covering the branches throughout the winter.

○ **P. 'Orange Glow'**
A free-flowering and fruiting pyracantha with masses of orange-red berries which again, birds permitting, last well into the winter.

○ **P. 'Waterer'**
Red berries with the added attraction of copper-coloured, young foliage. Dense, twiggy habit. Reaching 2.4-3m (8-10ft).

○ **P. 'Soleil d'Or'**
'Soleil d'Or' or 'Golden Sun' is a good variety with deep yellow berries, freely borne.

❧ SYMPHORICARPOS ❧

The common Snowberry *Symphoricarpos rivularis* was discovered on the banks of the River Columbia in Washington State by two American explorers, Merryweather Lewis and William Clark, who made an expedition to the Western USA in 1804-6. Seeds were sent to Britain and the shrub became immediately popular. It was once a familiar sight in cottage gardens, much planted in uninviting corners where its suckering ways could do little harm, and where the attractive white mothball-like berries would swing to and fro on twiggy stems during the winter months.

Symphoricarpos are hardy, deciduous shrubs with roundish, grey-green foliage and pink-tinted, bell-shaped flowers of little significance which appear in early summer. Whilst the common Snowberry is no longer encouraged in gardens, the various new varieties with better habits and pink as well as white berries are most certainly worth growing, along with the larger-berried ones which are much in demand by flower arrangers.

 The common Snowberry will grow anywhere and thrive where few other plants would survive but the new ones require rather better attention and a moist, loamy soil in an open sunny position to give of their best. Propagate by taking cuttings 20-23cm (8-9in) in length, of fully ripened, young growth in late summer, or increase by carefully removing sucker growth in the autumn.

○ *Symphoricarpos* x *doorenbosii* 'White Hedge'
A particularly good form, with large white berries which grow unusually close to the rather upright stems.

○ **S. x *d*. 'Magic Berry'**
A pink variety with deep cyclamen-pink berries. Much sought after for floral arrangements.

○ **S. x *d*. 'Mother of Pearl'**
A graceful shrub with white berries attractively flushed rose.

○ **S. *orbiculatus* 'Variegatus'**
An excellent foliage plant, good for cutting, with small gold-margined leaves and tiny red berries like red beads. May lose variegation in heavy shade.

CLIMBERS

❧ PASSIFLORA CAERULEA ❧

The Passion Flower is such an exotic-looking plant that it seems more suitable for a greenhouse or conservatory than a garden, but it is surprising how well it will grow out of doors in apparently cold areas, as long as it is planted against a sunny, sheltered wall. In the right situation it will flower for at least four months from early summer and in an exceptionally warm year will even produce orange-coloured fruits the size of bantams' eggs. It is a vigorous climber and clings by tendrils to natural or other supports, but is less successful when grown over open trellises or arbours. Apparently the heat generated by walls helps to ripen the wood and gives the plant a better chance of withstanding the winter.

The Passion Flower has been grown in England since before 1629 and in her book *Our Village,* the eighteenth-century writer Mary Russell Mitford describes it covering the white-washed walls of one of the cottages in the main street of her Hampshire village together with roses and clematis – not a labourer's house but 'a cot of spruce gentility'!

The story goes that these fascinating, slightly fragrant, blue and white flowers, made up of five sepals and five petals with a central corona of purplish stamens and pistils, were named the Passion flower by early Spanish missionaries to South America who saw the parts of the flower as representative of the Crucifixion. The ten petals and sepals represent the ten disciples, leaving out Judas who betrayed Christ and Peter who denied Him. The corona represents the Crown of Thorns, the five stamens, the Five Wounds and the three stigmas, the three nails. The hand-like leaves symbolise the hands of the tormentors of Jesus and the tendrils, the whips with which he was scourged.

Lovers of white flowers should look out for a beautiful, white-flowered variety, *Passiflora caerulea* 'Constance Elliot'.

A poor soil at the base of a sunny, sheltered wall is best, and the plants seem to flower better when their root run is restricted. Cover with sacking or bracken during the winter and cut back the secondary branches in late winter to within several buds of the base, allowing the new young shoots to take their place. Plant out pot-grown plants in the spring. Young shoots, 10-15cm (4-6in) in length, taken as cuttings in the spring with a heel of older wood and inserted in a sandy soil in a closed propagating frame, will increase stock. Passion flowers are very easy to raise from seed and very vigorous – given half a chance, they will quickly take over your greenhouse.

❧ CLEMATIS ❧
(AUTUMN-FLOWERING)

The all-time favourite amongst clematis is probably *Clematis* x *jackmanii,* which flowers from high summer well into autumn. It was introduced by George Jackman of Woking in the 1860s. A perfect companion for roses like the silvery pink 'New Dawn', its rich violet-purple flowers open in midsummer and stay in bloom till early autumn. The bad news is that it can succumb to wilt disease but, if it is planted deeply,

The small flowers and silky seedheads appear together on **Clematis orientalis**

there is every chance that it will recover and shoot from the base the following year.

Wilt is not a problem with the autumn-flowering species which scramble through the branches of trees, covering them with umbrellas of small, starry blossoms. A bonus is their almond scent, particularly noticeable on warm sunny evenings and, later in the season, their masses of fluffy, silver seed heads. They will climb to the top of large trees and are a good disguise for ugly walls and corrugated-iron roofs, but they are not for the border where the herbaceous clematis is a much better choice.

It is surprising that the blue-flowered herbaceous clematis, *C. heracleifolia davidiana*, known as the Abbé David's clematis is so rarely seen in cottage gardens. Its sweetly scented, hyacinth-like flowers on 90cm (3ft) shoots last well into the autumn. It doesn't take kindly to

staking, but looks good if allowed to sprawl over shrubs and sturdy herbaceous plants, and is a very strong grower.

Clematis are gross feeders and, as they are likely to stay where they are planted for many years, it is essential to prepare the soil thoroughly before planting out container-grown plants in spring and early summer, or after the heat of summer. A hole 45cm (18in) deep should be dug, the earth removed and replaced with a mixture of good top soil, well-rotted manure, old potting compost and some peat and grit with bonemeal or hoof and horn worked in, as well as a little lime. The plant should be removed from its container and the roots spread out, taking care to bury it well below its original planting level.

▪ Pruning consists of cutting back where new growth is visible in early spring. This is easier said than done, and a pair of shears will be more practical than secateurs for some of the more robust varieties. Finally, if you want to be really successful with these plants *water them copiously* throughout the spring and summer.

○ *Clematis* 'Jackmanii Superba'
The most popular variety ever raised, with dark, velvety, 12.5cm (5in) flowers which fade to purple. Although a hearty and prolific climber, it is subject to mildew in sheltered situations.

PLANT ASSOCIATIONS
A Gentle Autumn Scheme of Pink and Lilac

Eleagnus macrophylla, *has tiny, highly fragrant flowers and combines well with the soft green, pink and cream foliage of* Fuchsia magellanica 'Versicolor'. *In front of these, the flowers of pink Japanese anemones are surrounded by clouds of small, pale lilac daisies belonging to* Aster ericoides 'Ringdove' *while* Calamintha nepetoides, *with peppermint scented leaves and a mist of mauve-white flowers, covers their bare stems and is, itself, underplanted with* Ajuga 'Burgundy Glow' *with bright pink and cream foliage.*

BACK ROW *Eleagnus macrophylla.* 1.8x3m (6x10ft).
MIDDLE ROW *Fuchsia magellanica* 'Versicolor'. 1.2x60cm (4x2ft). Japanese anemones. 60-90cm (2-3ft). *Aster ericoides* 'Ringdove'. 75cm (2½ft).
FRONT ROW *Calamintha nepetoides.* 30cm (12in). *Ajuga* 'Burgundy Glow'. 15cm (6in).

○ *C. flammula*
Called the 'Fragrant Virgin's Bower' either in honour of the Virgin Mary or Queen Elizabeth I, the Virgin Queen, this is a vigorous species with myriads of small, white, almond-scented blossoms. Marvellous for growing through trees, where it will easily reach 4.5m (15ft) and bloom from late summer.

○ **C. rhederiana**
This is another strong species for growing in and over trees. It has straw-coloured, bell-shaped flowers which have a delicious, cowslip-like fragrance and it, too, is in bloom from late summer.

○ **C. orientalis**
This is known as the orange-peel clematis because the flowers, which start off yellow but fade to a soft orange colour, have 'petals' as thick as orange peel and are followed by feathery seed heads in the autumn. Little pruning needed.

𝒫ERENNIALS

❧ ANEMONE JAPONICA ☙

Anemone japonica, or Japanese anemone, is one of the oldest and best of the taller windflowers and is invaluable for late season colour. It was first seen growing in Japan by a seventeenth-century European visitor, hence the species name *japonica,* but was known only by its description. This very beautiful plant did not reach England until over 150 years later and it wasn't until 1908, when it was found growing wild in the Chinese province of Hupeh, that people realised it was a native of China. Most of the plants grown today are hybrids.

Spreading in habit, Japanese anemones are sometimes difficult to establish, although on sandy soil they can be invasive. Certainly once they have settled down you have them for life – but that's no hardship.

These plants will grow in any garden soil and thrive in partially shaded positions. They will even grow near large trees as long as they have some light. Plant the roots in autumn or spring, but try to find the right place for them first time as they resent being moved or divided and take some time to establish themselves again.

○ *Anemone japonica* 'Honorine Jobert'
Justifiably the all-time favourite, it was grown by a French nurseryman in the 1850s and his daughter is immortalised in its name. It has pure white, single flowers which look particularly lovely in the fading light of day. If you only grow one, this should be it.

○ *A. j.* 'White Giant' ('White Queen')
A large-flowered, strong-growing variety dating from before the First World War. Good for cutting.

○ *A. j.* 'Hadspen Abundance'
A modern variety which has fragile-looking single flowers with alternate petals of pale and deeper pink.

❧ ASTERS ☙
AND MICHAELMAS DAISIES

Think of autumn and immediately in your mind's eye you see Michaelmas daisies. Their botanical name is aster, the Greek word for a star, and in England they were originally called starwort or

*With its showers of tiny flowers, 'Silver Spray' is a
choice aster for the cottage garden*

and are the strongest-growing Michaelmas
daisies.

As different as can be are the *ericoides* and *cordifolius* species. With their cloud-like sprays of
tiny, star-like flowers and gentle colours they deserve to be more widely grown. The same can be
said for *A. corymbosus*, a spreading plant with
black wiry stems and masses of tiny, white, spiky-
petalled daisies, which look pretty growing
through more solid foliage at the edge of a path.
Aster linosyris, with minute, yellow flowers on
60cm (2ft) stems, is the plant which the Victorians
fondly called 'Goldilocks' and is worth growing in
a period garden.

We list a few good varieties, only an indication
of the vast choice of plants available today.

star plant. There are hundreds of them to choose
from, dwarf ones and tall ones, large-flowered and
tiny, and there are some treasures among them.

The first to be sent to England came from
North America around 1633 and was called *Aster
tradescantii* after John Tradescant, the earliest
English plant hunter and gardener to the King. It
is tall, with asparagus-like leaves and heads of
tiny, white, yellow-centred daisies and may have
been the first one to be given the name of
Michaelmas daisy since it was in flower on old
Michaelmas day, 18 September.

It was followed by the *amellus* group of asters
some twenty years later. None of them is more
than 60cm (2ft) tall. Then, at the beginning of the
eighteenth century came the *novi-belgii* (the New
York asters) and the *novae-angliae* (New England
asters). These two groups of indestructible plants
are so alike that they may as well be treated as one,

The *novii-belgii* and *novae-angliae* Michaelmas daisies flourish on clay or other moisture-retentive soils, and they do love the sun. *A. amellus,* also a sun lover, thrives better on poorer, drier soil. The *cordifolius* and *ericoides* types both prefer a dry open situation. Perennial asters are all easily increased by division, preferably in the autumn. The exception is the *amellus* group, which should be divided in the spring. It does not increase nearly so rapidly as the others and takes several years to grow into sizeable clumps.

ASTER AMELLUS

○ **A. a. 'Brilliant'**
A reliable new variety with bright pink flowers. 60cm (2ft).

○ **A. a. 'King George'**
An old favourite with bright violet daisies. 60cm (2ft).

A. NOVAE-ANGLIAE AND A. NOVI-BELGII

○ **A. n-a. 'Harrington's Pink'**
Pink with magenta buds. Good for cutting. 1.2m (4ft).

○ **A. n-b. 'Albanian'**
Lovely, creamy-white daisies with cream buds. 1.2m (4ft).

○ **A. n-b. 'Bridesmaid'**
Bright petunia-pink. Late. 90cm-1.2m (3-4ft).

○ **A. n-b. 'Helen Ballard'**
Semi-double, deep cyclamen. 90cm (3ft).

'Clara Curtis' a favourite 'cottage' chrysanthemum

○ **A. n-b. 'Blue Gem'**
Attractive, single-flowered violet-blue. 90cm (3ft).
○ **A. n-b. 'Blue Whirl'**
Lavender-blue with whorled petals. 90cm (3ft).

A. CORDIFOLIUS

○ **A. c. 'Silver Spray'**
Appropriately named. White feathery growth. 90cm (3ft).
○ **A. c. 'Photograph'**
An old variety with arching sprays of lilac-tinted flowers. 90cm (3ft).
○ **A. c. 'Elegans'**
Graceful, tall, upright sprays of soft lilac. 90cm (3ft).

A. ERICOIDES

○ **A. e. 'Vimmers Delight'**
Unusual stiff spikes of white flowers. 45cm (1½ft).
○ **A. e. 'Ringdove'**
A very attractive late variety with delicate, aster-violet flowers. 90cm (3ft).
○ **A. e. 'Golden Spray'**
White flowers, prominent, yellow centre. 60cm (2ft).

A. LATERIFLORUS (SYN. DIFFUSUS)

○ **A. l. 'Coombe Fishacre'**
Off-white rays, prominent centre. 90cm (3ft) plus.
○ **A. l. 'Horizontalis'**
Horizontal growth, prominent, chocolate-centred flowers, white rays. 60cm (2ft).

CHRYSANTHEMUM
❧ RUBELLUM ❧
AND OTHER COTTAGE TYPES

Chrysanthemums are now classified as *Dendranthema* but we have kept the old familiar name. *Chrysanthemum rubellum,* or Pompom Chrysanthemums, were an overnight success when they were first introduced to British gardens from the Far East as the 'Chusan Daisy' during the middle years of the nineteenth century, and within a very few years they were to be seen growing in virtually every small garden up and down the country. They came here via France where their small, round, many-petalled flowers reminded people of the pompons in the berets of French sailors. In both countries their sturdy

stems, which needed no staking, and their pretty cascading sprays of flowers in bloom when almost all the other border plants were past, guaranteed their popularity.

The later-flowering, taller cottage chrysanthemums should be grown more, but they flower later and have to contend with fiercer autumn winds, so staking is a necessity for them. One of the best of these is 'The Emperor of China', which has red buds followed by soft rose-coloured blooms and leaves which take on crimson tints at flowering time.

There are still many old varieties available, and again it is worth visiting a specialist nursery in autumn to see them. We list a few which are certainly worth considering.

 If they are to give of their best, chrysanthemums need a good, rich, deeply dug soil, well manured to retain summer moisture. Young plants should be planted out in beds or borders about 60cm (2ft) apart in late spring. After two or three years, division should be undertaken in the usual way by splitting apart with two forks. After discarding the old woody centres, over-winter the little plants in a cold frame where they can be moved to the garden during early spring.

○ *Chrysanthemum rubellum* 'Apricot'
Deep apricot flowers with yellow centre.
○ **C. r. 'Clara Curtis'**
Lovely, deep strawberry-pink flowers borne in great profusion.
○ **C. r. 'Duchess of Edinburgh'**
Large, globular, coppery-red flowers with golden centres.
○ **C. r. 'Mary Stoker'**
Reliable, with small, dainty flowers of a very pleasing shade of lemon-yellow.
○ **C. r. 'White Bouquet'**
Possibly the best white with large, pompon flowers shaded at the centre with green.

OTHER COTTAGE CHRYSANTHEMUMS FOR AUTUMN FLOWERING

○ **C. 'Anastasia'**
A delightful old variety of sturdy, upright growth

with double, rosy-crimson, semi-button flowers. Look out for the lovely variegated form of this plant.

○ **C. 'Innocence'**

An old cottage garden favourite with single pink flowers in mid- to late autumn. Needs staking.

○ **C. 'Mandarin'**

Bushy plants which smother themselves with small, double, orange-yellow flowers.

○ **C. 'Mei-Kyo'**

Delightful little pink pompons covering a tidy bush with small leaves. Among the last to flower in late autumn.

☙ CALAMINTHA ❧

Calaminthas are closely related to the thymes, and some are to be found growing wild on chalk downs and in hedgerows. They are plants for a sunny border and are useful in the rock garden or the front of a herb garden. If planted between paving stones where they are likely to be bruised or brushed against in passing, the neat little bushes, some 20-30cm (8-12in) high, emit a sweetly aromatic scent. The mauvey-white flowers, which form a cloud above the bushy growth, are loud with the buzz of bees, and butterflies hover over them throughout the late summer and autumn. A refreshing tea made from calamintha is said to be good for stomach disorders.

These plants are not difficult to please. They are hardy in all but the severest winters if you can give them a well-drained sandy soil. Propagation is by cuttings removed in mid- to late summer and rooted in a sandy compost, or by division.

○ *Calamintha nepetoides*

A charming, late-flowering variety about 30cm (12in) high with pale lavender-blue flowers, which does well in full sun or partial shade.

☙ DAHLIA ❧

This Mexican plant is named after a Swedish botanist, Dr Anders Dahl, and was originally pronounced dah-le-a and not day-le-a. The Spaniards brought it to Europe, but it wasn't until 1804 that it was grown successfully in Britain and it was only after the battle of Waterloo, when French varieties became available, that it took the country by storm.

The craze began amongst the aristocracy, and quickly took such a hold that by 1822 one nursery was selling 200 varieties. By the mid-1830s the Florists' Societies had added it to their lists and competitions were being held all over England. Then gradually its popularity waned, and even the introduction of the 'cactus' variety in 1872 caused only a temporary recovery. There are currently ten groups of dahlias recognised by the National Dahlia Society, and leading varieties of all sections are offered in spring catalogues.

William Robinson, the gardening guru of the 1890s, recommended that dahlias should be grown in the border in clumps with grey foliage plants as he had seen in Gertrude Jekyll's garden, or amongst Michaelmas daisies. Follow his advice and your dahlias will give you an unrivalled display of vibrant colour ranging from the creams and whites, through a whole host of gentle pastel shades to deep, thunder-like purples. Modern cottage gardeners with an eye to the species might like to try the fairly hardy *Dahlia merckii* with its small, lilac-coloured, single heads on long, slender stems, or the newer white-flowered 'Hadspen Snowflake' which has curved, slightly longer petals.

If you have visited the red border at Hidcote Manor Gardens in Gloucestershire, you cannot have failed to notice a scarlet dahlia with bronze foliage called 'Bishop of Llandaff'. Introduced in

1928 it nearly died out, but it is now more readily available. It is a spectacular plant, but unless you grow one produced by micro-culture it will be a carrier of dahlia wilt and a better choice would be the almost identical 'Bednall Beauty' which is healthy and virus-free.

 A well-drained, open site, in rich soil, trenched to a depth of at least 60cm (2ft), is the ideal situation for dahlias. A dressing of fine bonemeal forked into the top two inches (5cm) before planting out the tubers when frosts are over, will give them a good start, and twiggy sticks placed here and there will help to hold the plants up in windy conditions.

▪ Lift the tubers immediately after the first hard frost and allow to dry out naturally under cover, before trimming back and storing in trays in a frost-free and damp-proof place. In early spring, check and remove any damaged tuber 'fingers', cutting back to clean tissue.

❧ HELENIUM ❧

Helenium or Sneeze Weed, a native of North and Central America, is a vigorous and indispensable old favourite of the sunflower class with large, daisy flowers in bright yellow or good shades of bronze and bronzy-crimson.

Exceptionally free-flowering and good 'doers', heleniums grow strongly to a height of from 60cm-1.8m (2-6ft). The taller varieties tend to become lank and require staking, while the shorter ones will stay upright with the help of a few pea sticks. They are delightful border plants for a sunny position in ordinary soil and give a generous splash of colour to the autumn display.

Although heleniums prefer an open position, they will tolerate a certain

'Goldsturm', one of the most striking of the rudbeckias

Chinese Lanterns are beautiful in autumn but watch out, they can overrun a small garden

amount of shade. They can be grown in any ordinary soil but a little well-rotted manure dug into the border will pay dividends in extra-good blooms. Plants should be planted out in autumn or spring. As with rudbeckias, the clumps should be lifted and divided every third year to prevent overcrowding, and only the younger and more vigorous outer portions retained.

○ **Helenium autumnale 'Moerheim Beauty'**
A very popular variety and probably the best-known helenium with rich bronze-red daisies, growing to about 90cm (3ft).
○ **H. a. 'The Bishop'**
Another cottage garden favourite with big, yellow flowers which are excellent for cutting.
○ **H. a. 'Butterpat'**
A Bressingham variety with pure yellow flowers and a long flowering season.
○ **H. a. 'Bruno'**
Also from the Bressingham collection, 'Bruno' has crimson-mahogany flowers and a long flowering season.

❧ PHYSALIS ☙

The earliest species of physalis or Chinese Lantern to be grown in this country was *Physalis alkekengi,* also known as the Winter Cherry because of its edible fruit, which was thought to have curative properties. Nowadays we mostly grow *P. franchettii,* introduced in the 1890s from Japan.

Physalis can quickly become a nuisance when it settles down in a part of the garden it really likes. However, all is forgiven in early autumn when the balloon-like calyx, which surrounds the fruit after the creamy-white flowers are over, gradually starts to turn from a pale green through yellow and various shades of orange to a clear, bright mandarin-red which positively glows.

Chinese Lanterns are frequently seen in old gardens and very often used in flower arranging and for winter decoration. The sprays are cut just as the lanterns have ripened and before the colours start to fade. They are then hung up to dry, head downwards, perhaps retaining a few of the leaves which turn a delicate brown. If the

lanterns are left to skeletonise in the garden, the red berries will look as if they are suspended in filigree cages.

 This plant will succeed in any normal garden soil in a sunny, open position, but it does tend to roam and drastic action is required to keep it in check. It is easily grown from seed sown in spring, or increased by root division at the same time of year. Cuttings should be taken a little later.

❧ RUDBECKIA ☙
AND ECHINACEA

Both the annual and perennial rudbeckias are a very showy race, with enormous, bright yellow daisies and a conspicuous black cone in the centre which gives the flower its common name of Black-eyed Susan. The rudbeckias flower in early autumn, give useful height to the border and, with their long, strong stalks, make excellent cut flowers. When the flowers are over, the cones remain, looking like miniature bulrushes, and these, too, can be used by the flower arranger.

The closely related but purple-flowered *Echinacea purpurea,* or purple coneflower, has rose-purple blooms, fully 10cm (4in) across on 90cm-1.2m (3-4ft) stems, and looks well planted in groups at the back of the border. The white form, *Echinacea purpurea* 'White Lustre' has considerable charm and contrasts well with the darker mass of the others.

 Coneflowers are content in an average soil with a reasonable humus content.

They are sun-loving plants, but accommodating, and will easily adapt to semi-shade. They should be planted out in the winter or spring. Because of their vigorous growth they will need to be divided up about every third year during autumn. Annuals may be sown in a cold frame in spring for planting out a month or two later, or the seeds scattered where they are to flower in late spring.

○ *Rudbeckia fulgida*
A Black-eyed Susan with flowers of a warm yellow from late summer onwards.

○ *R. f.* 'Goldsturm'
A fine plant for the border with a profusion of golden-yellow flowers which give of their best in semi-shade or full sun.

○ *R. nitida* 'Herbstsonne' (Autumn Sun)
A variety with large, bright gold, single flowers, and petals that hang down and show off the central green cone to great advantage.

○ *R. hirta* 'Gloriosa Daisies'
Enormous, single, daisy-like heads averaging 13cm (5in) across on long stems – perfect for cutting. Colours include golden-yellow, mahogany and well-defined bi-colours. The double variety also has large, rich golden-yellow flowers, but because they are double the distinctive black cone in the centre is missing.

○ *R. amplexicaulis*
A very useful and attractive annual rudbeckia with

numerous flowers of the typical golden-yellow, each 5cm (2in) or so across, with a very prominent black central column 2.5cm (1in) or more in height. The plants grow to about 60cm (2ft) and are particularly useful for the smaller cottage garden.

○ *Echinacea purpurea* 'Robert Bloom'
A fine, named variety of the purple cone-flower with red-purple daisies on erect stems and with a long flowering period.

❧ SEDUM ❧

After the Michaelmas daisy, the sedum is one of the best-known plants in the late autumn garden. The large, plate-like heads in rich, rose-red colours have turned to a deep bronze by the end of the season and can be left to stand as winter decoration in the garden. Their flowering season starts in late summer, but they also have fleshy leaves which appear as tiny rosettes in the spring and then develop into upright decorative stems.

They will grow in a sunny spot in any soil, even builder's rubble. The tiniest bit will root, too, so it is easy to build up a stock of them to grow or give away. Yet they shouldn't be despised for their good nature. They are wonderful butterfly plants and their architectural form makes them ideal for the edge of a path or in paving.

Sedum telephium is one of our native stone-

PLANT ASSOCIATIONS

Lively Pinks and Blues for Late Summer to Early Autumn

Lavatera 'Barnsley', with pink-eyed flowers in white or blush pink, blooms throughout summer and autumn. Callicarpa giraldii 'Profusion' is noted for its masses of violet-mauve berries, while in front, Aster ericoides 'Pink Cloud' produces dense sprays of small, pale rose daisies. Caryopteris 'Kew Blue' or 'Ferndown' contributes fluffy blue flowers and grey-green foliage, underplanted with Teucrium chamaedrys which has small, dark green leaves and stems of bright pink flowers. Salvia 'East Friesland' displays its spikes of deep purple flowers for a long period in summer.

BACK ROW *Lavatera* 'Barnsley'. 2.1x1.2m (7x4ft). *Callicarpa giraldii* 'Profusion'. 3x2.4m (10x8ft).
MIDDLE ROW *Aster ericoides* 'Pink Cloud'. 75cm (2½ft). *Caryopteris* 'Kew Blue' or 'Ferndown'. 90cm (3ft). *Salvia* 'East Friesland'. 90cm (3ft).
FRONT ROW *Teucrium chamaedrys*. 15-23cm (6-9in).

Sedums, easy and beautiful, turn pink and red in autumn and fade to a rich brown in winter

crops. The colour of its flower heads ranges from dull red to a deep velvety mahogany, and it has heavily notched leaves in various shades of pink which eventually darken to green with age. Grow one of the varieties listed rather than the species.

Sedum spectabile, or the Ice Plant, is a first class garden plant, with very distinctive and beautiful upright, broad, glaucous leaves. It bears flat, pink flower heads from late summer till almost the end of the year. There are several named varieties which are a great improvement on the old-fashioned plant, with deeper, richer colours and taller, straighter foliage.

These plants thrive in a sunny position and are ideal for droughty conditions. It is best to divide them fairly frequently to keep the clumps to a manageable size, and every little scrap will grow. The larger-flowered sedums can also be propagated by cuttings taken during the summer and inserted in sandy soil in a cold frame.

○ **S. telephium 'Munstead Red'**
Miss Jekyll's dark red-flowered form.

○ **S. t. x 'Vera Jameson'**
An interesting hybrid which has spreading clumps of 23cm (9in) dusky purple leaves, which keep their colour all summer, and reddish-pink flowers in the autumn.

○ **S. t. 'Variegatum'**
This sedum has buff-yellow, variegated, glaucous foliage, with pink-tinged flowers. Care should be taken to ensure that any stems which revert to green are removed immediately.

○ **S. t. *maximum* 'Atropurpureum'**
This magnificent plant, with deep purple foliage and creamy-rose flowers, grows twice as tall as most other sedums but will probably need staking in an exposed situation.

○ **S. spectabile 'Brilliant'**
Very striking, bright pink flowers.

○ **S. s. 'Carmen'**
A scarce variety with soft, mauve-pink flowers.

○ **S. s. 'September Ruby'**
A dwarf cultivar with a deep rose-pink head.

○ **S. s. 'Iceberg'**
A fine white-flowered variety.

○ **S. 'Autumn Joy'**
A hybrid whose large flower heads change from salmon pink to coppery rose as the flowers fade.

❧ SOLIDAGO ❧

Golden Rod is a bee plant and, as such, must have been grown in cottage gardens. Its botanical name comes from the Latin solidare, to heal, and it was credited with knitting together wounds. There is also a legend that, when held in the hand it would lead to gold, rather like a diviner's rod!

The old-fashioned Golden Rods are rough, tough plants. They can survive years of neglect but quickly become a menace on sandy soil. Only drastic treatment will keep them in check. They are gross feeders, impoverishing the surrounding soil, are not particularly beautiful, and should never be allowed in the garden proper. The place for these 'toughs' is in rough scrubland or woodland, where their pretty silk seed heads, which dry well, are attractive far into the winter.

The new varieties are quite another story. Inheriting many of the virtues, they have few of the faults of the older ones. Their short, bushy growth with many more flowering spikes makes them ideal for brightening dark corners among shrubs and they are very effective combined with Michaelmas daisies. They quickly form large clumps which should be divided up and replanted regularly.

Any reasonable garden soil, enriched with manure, will produce excellent plants. They do prefer a sunny position, but will grow and flower quite satisfactorily in shade. Plants are increased by division in the spring and autumn as soon as there is something to divide. One of the advantages of the solidagos is that they re-establish themselves very quickly, and quite small pieces planted out in the spring will be in flower the following autumn.

○ *Solidago* **'Goldenmosa'**
A well-named variety with deep golden-yellow, mimosa-like flowers. Neat of habit.

○ **S. caesia**
A quite distinctive and very old Golden Rod with wavy black spikes of small, deep yellow flowers which make an attractive and graceful appearance in autumn. Growing to 90cm (3ft).

○ **S. 'Golden Thumb' ('Queenie')**
A pygmy solidago with neat little bushes of soft yellow flowers growing no more than 30cm (12in) tall. Looks well when grown with autumn-flowering sedums.

○ **S. 'Cloth of Gold'**
Another dwarf but robust variety with deep yellow flowers.

Colchicum speciosum *'Album', one of the loveliest of autumn-flowering bulbs*

AUTUMN-FLOWERING BULBS

❧ COLCHICUM ❧

The popular name for colchicum, a group of mainly autumn-flowering bulbs, is Naked Ladies, because of the way the flowers seem to spring up suddenly on their pale, tubular stalks without any leaves to clothe them. Their other name is Meadow Saffron and the French called them Tue-Chien (Kill-Dog) because the whole plant is extremely poisonous. Its juice was sometimes used to kill head lice and a drug extracted from it was recommended as a cure for gout. Colchicums are often mistaken for autumn crocuses, but if you count the stamens you will find that the colchicum has six stamens and the crocus only three.

Requiring no special culture, the species colchicums in particular are probably best grown in the margins of shrubberies or in a woodland or wild-garden setting where they can be left undisturbed. In this situation their flowers receive some protection from wind and soil splash and there is less danger of their rather coarse leaves, which come in spring, smothering choicer plants. The disadvantage of these plants is that after a few days their blooms are often flattened by wind or rain.

Although colchicums are naturally meadow plants, the hybrids, if grown in long grass or woodland, will produce all leaf and little flower. They should be planted in open spaces where they can enjoy some afternoon sunshine, preferably in well-nourished, moist soil. The smaller types may well benefit from the weather protection offered by unheated glass.

■ The easiest way of increasing stock of all types is to take up and divide the bulbs every few years. However, they may be increased by seed sown in a frame or greenhouse as soon as it is ripe, although plants may not come true to type. High summer is a good time for planting, and the bulbs should be planted at least 15cm (6in) deep and covered with at least 5cm (2in) of soil.

○ ***Colchicum autumnale***
A free-flowering native, frequently seen growing in wide drifts in grass or woodland and flowering in late autumn. The albino form, *C. autumnale* 'Album', produces its cluster of white flowers slightly earlier than the species.

○ **C. a. 'Alboplenum'**
The beautiful white form with large, fully double, milky-white flowers which bear a striking similarity to the starry blooms of *Magnolia stellata*. Bulbs are expensive, but it does pay to buy from a reliable source as there are inferior forms around.

○ **C. a. 'Pleniflorum' (syn. *roseum plenum*)**
This has numerous, dainty, double, amethyst-violet flowers. During heavy frosts, the petals often tend to develop stripes – this is not unusual and does not mean the bulbs are affected with virus.

○ **C. agrippinum**
A vigorous *variegatum* x *autumnale* hybrid with attractively chequered, reddish-purple flowers followed by tidy, blue-green leaves in the spring.

○ **C. speciosum**
Possibly the best and largest flowered of the colchicum species with showy, red-purple blooms on sturdy, reddish stems and a clear white patch in the throat. Good, early autumn flowerer.

○ **C. s. 'Album'**
Described by E. A. Bowles, the celebrated plantsman, as 'one of the most beautiful of hardy bulbous plants', it is the white form of *speciosum* with snow-white 'goblets' on soft emerald-green stems.

○ **C. 'Lilac Wonder'**

A hybrid with very slight chequering on the deep amethyst-violet flowers. Easy, vigorous and free-flowering.

○ **C. 'Waterlily'**

Surprisingly, a cross between the double white *C. autumnale* and *C. speciosum* 'Album' produced this magnificent, fully double, deep rose-pink beauty which more than compliments its namesake. It flowers for several weeks in late autumn. 'Waterlily' does require a sunny position as it can suffer from the weather if badly sited.

❧ CROCUS ❧
(AUTUMN-FLOWERING)

Autumn-flowering crocuses begin to flower in early to mid-autumn and various species carry on until midwinter. Perfectly hardy, but preferring a well-drained, sunny position, the autumn crocuses are easy-going and their purples and blues, ambers and golds are in complete harmony with the colours of the 'season of mists'.

Autumn crocuses enjoy an open, well-drained soil improved with liberal help-ings of moss or leaf mould. Bulbs should be planted 8cm (3in) deep in summer. Most

gardeners will be content to increase their stock by division or removal of the offsets when the old clumps are lifted. Fresh ripe seed sown in pans or sandy soil and left to germinate in a cool greenhouse or cold frame will produce flowering corms in about four years.

○ **Crocus speciosus**

One of the best known of the autumn crocuses with large flowers of bright violet-blue set off by rich orange stigmas. It is usually in flower during early to mid-autumn.

○ **C. kotschyanus (syn. zonatus)**

An easy, early-flowering autumn species with dainty, lilac flowers and a zone of golden spots in the throat.

○ **C. sativus**

The famous Saffron Crocus, which takes time to establish, has lilac flowers with brilliant red pistils and requires a sunny position to flower well. It is this crocus which yields the saffron used in the preparation of dye and drugs. No wonder it is expensive, as 8000 flowers are needed to produce 100g ($3^{1}/_2$oz) of saffron. There is a free-flowering pure white form, *C. s. cartwrightianus* 'Albus'.

○ **C. goulimyi**

Although a comparatively recent discovery, this species has quickly established itself as one of the best autumn crocuses. Soft pale lilac flowers are

PLANT ASSOCIATIONS

A Mixture of Pink, Bronze and Purple Highlighted with White

The rich autumn foliage colours and small mop-heads of Hydrangea *'Preziosa', changing from light pink to deep bronze-pink with the season, contrast well with a background of the semi-evergreen shrub* Cotoneaster simonsii *which has long-lasting, orange-red berries.* Aster tradescantii, *a tall, slender, branching perennial with a long succession of small white daisies and* Fuchsia *'Sharpitor', with pale green and creamy-white variegated leaves and pale shell-pink flowers, complement the hydrangea. Underplant with purple-leaved ajuga and white autumn crocuses. Add white crocuses and* Anemone blanda *for spring colour.*

BACK ROW *Cotoneaster simonsii.* 2.7x2.1m (9x7ft). **MIDDLE ROW** *Hydrangea* 'Preziosa'. 90x90cm (3x3ft). *Aster tradescantii.* 1.2m (4ft). *Fuchsia* 'Sharpitor'. 60x60cm (2x2ft).

FRONT ROW *Ajuga reptans* 'Atropurpurea'. 15cm (6in). White autumn crocuses, white crocuses and *Anemone blanda* 'White Splendour': all about 15cm (6in).

White **Cyclamen hederifolium** *are rarer, and so more sought after than the pink ones*

borne on a very characteristic long tube in late autumn. *C. g.* 'Albus' is the pure albino form with bridal-white flowers without a trace of yellow on the petals.

○ ***C. laevigatus fontenayi***

A late-flowering autumn crocus with beautiful, pale lilac flowers which are prominently striped on the outside, producing a succession of flowers well into the winter months.

❧ HARDY CYCLAMEN ❧

Hardy cyclamen, or sowbread, are first-class plants which require little or no attention after planting, thriving in the poorest of soils, about the roots of trees, in woodland and borders and yet, sadly, are rarely seen in the average garden.

The old name, sowbread, suggests that they were the main food for wild boars and that they are natives of British woods. They have been found growing wild but are more likely to have been brought to Britain first in dried form from the Mediterranean as remedies for all sorts of ills,

and were probably not cultivated until the end of the sixteenth century. Their uses were numerous and surprising. Stuffed up a bald man's nose, the roots might encourage a new growth of hair; they were taken very seriously in bringing on labour, and pregnant women were warned not to walk over them; they were also considered an aphrodisiac.

With just half-a-dozen or so of the cyclamen species, cyclamen can be enjoyed in every season of the year, spreading by seed and living to a ripe old age. There are even records of cyclamen corms the size of bowler hats, flowering away vigorously after more than eighty years.

○ ***Cyclamen hederifolium*** (syn. *neapolitanum*)

The dainty, 'shuttlecock', pink and white flowers of this autumn-flowering cyclamen appear before the leaves and look best planted in a mass where the

---

Nerine bowdenii *flowers late in the year but needs a sunny spot*

PLANT ASSOCIATIONS
A Purple-Red, Orange, White and Lime Green Colour Scheme

For the background choose Berberis x ottawensis *'Purpurea' or* Cotinus coggygria *'Royal Purple'. Both have mahogany-coloured foliage in spring and summer, mixed with gold and flame in autumn. In front of them, white-flowered Japanese anemones and* Aster ericoides *'White Heather' stand out well. Add bright orange Chinese Lanterns (*Physalis franchettii*) and red and orange* Euphorbia dulcis.
To extend the interest to other seasons, Kniphofia *'Green Jade' brings fresh colour and dramatic form in summer and contrasts with the branching heads of soft orange-red trumpets of* Phygelius *'African Queen', which blooms for a long period.* Euphorbia polychroma *and orange tulips would give late spring colour, with* Alchemilla mollis *and* Tellima grandiflora *filling any foreground gaps.*

BACK ROW Berberis x ottawensis *'Purpurea'*. 2.4x2.4m (8x8ft). *Cotinus coggyria 'Royal Purple'.* 4.5x3.6m (15x12ft).
MIDDLE ROW *Kniphofia* 'Green Jade'. 1.2m (4ft). Japanese anemones. 90cm (3ft). *Phygelius* 'African Queen'. 90cm (3ft). *Aster ericoides* 'White Heather'.

75cm (2½ft). *Physalis franchettii.* 45cm (1½ft).
FRONT ROW *Euphorbia dulcis.* 30cm (1ft). *E. polychroma.* 45cm (1½ft). Orange tulips. 35-55cm (14-22in). *Alchemilla mollis.* 45cm (1½ft). *Tellima grandiflora.* 45cm (1½ft).

---

mottled ivy-shaped leaves which follow will make a handsome winter carpet.

○ **C. purpurascens** (syn. *europaeum*)
A late summer to autumn bloomer it produces its rose-crimson, scented flowers for many weeks with the added bonus of almost evergreen foliage.

○ **C. cilicium**
C. cilicium whose shorter, heather-scented, bright pink flowers precede its rounded leaves, puts in a rather later appearance and, barring an unusually severe spell of weather, will bloom until the winter-flowering cyclamen start to take over.

○ **C. coum and C. c. 'Atkinsii'**
These are both winter-flowering, although the little pink buds are usually detectable by the end of autumn. The flowers of both are similar and quite delightful. Shorter and much chubbier than their autumn-flowering counterparts, they emerge at the same time as the leaves, which are smaller and less abundant than those of the autumn-flowering cyclamen.

○ **C. c. album**
The white-flowered form, which retains a carmine 'nose'.

○ **C. repandum**
Flowers in late spring. Its rather fierce magenta colour is not to everyone's taste. The leaves are a deep green,

almost heart-shaped, and lightly patterned.
C. repandum will put up with most conditions, and its rosy-purple flowers are in bloom for several months.

❧ NERINE ❧

The nerine has flowers which are basically trumpet-shaped, with narrow segments which are recurved and frilled at the tips, giving the plant its characteristic spidery look. It was called the Guernsey Lily because its roots were believed, wrongly as it turned out, to have drifted ashore on Guernsey from the cargo of a shipwreck in the reign of Charles II, and in due course flowered there.

Nerines need to be starved on poor soil at the base of a sunny, sheltered wall with the neck of the bulbs just showing at ground level. Give some protection during severe frost. Bulbs should be planted 15cm (6in) deep in early spring just as the strap-like leaves are pushing up. Within a year or two the bulbs will have multiplied many times and will have worked their way to the surface, which is where they like to be, provided they are protected with a covering of old ferns or bracken fronds in the winter.

○ *Nerine bowdenii*
Originally introduced by Mr Cornish Bowden from his mother's garden at Newton Abbot in Devon, it is the hardiest of these beautiful South African plants which produce most of their strap-like leaves in the spring and their rather exotic-looking flowers in autumn.'
○ **N. b. 'Mark Fenwick'**
A taller, more vigorous form with larger flower heads of a deeper pink than *N. bowdenii*.
○ **N. b. 'Pink Triumph'**
A beautiful, free-flowering hybrid with silver-pink flowers which bloom rather late.
○ **N. flexuosa alba**
The best pure white species with beautiful, frilled blooms which are excellent for cutting. It prefers a warm situation.
○ **N. masonorum**
A dwarf form with narrow, almost evergreen leaves and small, pale pink flowers with crinkled petals on narrow stems up to 15cm (6in). Probably best in a raised bed.

❧ SCHIZOSTYLIS ❧

Occasionally referred to as the Winter Gladiolus, schizostylis or Kaffir Lilies, as their name suggests, are natives of South Africa, introduced here in 1864. They are described as hardy, but are really only safe in the mildest districts and even there they should be given winter protection. Handsome plants, with sword-shaped leaves and spikes of splendid deep red flowers, the Kaffir Lilies enjoy a rich diet, plenty of moisture and plenty of sunshine. They begin their flowering season in early autumn and in a mild season in Britain offer the tantalising prospect of flowers picked on Christmas Day.

There are several forms of *Schizostylis coccinea* in various shades of pinks and reds. The newest introduction is a white schizostylis, but as yet it is not widely available.

 Kaffir Lilies prefer a rich, well-drained soil and a sunny position but, most of all, copious amounts of water during the summer months. In the winter the soil must be warm and dry, and protection given against severe frosts. Stock is easily increased by dividing up the leek-like roots and stolons and replanting them with some dried blood.

○ *Schizostylis coccinea* **'Major'**
Usually the earliest to flower, with extra-large scarlet flowers on strong spikes.
○ **S. c. 'Professor Barnard'**
An attractive shade of dusky red with more open, starry flowers.
○ **S. c. 'Viscountess Byng'**
A lovely old pale pink variety which is the last to flower, continuing through until winter begins in earnest.
○ **S. c. 'November Cheer'**
A charming deep pink 'sport' from S. c. 'Major', equally as strong and free flowering.
○ **S. c. 'Sunrise'**
A vigorous, new variety with large, glowing, pale pink flowers.
○ **S. c. 'Pallida'**
A rare form with very large, pale pink flowers.

WINTER

Gradually winter establishes itself in the cottage garden. The first thick, cold fogs of the season wrap the familiar surroundings in veils of grey, moisture laden air and transforming the friendly bulk of laurel, box and yew into strange and menacing shapes. Then a change in the weather brings days of pale sunshine, highlighting the polished bark of cherry, dogwood and willow. At dusk, and in the morning, hoar frost etches every twig, leaf, and berry in crystalline white.

A SEASONAL PICTURE

The blaze of autumn foliage may be gone, but there is no lack of colour in the winter garden. The beauty of form and texture in bark, stems and seeds is highlighted and the diversity of evergreen leaves brought into focus, adding emphasis to the season's few but lovely blossoms. Evergreens, in particular, come into their own, their solid shapes giving weight among the naked branches of lilac, weigela and rose and all the other favourites of spring and summer. The variegated forms are some of the most colourful shrubs for the winter garden, but even the common green holly has a glitter to its dark, prickly-edged leaves that is cheerful and encouraging on even the gloomiest of grey, wet days, and it makes a perfect background for the fragile flowers of the winter cherry and viburnum.

The flower borders, brown and grey after the summer-long pageant of bright blossoms and butterflies, now play host to different visitors. Redpolls and linnets explore the fluffy

seedheads of aster and onopordon and *Sedum spectabile* with its broad heads of darkened rose, while the seed-filled spikes of lavender and agastache and the spiny domes of teasels are particularly attractive to goldfinches. Numerous insects hide in the withered leaves of achilleas, echinops, fennel and others, and tits and warblers visiting the garden search these hiding places over and over again. They are the cottage gardener's friends, and an effective natural control of aphids and scale insects that overwinter on the bark and dormant buds of shrubs and trees.

The round shapes of santolinas, artemisias and helichrysums in grey and shining silver give colour and substance to the borders, as do *Dorycnium hirsutum,* with softly woolly leaves in grey-green, *Salvia icterina,* in muted shades of green and yellow, and the ice-blue of rue, contrasting with the angular dried stems of herbaceous perennials in varied shades of brown.

In the front of the border the broad, leathery leaves of bergenias create a patch of vibrant green, scarlet and mahogany tones beside the golden tan of molinia, while behind them a tangle of nut-brown twigs waits for spring to transform it once more into a potentilla, with small grey-green leaves and a summer-long succession of cream flowers. The hardier varieties of hebe and cistus also mix well with clumps of herbaceous perennials, and their evergreen foliage, in shades of green, bronze-purple and blue-grey, keeps the flower border furnished during the threadbare weeks of the year.

In shady areas to the cool, exposed side of large shrubs, or beneath the branches where rowan or cherry spread their summer leaves, the fresh green ribbons of Hart's Tongue ferns and the marbled arrowheads of arums defy the weather. Epimediums guard their emerging buds with foliage of glowing copper-red or mottled green and leather-brown, and the fat flower buds of hellebores begin to show their colours. Under the pale pink lace of a winter-flowering cherry, pulmonarias and irises weave a tapestry of spots and stripes, and against a cool, shady wall *Garrya elliptica* punctuates its dark foliage with tassels of grey-green. Here, as the cold grey weeks pass slowly by, the first snowdrops and snowflakes pierce the soil, and winter aconites open their glossy yellow cups to the pale sun, with a promise that spring is on its way.

Seasonal Tasks

FOR WINTER

Lift dahlia and begonia tubers, bedding gladiolus and pelargoniums and store in a frost-free shed or garage. Check occasionally for signs of mould and remove affected tubers or corms. Cut out any badly affected parts, dust with flowers of Sulphur and allow to dry thoroughly before returning to storage.

Protect plants on the borderline of hardiness by covering with a good blanket of straw, fern or conifer fronds, peat substitute, bubble plastic or fine-mesh horticultural netting. It is a good idea to cover loose, light material with wire netting and peg this down round the edges to keep it in place.

Cut back dead stems of perennials, and tidy borders by removing dead leaves and weeds, then lightly fork over the surface of the borders to incorporate any previously applied mulch and break up any surface crusting. Alternatively, leave until spring and enjoy the shapes and colours of the stems and seedheads, and the contribution they make to the winter garden, – and buy a book on bird recognition and a pair of binoculars! Bird watching from the window is often very rewarding (and comfortable) on a snowy winter day.

If planning a new border, dig the whole area roughly and leave it exposed to the weather. Frost will break heavy soil into a fine crumbly texture, making planting and sowing much easier in the spring.

Sow berries and hard-coated seeds of trees, shrubs and bulbs in pots of sand and leave exposed to the action of frost. This is known as 'stratification' and helps germination.

In frost-free weather continue pruning trees and shrubs where desirable. Evergreens and spring-flowering shrubs should not be pruned in winter unless unavoidable. Dead wood can be removed at any time, and branches or twigs affected by coral spot fungus should be cut out and burned as soon as possible. Winter is also the best time to thin out unwanted or badly placed stems from trees and shrubs to improve their balance or general appearance.

Put out water and food for the birds, especially in frosty weather. Water should be put in a shallow container wide enough to allow birds to bathe, which is vital to keep their plumage in good condition to insulate against the cold. Empty the water in the late afternoon (or you will have to chip it out next day!) and refill as early as possible in the morning. Food is best on a bird table or window sill, out of the way of vermin. Peanuts and sunflower seeds should be placed in special hanging containers. Any food which is scattered on the ground should be put out in the morning, so that the birds will clear it all before dusk.

Make sure that a small area of water in the garden pond is kept clear of ice so that gases from rotting vegetation can escape, or fish may be poisoned.

Spend some happy evenings browsing through seed catalogues and plan (and order!) for next spring and summer, remembering that some seeds need to be sown in warmth in late winter. This applies mainly to half-hardy annuals, many of which are favourite bedding and container plants.

By early winter, bulbs to force for Christmas flowering should show 2.5-5cm (1-2in) of leaf, and can be brought indoors into a cool room. Stand in a shaded position at first, then provide more light, but keep out of direct sunlight and away from sources of heat, such as fires and radiators. Keep compost moist and feed with liquid fertiliser. After flowering, allow foliage to die down naturally, then dry bulbs and store ready to plant in the garden in the early autumn, as they won't succeed again in bowls.

Clear fallen leaves from plants such as arabis, aubrieta, mossy saxifrages and dianthus. If they are allowed to collect on the foliage they cause excessive wetness and rot, and harbour slugs.

TREES FOR WINTER

In a corner of the winter cottage garden, **hazels** (*Corylus avellana)* which grow up to 6m (20ft) high look well underplanted with purple and yellow primroses, their long yellow catkins one of the first signs of approaching spring. There is a variety with yellow leaves, *C. a. 'Aurea'*, and a purple one, *C. a. 'Purpurea'. C. a.* 'Contorta' is the hazel with grotesquely twisted branches loved by flower arrangers and its bare branches look attractive against the winter sky, but once the leaves appear it has a lumpy, graceless look.

Arbutus unedo, the **Strawberry Tree**, 4.5-6m (15-20ft) high, with its rich reddish bark and branches, is an evergreen tree or shrub which produces hanging clusters of lily-of-the-valley-like flowers during the winter after its 'strawberry' fruits have gone. It is a native of Ireland and grows best in mild, frost-free areas.

Prunus subhirtella 'Autumnalis' or the **Winter Cherry, 6-9m (20-30ft)** tall, is deservedly the most popular winter-flowering tree. It starts its flowering season in the autumn, blooms intermittently throughout the winter and then gives a final show of its delicate blossoms in the early spring. Its sprays of pink or white brighten dingy city streets and overhang suburban walls or country hedges on grey days. Frost sets it back for a while and then milder weather encourages it to flower again. The Winter Cherry can be grown either as a tree with a single trunk or as a shrub with two or three main stems. For white flowers, the form to choose is *P. s.* 'Autumnalis', and for pink ones, 'Autumnalis Rosea'. Both have semi-double flowers just 2cm (½in) wide. There is also a weeping form, *P. s.* 'Pendula', a small umbrella-like tree with pink flowers.

EVERGREEN SHRUBS FOR WINTER

In our imagination we always see the cottage garden as a summer garden crammed full of flowers. We forget that the same garden in winter will look dreary, bare and formless without a few evergreens planted at either side of a front gate or arch, against back walls and fences or in the angle between two paths, to give structure to the garden, and as a gentle background for summer colour.

The most traditional plants for this purpose are British natives – **box, holly, ivy** and **yew** – but there are others such as *Viburnum tinus,* **aucuba, skimmia** and **laurel** which, although over-planted by the Victorians, can still make an attractive winter backbone of different greens.

Choisya ternata, a native of Mexico which bears white scented flowers in early summer, was thought for many years after its introduction in 1825 to be too tender for outdoors, as were camel-

lias. But in a sheltered spot, particularly in a town garden, both are fairly reliable. Crush the leaves of the **Mexican orange blossom** to enjoy their spicy fragrance. The legendary **Sweet Bay,** *Laurus nobilis,* although it may succumb to frosts in a bad year, has been growing in sheltered gardens since the sixteenth century, when it was considered protection against thunder and lightning and, grown as a shrub, as Parkinson wrote in 1632, serves 'both for pleasure and profit'.

Rosemary, in both its tall and low-growing forms, keeps its narrow needle-like foliage, dark green above and greyish beneath, all winter as does *Teucrium chamaedrys,* the **Wall Germander,** with its small, evergreen toothed leaves. It has

It is important to grow shrubs and trees with berries, like this cotoneaster, to give interest to the winter garden

been grown in British gardens since Tudor times and is still useful to clothe raised beds or low retaining walls or to edge a path. In late summer it has purple flowers like miniature antirrhinums. There are rarer variegated forms of both rosemary and teucrium, and if you live in a mild area or can give it the protection of a sunny, sheltered wall, *Teucrium fruticans* will keep its arching sprays of oval leaves, grey-green on top and a soft silver underneath, all winter.

Another low-growing plant with insignificant but fragrant cream flowers in winter is the Sarcococca or **Sweet Box**. S. *humilis,* which grows to about 45cm (1½ft), has pointed, glossy dark green leaves and shiny black berries later in the year, but it may give up the ghost in a very severe winter. S. *hookeriana digyna*, with reddish stems, has narrower leaves and its strongly scented flowers have a tasselled look with their pink tinged anthers. It makes a taller shrub and is hardier. The Sweet Box has never really caught on in spite of its sweet scent but the ordinary box is one of the most popular of winter evergreens, especially in the cottage garden.

❧ BUXUS SEMPERVIRENS ❧

The common box may have been introduced into England by the Romans, who were as dedicated to topiary as the nineteenth-century creators of shrubby peacocks or misshapen doves, and it has been in and out of fashion ever since. The Romans loved box but didn't like yew which, for them, smacked of mourning. However, in Wordsworth's day sprigs of box were given to the guests at funerals in the north of England to throw on the coffin, and in the Second World War it was sometimes handed out in church on Palm Sunday instead of palm leaves.

In the seventeenth century, knot gardens, those intricate patterns laid out in front of grand houses, were outlined in box. It was the most popular edging plant for borders in the eighteenth century but even then some people complained about its 'foul' smell, while for others the scent of cut box is as evocative of happy childhood summer days as new mown grass. The great gardener, William

Robinson, condemned it for harbouring slugs and weeds and for the time it took to trim.

Groves of box grew wild to a height of 9m (30ft) at Box Hill in Surrey and ladies and gentlemen went there to 'divert themselves unperceived' in these 'pretty labyrinths of Box-wood' but, because it was in such demand for making musical instruments and for furniture inlays, since it does not warp, it was cut as timber and gradually disappeared. Concoctions made from box featured as a purgative in old wives' lore and it is also a bee plant.

 There are many varieties but the most common is the dwarf box, *Buxus suffruticosa.* 'Elegantissima' has grey-green leaves edged with silver, 'Maculata' makes a compact bush with broader leaves, variegated yellow, and 'Pyramidalis' has a more upright habit. The tallest box commonly available is 'Handsworthiensis', which is suitable for taller hedges.

■ Box is easy to grow from cuttings taken in late summer and left in a mixture of equal parts peat, or peat substitute, and sand in a cold frame until late spring when it is a good idea to knock the cuttings out of their pots and take a look at the base of the stems. If no roots have formed but the ends of the stems have swollen and look bumpy, put them back in the compost for another month. Then the rooted cuttings should be set out in a nursery bed or potted on individually.

LIGUSTRUM
❧ OVALIFOLIUM ❧

Say the word privet and many gardeners sniff with disgust at its dull green foliage and hungry roots. Out of fashion now, it was the everyday hedging plant in cottage gardens and its variegated form, slow-growing and more difficult to propagate, was a great favourite. Privet was the poor man's topiary plant, quick growing and easy to shape and, as well as being excellent for making arbours where the cottager could sit out of the wind on a cool sunny day, it was, and is, a haven for birds and insects, its insignificant creamy flowers food for the Privet Hawk Moth and the bees, and its berries cropped by birds.

The native British shrub, *Ligustrum vulgare,* was popular in the seventeenth century but was gradually superseded by other forms which were more reliably evergreen, especially *Ligustrum ovalifolium,* introduced in 1842 and impervious to a polluted atmosphere. *L. lucidum* should be left unclipped since it makes a fine shrub with its fragrant panicles of little, white tubular flowers. *L. o.* 'Aureum' is the golden privet of Victorian cottage gardens with wide irregular, gold-splashed margins to the leaves, while *L. o.* 'Variegatum' has variegated edges of a gentler yellow. Both give the effect of bright sunlight in the winter garden and are just the thing for a dull shady spot, surrounded perhaps by dark-petalled hellebores with creamy-yellow stamens.

❧ TAXUS BACCATA ❧

The yew, as well as having churchyard associations, was grown in farmhouse or large cottage gardens close to the south-west side of the house as protection from evil spirits, and possibly from the prevailing wind! A yew hedge is the perfect background for a herbaceous border but it was rarely used as hedging in cottage gardens, perhaps because it was too grand or perhaps because every part of it except the pulp surrounding the seed is poisonous. It is a first-class material for topiary, though box, with its lighter, fresher green, is much more cheering on a winter day.

❧ ILEX ❧

The common holly, *Ilex aquifolium,* with its fine dark glossy-green foliage is, without doubt, one of the best evergreens, and a well-berried shrub or tree is certainly one of the joys of the winter garden, although too big for a small cottage garden. As a hedging plant it has few equals, making a very close, impenetrable hedge anything up to 6m (20ft) high, dense right down to the ground, and keeping fresh and green for years.

There are many varieties of holly which are suitable for the smaller garden, including the beautiful gold- and silver-variegated forms which

are slower growing and more compact than the common holly, and a green-leaved weeping form, *I. aquifolium* 'Pendula' which makes an elegant bush, producing berries all on its own.

All hollies are shade tolerant, though the variegated forms will have a poor colour in dense shade. Male and female flowers are normally borne on separate trees, and female trees will only bear berries if there is a male tree in the vicinity. The hermaphrodites, which include 'J. C. van Tol', 'Pyramidalis' and *I. a.* 'Pendula' will set berries on their own.

■ Hollies are not easily transplanted as they resent root disturbance. For this reason it is advisable to plant quite small plants which can be lifted with their root systems more or less intact.

○ *Ilex altaclarensis* **'Golden King'**
One of the best golden-variegated hollies with well-rounded, spineless, shiny leaves, margined bright yellow-gold, and producing bright red to orange-red berries. Contrary to what the name implies, this is a female form. Vigorous.
○ *I. aquifolium* **'J. C. van Tol'**
One of the best berrying forms. Hermaphrodite, so it will set berries on its own. Almost spineless, dark green leaves, good for hedging.
○ *I. a.* **'Ferox Argentea'**
Known as the Silver Hedgehog Holly, with curious leaves, variegated cream, with cream spines on the surface as well as on the edges. Will make a small, compact little bush with all-year-round interest. There is a gold variegated form, *I. a.* 'Ferox Aurea'. Male.
○ *I. crenata* **'Golden Gem'**
This is a delightful, small-leaved, dwarf holly which

Privet 'doves' at Stretton Cottage in north-west England

Variegated shrubs like holly cheer a winter garden

forms a flat-topped bush with bright golden-yellow leaves particularly good in winter and spring.

○ *I. x meservae* **'Blue Angel'**

The slowest growing and most compact of the blue hollies. Its crinkled foliage, glossy deep blue in summer, turns a stunning deep purple-green in winter, with large scarlet berries.

❧ HEDERA ❧

Ivy, botanically known as *Hedera,* is indispensable in the cottage garden. The leaves of the variegated and unusual forms, quite as colourful and interesting as any flowers, enliven a winter wall with their bold patterns and branching growth, or contrast beautifully with winter-flowering crocuses, snowdrops and irises.

The common ivy, *Hedera helix,* will grow in almost any soil and situation, including deep shade. In the cottage garden it is frequently seen wandering over old tree stumps, walls and into trees, where its unrestricted growth will reward the cottager with a very attractive display of green flowers in high summer, a paradise for insects including the Holly Blue butterfly whose second-brood eggs are generally laid in the ivy. Although not a true hedging plant, it can be trained very effectively up wattle hurdles with the ivy planted on one or both sides to make a very dense narrow 'fedge' (a corruption of fence and hedge), particularly useful for partitioning and screening off two houses where space is strictly limited.

Ivy grown against a wall, used as a 'fedge', or trained over pergolas and arches, should be trimmed annually in spring. Propagate by cuttings taken in late summer or early autumn. Container or pot-grown plants should be planted out during the winter months.

○ *Hedera helix* **'Goldheart'**
A small-leaved form with a rich golden-yellow irregular centre and a deep green border. Excellent for walls.

○ *H. h.* **'Hibernica'**
Known as the Irish Ivy, it has handsome, large dark green leaves 10-12cm (4-5in) wide. A vigorous climber, quickly covering walls, fences and bare ground.

○ *H. canariensis* **'Gloire de Marengo'**
The variegated Canary Island Ivy or *H. c. variegata*. Very attractive, large dark green leaves with patches of silvery-grey and an irregular cream margin, sometimes flushed pink.

○ *H. colchica* **'Sulphur Heart'**
'Sulphur Heart' or 'Paddy's Pride', also known as the Persian Ivy, is a vigorous grower and one of the most colourful and handsome of ivies. The leaves are yellow edged with irregular splashes of pale and darker green. Highly recommended.

In the dead of winter, snow-laden branches make interesting shapes and patterns

WINTER-FLOWERING
SHRUBS AND CLIMBERS

The cottage garden in late autumn and winter can still provide many visual treats, and a few surprises. None are more welcome than the winter-flowering shrubs and climbers.

❧ DAPHNE MEZEREUM ❧

Daphne mezereum has been grown in cottage gardens for generations and may even be a native wild plant. It is a small, rather stiff, branching shrub which produces mauve-pink flowers on its bare branches towards the end of the winter. Later on, the flowers are replaced by large bright red berries amongst the leaves, when the plant has the rather formal look of a wood engraving in an early herbal. There is a white variety, *D. m. alba,* with narrower leaves of a fresher green and yellow fruits. Variegated and double-flowered varieties were known in the past but, alas, no longer. The chief reason, however, for growing the Mezereon is its wonderful heady scent.

Another winter-flowering daphne with a fragrance like some rare and exotic perfume is *D. odora.* The variegated form of this plant, *D. o.* 'Aureo-marginata', is very attractive with its dark green, oval leaves rimmed with gold, and it is possibly more hardy than the type. More ungainly in habit than the Mezereon, it tends to produce its foliage and flowers together near the top of the

shrub, leaving the lower branches bare. The flowers are produced in tight clusters, the individual four-lobed blossoms being a redder-pink than *D. mezereum* on the outside and white within.

Daphnes generally are considered difficult to grow, though, like the Madonna Lily, *Daphne mezereum* is supposed to prefer the humble cottage garden. It will tolerate almost any soil provided it is well drained, but is often short-lived. Look out for seedlings underneath the parent shrub. Otherwise, best results come from seeds sown in the summer, as soon as they are ripe, in a shady part of the garden. The white variety will come true from seed. The whole plant is very poisonous, though the birds eat the seeds without ill effects.

❧ MAHONIA ❧

Mahonia aquifolium, or the Oregon Grape, was first discovered on the Pacific coast of America and introduced to Britain by the Scottish plant hunter David Douglas, after his plant-hunting expedition there in 1825-27. This easy, workaday mahonia will flower almost anywhere, on a sandy bank or in full sun, next to a wall or in deep shade, and is the mahonia most closely associated with cottage gardens.

The vigorous mass of handsome dark, shiny, holly-like leaves takes on a distinct bronzy tint at the onset of winter and on a very poor soil will often turn bright red, almost scarlet, one of the joys of the winter garden. Come the spring, the leaves will return to their bright polished green, and will be topped with bunches of erect golden-yellow flowers which are delicately scented. Later the shrub is loaded with masses of large black berries with a heavy violet bloom which look like miniature grapes, hence the 'Grape' of Oregon Grape. They make an excellent jelly tasting of blackcurrant. There is a superior variety of Dutch origin named 'Apollo' which is well worth growing.

The more elegant *Mahonia japonica* will make a sturdy upright shrub some 2.1m (7ft) in height and as much as 3m (10ft) in width. It has deep green, palmate leaves 45cm (1½ft) long, each composed of up to nineteen sharply-toothed leaflets borne in a whorl like a windmill. They make a perfect backdrop for the long strings of pale yellow, scented flowers like lilies of the valley, which appear in succession throughout the long winter months, filling the garden with a delicious fragrance, particularly during a mild damp spell. Although *Mahonia japonica* is quite hardy and happy in all soils, it is best planted in partial shade as exposure to full sun very often results in discolouration of the leaves.

The upright *Mahonia media* hybrids, with their tier upon tier of magnificent dark green foliage and showier, more erect flowers of a richer yellow, owe their existence to a chance cross between *M. japonica* and the rather tender but delightful *M. lomariifolia*, which was discovered in a batch of *M. lomariifolia* plants sent to a Surrey nursery by the Slieve Donard nursery in Northern Ireland. The first of these hybrids was named 'Charity', followed by 'Faith' and 'Hope', with eleven superb hybrids now available from specialist nurseries including 'Lionel Fortescue', with outstanding foliage and flowers, 'Underway', 'Buckland' and 'Winter Sun'.

 Mahonias do not need regular pruning. However, over the years they do tend to get a bit leggy, showing rather too much bare wood, but can be improved by cutting back quite severely in spring as soon as flowering is finished. New growth will break from the old wood and the mahonia will continue to flower in the next season, almost unaffected by the drastic action taken in the spring.

✿ VIBURNUM TINUS ✿

Once a great favourite, but underrated today when there are so many more glamorous viburnums to give winter fragrance, summer flowers, and autumn colour, *Viburnum tinus,* the Laurestinus is a sympathetic plant in the cottage garden. It has smooth, pointed dark green leaves, reddish stems and heads of tight pink buds which open into umbel-like clusters of tiny white-petalled flowers followed by blue-black fruits. However, its quiet charm is often overlooked in favour of the richly scented, winter-flowering hybrids of *Viburnum fragrans* like V. x *bodnantense* 'Dawn' or 'Deben' or the less well known but equally beautiful 'Charles Lamont'.

One of the best ways of using V. *tinus* is as an informal leafy hedge which will flower generously from autumn to spring. It grows remarkably quickly and will reach 3m (10ft) in 10 years. A number of slightly differing forms exist, like V. *t.* 'Lucidum', which is a larger more open shrub, and 'Gwenllian', with pale pink flowers and smaller leaves. V. *t.* 'Eve Price' is a more compact and free-flowering variety with darker green leaves, a deeper pink in bud, and white flowers. There is also a variegated form, which is slower growing and not quite as hardy. Cuttings should be rooted in the usual way and grown on in a nursery bed for two years before planting out.

JASMINUM ✿ NUDIFLORUM ✿

The winter-flowering jasmine with its five-pointed, yellow star-like flowers was introduced to Britain from China in 1844 by the plant hunter Robert Fortune, who was paid the sum of £100

MORE FRAGRANT WINTER-FLOWERING SHRUBS

Chimonanthus praecox
WINTER SWEET

3x3m (10x10ft). Deciduous. Leaves dark green, oval and scented. Flowers cup-shaped, outer 'petals' yellow, inner ones purple on bare branches. Takes some years to flower. Sunny, sheltered position.

Cornus mas 'Variegata'

3x2.4m (10x8ft). Deciduous tree or shrub. Hardy. Leaves dark green edged with white, oval. Flowers yellow, in clusters on bare twigs. Thin, sharp scent. Red berries. Late winter to early spring. Suited to wild garden.

Hamamelis mollis 'Pallida'

3x2.4m (10x8ft). Deciduous. Hardy. Leaves mid green. Flowers soft yellow, spidery, on bare branches. Prefers acid soil but will grow on any well-drained good humus. Shelter flowers from wind.

Lonicera purpusii

1.5x1.5m (5x5ft). Shrub not climber, though can be grown against a wall. Semi-evergreen, hardy. Leaves oval, dark green. Flowers creamy-white, short, wide-mouthed tubes with yellow anthers unlike familiar honeysuckle. Though small, very fragrant. Ordinary garden soil.

Viburnum farreri (syn. fragrans)

3x1.8m (10x6ft). Deciduous, upright habit. Foliage dark green, bronze when young. Flowers in clusters at end of branches, pink. White form 'Candissimum' has light green leaves. Good moist soil.

for it by the Council of the Horticultural Society of London (now the RHS). The plant quickly established itself as a cottage garden favourite and today there can be few cottage gardens without at least one of these rambling shrubs, covering walls and showering sunshine into the winter gloom.

From early winter until early spring, before its leaves appear, *Jasminum nudiflorum* studs its bright green stems with primrose flowers, and in British gardens shares the honour as a Christmas flowering plant with the Christmas rose. Sprays cut at this time of year and arranged with some evergreen foliage make superb table decorations, whilst a few sprigs placed in a simple dark chocolate-brown vase look particularly attractive and cheerful throughout the dark winter months. Nor is there any need to feel guilty about denuding the shrub, as the more the bare twigs are cut, the better it will flower the next year.

Although not a true climber, the rambling habit of the winter-flowering jasmine makes it suitable for training up walls and over fences or for disguising unsightly out-buildings. It can be trimmed to make a good bush or hedge, and a bare bank can be improved by planting and pegging down the shoots, allowing the jasmine to sprawl down and carpet the slope.

There is a variegated form for connoisseurs, *J. n.* 'Aureum'. The normally bright green summer foliage has a rich yellow variegation which, from a distance, gives the appearance of a flowering plant.

 Given a well-drained soil, the winter jasmine will bloom freely on walls facing any direction. To avoid a tangle of bare lengths of old wood, all shoots that have been flowering through the winter should be sheared back in the spring, thus stimulating the plant into producing a generous new crop of green wands on which to flower in the following season.

■ Few shrubs are easier to propagate, and perhaps one of the reasons for its popularity in cottage gardens is that every strand that strays and happens to touch the ground will root in a few weeks, supplying an abundance of free plantlets for use elsewhere or to be given as a present to visitors.

WINTER-FLOWERING
*B*ULBS AND *P*ERENNIALS

❧ CROCUS ❧
(WINTER-FLOWERING)

Crocuses bring a welcome touch of spring to the winter garden. They are the most colourful of all early-flowering bulbs, with endless varieties and species in bloom at a time when every flower is a bonus.

They do make a bit of a nuisance of themselves in the borders with seedlings coming up everywhere except, of course, where you want them, but who can resist the charm of *Crocus tommasinianus* or old 'Tommy' as it is affectionately referred to by cottage gardeners. Old 'Tommy' is a wilding and is probably happiest when grown in grass or around the base of trees, where the bulbs can be allowed to seed and spread to their hearts'

Crocus tommasinianus *growing through* Lamium galeobdolon

content. The flowers of *C. tommasinianus* seem to come up overnight and, following an hour or so of sunshine, produce a shimmering haze of hundreds of stars, in colours ranging from palest lilac to mauve and deep purples. If the air is warm enough, the bright orange stamens will attract bees in great numbers.

It is a rather curious fact that the sparrows and other birds seem to prefer yellow crocuses and leave the purples, blues and whites, to flower undisturbed. Although it is tempting to purchase the mixed collections of the larger-flowered crocuses often offered very cheaply, it is definitely advisable to pay a little more and buy individual varieties, as the mixture almost invariably has a preponderance of one colour – and that is nearly always yellow.

Crocuses respond well to an open, well-drained soil but not one that dries out during the summer months. Winter-flowering crocuses should be in the ground by the end of the summer or early in the autumn.

■ Crocuses scarcely need any attention, and with a little cunning, it is possible to obtain colour for six weeks and more by planting the larger-flowered varieties at different depths, some at 10cm (4in) and some at 15cm (6in). By this method of planting it is possible to change the flowering periods so that in any one group, the flowers will come out in succession.

○ **C. crysanthus 'Cream Beauty'**
Lovely pale creamy-yellow blooms with a bright orange centre. Very floriferous.

○ **C. c. 'Zwanenburg Bronze'**
Raised at van Tubergen's famous nursery at Zwanenburg in Holland, this hybrid has golden-yellow flowers with the exterior heavily marked dark bronze.

○ **C. c. 'E. A. Bowles'**
One of the largest forms, with rich buttery-yellow globes stained brownish-grey at the base on the exterior.

○ **C. c. 'Blue Pearl'**
A soft, delicate blue. Bronzy base and silvery-blue interior.

○ **C. c. 'White Triumphator'**
Pure white flowers with pale yellow centres. This

comparatively recent introduction is already proving to be very popular.

○ **Crocus tommasinianus 'Albus'**
A robust white form of old 'Tommy'. Easy, and makes masses of offsets. Late-flowering.

○ **Crocus sieberi 'Violet Queen'**
This beautiful form has many rounded violet-blue flowers on short stalks. Very easy and free-flowering.

○ **C. s. 'Bowles White'**
Raised by E. A. Bowles in 1923 and still regarded as one of the best white crocuses, with pure white flowers, a lemony-yellow centre and scarlet stigmas.

❧ ERANTHIS ❧

Eranthis hyemalis, or Winter Aconite, is one of the earliest bulbs to flower in the cottage garden and is perfect for naturalising in grass around the base of deciduous trees or in banks and borders, where the bright lemon-yellow flowers set off by a green collar make a very welcome show in late winter.

Eranthis cilicica, a form of *E. hyemalis* with larger, more butter-coloured flowers over bronze-tinted foliage, prolongs the flowering season, and a cross between *E. cilicica* and *E. hyemalis, Eranthis tubergenii* 'Guinea Gold' which flowers in late winter and early spring, is the finest eranthis, with large golden-yellow flowers on long stems and noticeably bronzed foliage.

The rare miniature white Japanese aconite, *Eranthis pinnatifida,* is less easy to grow than the others, but still far from difficult. It does require protection from slugs and is probably best for a raised peat bed or a pot where one can keep an eye on it. A ruff of thick green leaves sits under a flower of white with purple anthers.

Aconites enjoy a well-drained soil, especially if leaf mould can be worked into the soil and light shade provided. The best effect is obtained by planting fairly thickly in early autumn. Once established the plants should not be disturbed unless required for propagation. The easiest and simplest method of propagation is to divide the tuberous roots during early autumn just as the plants restart into growth. Stock can also be increased by seed, if you have the patience to wait three or four years for flowers.

❧ GALANTHUS ❧

The harbingers of spring, snowdrops are highly prized by cottage gardeners. Although acquaintance with them is all too often limited to the common snowdrop, *Galanthus nivalis*, there are at least ninety varieties available. *Galanthus nivalis* is to be found all over Europe and, whilst the charm of its dainty flowers is undeniable, there are many other species and varieties to recommend to the budding galanthophile.

In the Middle Ages the 'white bulbous violets' (an early name for snowdrops) were also known as St Mary's Tapers and Candlemas bells, flowering first, according to tradition, on Candlemas Day, 2 February, the feast of the Purification of the Blessed Virgin Mary. At the Feast of Candlemas, it was the custom to remove all the Virgin's pictures from the altars of churches and to strew snowdrops in their place.

The common snowdrop is ideal for naturalising in grass or woodland, but to be really effective the bulbs should be planted in fairly extensive drifts, as clusters or small isolated clumps dotted here and there in the grass can look rather silly. In the border among the hellebores and pulmonarias, groups of the double form, *G. n. plenus*, and the named varieties, which in any case require better treatment, make excellent companions for winter aconites, early crocuses and the many different types of *Viola odorata*, as well as the deep blue forms of *Anemone blanda*.

With such a wide choice of varieties and species to choose from, it is comparatively easy to build up a wide collection of snowdrops to extend the flowering season. When one form fades away there will be another to take its place and brighten the winter scene.

Snowdrops flourish in any well-drained soil, but as a general rule most species which have a glaucous leaf prefer a drier situation than those with a shiny green leaf, which are natives of shadier, damper habitats. When planting in grass, the turf need only be lifted to a depth of 5-7.5cm (2-3in) and the bulbs set in position. A top dressing of bonemeal and perhaps a little compost or leaf mould in the autumn is all the attention they require once planted.

▪ Bulbs multiply quite rapidly by means of offsets, and clumps should be divided 'in the green' either whilst still in flower or as soon as possible after flowering. Most nurseries send out orders 'in the green' and dried bulbs are best avoided as they take such a long time to establish.

○ *Galanthus byzantinus*
One of the earliest snowdrops to flower, this is one of the more instantly recognisable species with large white flowers about 3cm (1¼in) long, with the inner segments heavily marked with green at the tip and the base. The flowers are held on long stems and the edges of the leaves are turned back. It flowers best in a sunny position.
○ **G. 'S. Arnott' (also known as 'Sam Arnott' or 'Arnott's Seedling')**
This well-known snowdrop is named after a nineteenth-century galanthophile who was Provost of Dumfries. It was considered by E. A. Bowles to be one of the best and boldest of snowdrops. The large, rounded flowers, the outer segments pure white and

Galanthus lutescens, *a rare snowdrop with yellow markings*

the inner ones margined with green, are strongly scented and carried on tall sturdy stalks.

○ **G. 'Lady Elphinstone'**
The fabulous double yellow snowdrop in which all the normally green markings on the flowers are yellow, including those of the inner double frill. Occasionally, when the plant is disturbed or transplanted, these markings may revert to green, however, once settled down again, 'Lady Elphinstone' will revert back to her yellow markings. This snowdrop was found growing at Heawood Hall in Cheshire by Sir Graeme Elphinstone when he moved there in 1890 and was subsequently passed on to Samuel Arnott.

○ **G. elwesii**
A late-flowering species introduced in 1874 by H. J. Elwes of Colesborne from the mountains around Smyrna in Turkey, this species has large almond-scented white flowers and green markings on the inner segments at the tip and the centre, similar to G. byzantinus. The erect, broad, hooded leaves are bright green.

○ **G. 'Straffan'**
A magnificent late-flowering snowdrop with glaucous foliage and pristine white flowers with an inverted green horseshoe on the inner segments. It often produces a second, later flower, which considerably extends the flowering period. This snowdrop originated at Straffan, County Kildare, Ireland in 1858 amongst a batch of G. caucasicus collected by Lord Clarina in the Crimea two years previously.

❧ HELLEBORUS ❧

Helleborus niger gets its name from its black root, and was used by the Greeks as a cure for insanity. The Romans introduced this species to Britain and in medieval times it was planted near the door of the house as a safeguard against witches and evil spirits. It is better known as the *Christmas Rose* and is an indispensable plant in the winter cottage garden. Large, snowy-white, single flowers are produced in profusion on established plants, and the challenge for the British gardener is to get them flowering on Christmas Day and pick a few for the table. To make them last more than a few hours, immerse the stems to the neck in water overnight before arranging them.

Christmas roses vary enormously in size, whiteness, or lateness in flowering, with good forms much in demand. Two named varieties, particularly sought after but well worth the hunt, are *Helleborus niger* 'Potters Wheel', the Christmas Rose with the largest blooms, and *H. n.* 'St Brigid', a very rare old hybrid with twin-borne flowers of the purest white held above a brighter green foliage than other forms.

Helleborus foetidus, a British native, owes its name to the very unpleasant odour released on squeezing unripe seed heads, and not to the scent of the flowers or the leaves. A shrubby evergreen plant, *H. foetidus* is particularly valued for its attractive, finely-divided dark foliage and the small cup-shaped blooms of pale green which develop a maroon edging after they have been out a little while. Although short-lived, *H. foetidus* seeds prolifically, and can be a nuisance in smaller gardens. However, the plant is quite at home in a wild corner of a garden or planted in a shrubbery, where its rather lax form of growth can be supported. There is an Italian form, simply called 'Italian Form', which is more upright in growth, and a named form, *H. f.* 'Westerflisk' which has glaucous foliage and very attractive red stems.

H. orientalis, or the Lenten rose, seems to have been introduced from Asia Minor towards the middle of the nineteenth century. Today, thanks to hybridisation, there is a vast number of varieties of these free-flowering perennials to choose from, in colours ranging from pure white through various shades of red, pink, mauve, green, spotted, deep chocolate and black. With their dark evergreen leaves they are a perfect foil for snowdrops, primroses, aconites and violets. Crossing and careful selection have produced clearer and more distinct colours, more upright flowers and a rounded petal shape, with named clones appearing regularly at the Royal Horticultural Society Spring Show.

Of the older named varieties, *H. o.* 'Black Knight' and 'Apple Blossom' are still obtainable, although you usually have to go to an enthusiast to find them, but a superb selection of modern named varieties are available from specialist nurseries, including 'Rubens' with large deep-red flowers, 'Helen Ballard' with vivid green outward-looking flowers, 'Ingot' which has the deepest yellow yet, and 'Philip Wilson' with clear pink spotted flowers. Double and semi-double forms are grown but are rare, and a recently discovered variegated form in Ireland with speckled foliage has been named *H. o.* 'Graigueconna'. A rare beauty to look out for in the future.

 Perhaps the greatest secret of success with hellebores is to leave them well alone. They prefer a shady, cool position and humus and moisture in hot weather, but greatly resent disturbance. Light, dry soils should be improved with well-rotted manure.

■ Division, usually carried out in the spring, must be undertaken with great care to avoid injuring the roots more than is absolutely necessary. Clumps must not be split up into too small sec-

A speckled, deep rose-coloured Oriental hellebore

tions and some years will elapse before the new plants settle down to proper flowering. Seeds sown in a cold frame as soon as they are ripe will take a year or more to germinate but offer the chance of some exceptional seedlings. Do not spray the pots against mosses and liverworts or the seedlings will die. Named varieties must always be propagated by division.

❧ IRIS RETICULATA ☙

Flowering bravely when the rest of the garden is sparkling with frost, the dainty, smaller bulbous irises of the *reticulata* group are undaunted by bad weather and make excellent companions for the other harbingers of spring, the crocuses and the snowdrops. They are sometimes known as the netted iris because of the net-like markings on the bulb. *Iris reticulata*, one of the earliest bulbs to flower, with its different colour forms ranging from pale blue through red-purple to deep violet-blue, is a little treasure. It is, however, frequently difficult to establish in gardens, providing a dazzling display one year and disappearing the next.

Bulbs of the *reticulata* group, including various named forms are easily obtainable, and frequently sold in supermarkets as well as nurseries. A few bulbs potted up in early autumn and brought indoors six to eight weeks later to flower, make excellent winter-flowering pot plants. Their rich dark purple flowers emit a strong violet perfume quite capable of scenting a large room.

Iris histrioides major which flowers earlier than *I. reticulata* has deep gentian-blue flowers with bold markings, bursting open 2.5cm (1in) or so clear of the ground before the leaves appear. Excellent for a sunny rockery where the bulbs can remain undisturbed for years and where the flowers can receive some protection from the cold buffeting winds, *I. h. major* will increase quite rapidly to create a brilliant display in the winter sunshine.

I. danfordiae, another gem of the *reticulata* group is named after its discoverer, Mrs Danford, an intrepid Victorian traveller and plant collector. Reaching 7.5cm (3in) high, the rich golden-yellow flowers speckled with brown appear at the same time as the strong, sturdy, 30cm (12in) long leaves. Another iris for the sunny rock garden or front of the border, *I. danfordiae* is best treated as an annual and new bulbs planted every year as, after flowering, the bulbs disintegrate into tiny bulbils the size of 'hundreds and thousands', which take several seasons to reach flowering size again.

 All members of this group enjoy a good summer baking in a well-drained, limey soil and are well suited to growing in a raised bed or sink in a sunny sheltered position, where they seem to thrive and increase far better than in the open garden, and where the lovely flowers and scent can be enjoyed at waist level. The 45cm (18in) high leaves which follow the flowers should be encouraged to grow and die back naturally.

■ All irises of the *reticulata* group are early-flowering and quite hardy, even flowering in the snow. They should be planted deeply in clumps in a sunny, well-drained, well-limed soil with plenty of peat and leaf mould. Most grow to about 15cm (6in) and are quite charming in the rock garden or in pots. Carefully collected, well-ripened seed, sown at once, will produce strong flowering bulbs in about three years.

○ **Iris reticulata 'Cantab'**
Raised in 1914 by E. A. Bowles, 'Cantab' has Cambridge-blue flowers crested in orange. A neat plant, smaller than *I. reticulata*, it is ideal for the rock garden or a raised bed.
○ **I. r. 'Harmony'**
Bred by C. J. Hoog from a cross of *I. reticulata* with *histrioides major*. Short, tiny leaves and sky-blue flowers crested with yellow on the falls.
○ **I. r. 'J. S. Dijt'**
Raised by the Dutch grower of the same name on the island of Texel, this clone has deep purple standards with reddish-purple falls crested in vivid orange, and with a sweet scent. Not as fussy about soil as the others, and a favourite of the honey bee on a mild sunny day.

❧ IRIS UNGUICULARIS ☙
(SYN. STYLOSA)

One of the most exciting of all the irises is the species now known as *Iris unguicularis*, although more often than not still referred to by its old name of *I. stylosa,* the winter-flowering iris. It is also called the Algerian Iris.

Iris unguicularis will flower best after a summer baking in a poor soil, the poorer the better, and sheltered from cold, frosty winds at the foot of a sunny wall, it will reward the cottage gardener with an early display of mauve-blue flowers in profusion throughout the bleakest of winters. A common complaint, frequently heard, is that this iris is difficult and shy to flower. Certainly patience is required as a newly planted iris will take a long time to establish, and it may be several years before it can be said to be blooming freely. However, by starving the plant and avoiding the temptation of providing it with rich moist soil, which will only serve to produce an abundance of dark green leaves but precious few blooms, the patient gardener will be rewarded by a bumper crop of beautiful scented flowers. E. A. Bowles once wrote that any garden large enough to grow two plants should be devoted to the culture of *Iris stylosa* and *Chimonanthus praecox,* and to *Iris stylosa* he accorded first place.

There are several forms and varieties available including an albino form, *I. u.* 'Alba', which can be variable, with the white not always a good white and the yellow crest on the falls decidedly dingy, but there are good forms to be found and the search, after all, is part of the fun.

In addition to a poor soil, a restricted depth will help to reduce leaf growth and produce flowers instead. Cutting back dead and unsightly foliage in early summer will not only assist the sun to ripen the rhizomes but also make the plant a less desirable habitat for snails and slugs, which eat the flower buds in winter. Rhizomes can be increased by careful division, preferably as soon as the flowers begin to fade. However, it should be stressed that it is not advisable to split up the clumps into very small pieces, as they are less likely to survive and will certainly take much longer to establish.

○ *I. unguicularis* 'Mary Barnard'
An excellent and vigorous free-flowering variety with

an unequalled, rich violet-blue colour. The late Mary Barnard of Honiton collected it in Algeria and the discriminating plantsman E. B. Anderson, who throughout his long life (1886-1971) introduced many choice plants to general cultivation, was largely responsible for its distribution. It comes fairly true from seed.

○ *I. u.* 'Walter Butt'
Another plant collected in Algeria this time by a friend of Walter Butt, the previous owner of E. B. Anderson's garden at Porlock. This variety has large, very pale lavender flowers which look almost white in the sun, and a strong fragrance.

○ *I. u.* 'Cretensis'
G. P. Baker, who collected the plant in Crete, told the story of how he looked everywhere for this iris and could not locate it till he sat down to lunch and found he was sitting on it. Good violet falls with a large central white patch, crested yellow and with a few violet lines. Tough, short, wiry grey-green leaves. Can be difficult.

❧ PULMONARIA ❧

Although strictly speaking early spring-flowering plants, pulmonarias, or Lungwort, sheltered and protected as they often are in the cottage garden by other closely planted companions, rarely wait till spring before flowering, and the little pink and blue flowers in tight bunches held high above the spotted leaves can usually be relied upon to bring a touch of early colour to the mid-winter garden.

Pulmonaria rubra, the distinctive red pulmonaria with unspotted, soft green foliage and lovely bright coral-pink flowers, will have been flowering on and off since midwinter, which would no doubt account for its British country name of the Christmas Cowslip, while the form known as 'Mr Bowles' Red' with bigger and much brighter flowers and spotted instead of all-green leaves, puts in a slightly later appearance.

The common *Pulmonaria officinalis* and its various forms are next to flower. These tough cottage garden favourites, often seen in old gardens, will not be deterred by bad weather and the jaunty little blue and pink flowers flutter bravely above heart-shaped, spotted leaves during the worst of winter's storms. The leaves are bristly and rasping to the touch.

Pulmonarias have been graced with many names over the years, with interesting regional differences. Amongst them are Joseph's Coat, William and Mary, Joseph and Mary, Soldiers and Sailors, Hundreds and Thousands, Jerusalem Cowslip, Adam and Eve, and so on. Most, but not all, allude to the flowers which are pink at first, changing through mauve to blue when fully mature, a characteristic trait of many members of the borage family.

The current vogue for handsome foliage and good ground cover has created a demand for unusual forms with attractive leaves, and *P. saccharata* varieties with silvered and heavily spotted or blue-grey leaves are much sought after by the plant collector.

Pulmonarias and hellebores bridge the gap between winter and spring at the Old Rectory, Burford

 Pulmonarias will thrive in any ordinary garden soil. They prefer a position in

partial or full shade and grow approximately 30cm (1ft) high and 60cm (2ft) wide. Since the leaves of the pulmonarias get bigger and coarser as the season progresses, these are not plants for the front of the border and it is better to grow them farther back where other perennials will mask them later. They are, of course, perfect for a wild or woodland garden.

They can be propagated, preferably in damp weather, by division of rootstock after flowering, or in the autumn.

○ *Pulmonaria vallarsae* **'Margery Fish'**
Mottled silver and green foliage with pink and blue flowers. Ideal for a dry shady position and with shrubs.

○ *P. officinalis.* **'Sissinghurst White'**
Fresh green palely spotted leaves and an excellent show of white flowers, which contrast beautifully with the blues and reds.

○ *P. rubra* **'Redstart'**
A splendid variety with long, soft green leaves all year round and rosy-red flowers over a long period.

○ *P. angustifolia* **'Mawson's Variety'**
A beautiful variety with dark purple-blue flowers and green leaves. Taller than the popular form, *P. a.* 'Azurea'. The pink-flowered winter heathers make excellent companions for the *angustifolias*.

❧ VIOLA ODORATA ❧

Viola odorata, the ever popular sweet violet, is one of the oldest of garden plants. The ancient Greeks cultivated it with enthusiasm, while in France violets are still grown in vast quantities, as they have been for centuries, not only for the flower markets but also for the valuable perfume industry. Napoleon always gave a bunch of violets to Josephine on their wedding anniversary, and after he died a few dried violet flowers were found in his locket along with a lock of her hair. In folklore the violet is the symbol of fidelity.

In flower from early winter till almost midsummer, these exquisitely scented flowers make a welcome contribution to the winter scene, and a

Sweet violets will spread happily under hedges and amongst shrubs

posy of violets picked in the depths of winter will scent the largest of rooms with a delicious breath of spring.

Scented, single, semi-double and fully double-flowered forms in purples and whites, blues and reds, have gradually evolved from a small wild species botanically known as *Viola odorata* and violet hybridisers have raised numerous choice cultivars.

Deciding which of the many lovely violets to choose for the garden is difficult. However, a collection of the single-flowered cultivars of *Viola odorata* would be incomplete without 'Coeur d'Alsace' an early-flowering French cultivar of great charm with sweetly scented rosy-pink blooms on long stems, or 'California' the largest-flowered sweet violet with giant dark blue flowers and a rich perfume, introduced from the United States at the end of the nineteenth century. 'Alassio', also known as 'Mrs R Barton', a firm favourite during the 1920s and '30s, has very large white flowers. 'John Raddenbury', a nineteenth century Australian introduction, has bright china-blue flowers and a strong scent. The same, unfortunately, cannot be said of the so-called yellow sweet violet, 'Sulphurea', which is neither scented nor yellow, but a soft cream colour with an apricot centre. The blooms of the form called 'Irish Elegance' are of a slightly deeper shade of cream-buff and do carry a faint fragrance.

Of the double-flowered, scented hardy sweet violet, only three out of the thirty or so originally listed are available today and these are only available from specialist nurseries. They are 'Double Rose', with lavender-rose buds and flowers on long stems, 'Comte de Chambord', an old Victorian double with large off-white flowers, and 'Double Russian', with deep purple flowers. Sadly, only one semi-double is still offered for sale in Britain. It is called 'Mrs David Lloyd George'.

Today the old double violets are much more likely to be found in the US and Australia, where they were taken by immigrants as a memory of home and looked after lovingly, whereas in Britain they went out of fashion and were neglected.

Violets enjoy a situation shaded from the summer sun, where protection is given from winter and spring winds. Soil improved with humus and farmyard manure, so that it remains reasonably moist in summer, will pay dividends in healthier plants with an abundance of free-flowering blooms. Stock can be increased by runners taken during late spring, preferably during a showery period of weather, and planted 30cm (1ft) apart, or by division, although it should be pointed out that it is useless to keep old plants or old portions of a plant.

SELECTED READING LIST

BROWNLOW, MARGARET. *Herbs and the Fragrant Garden* (Darton, Longman & Todd, 1963)

CLAPHAM, A.R., TUTIN, T.G. & WARBURG, E.F. *Excursion Flora of the British Isles* (Cambridge University Press, 1959)

COATS, ALICE M. *Flowers and their Histories* (Hulton Press, 1956)

○ *Garden Shrubs and their Histories* (Vista Books, 1963)

COOMBS ROY, E. *Violets* (Croom Helm, 1981)

FISH, MARGERY. *Cottage Garden Flowers* (Faber, 1980)

FLETCHER, H.L.V. *The Fragrant Garden* (Newnes, 1965)

GENDERS, ROY. *Scented Flora of the World* (Granada Publishing, 1978)

HADFIELD, MILES. *One Man's Garden* (Dent & Sons, 1966)

JOHNSON, A.T. *The Garden Today* and *My Garden* (1938)

LLOYD, CHRISTOPHER. *The Well-Tempered Garden* (Collins, 1970)

MACSELF, A.J. *The Gardener's Treasury of Popular Plants and their Cultivation* (Amateur Gardening, 1934)

PANKHURST, ALEX. *Who Does Your Garden Grow* (Earl's Eye Publishing, 1992)

POWELL, CLAIRE. *The Meaning of Flowers* (Jupiter Books, 1977)

PROCKTOR, NOEL J. *Climbing and Screening Plants* (Collinridge, 1983)

PROCTOR, ROB. *Antique Flowers: Perennials* (Harper and Row, 1990)

○ *Antique Flowers: Annuals* (Harper Collins, 1991)

READER'S DIGEST *Encyclopaedia of Plants and Flowers* (Reader's Digest, 1978)

STREET, JOHN. *Plants for Performance* (David & Charles, 1974)

STUART, D. and SUTHERLAND, J. *Plants from the Past* (Penguin, 1989)

WOODWARD, MARCUS. *How to Enjoy Garden Flowers* (Hodder & Stoughton, 1928)

SOURCES OF PLANTS

UK
SEEDS

○ Chiltern Seeds, Bortree Stile, Ulverton, Cumbria LA12 7PB

○ Suffolk Herbs, Monks Farm, Pantlings Lane, Kelvedon, Essex CO5 9PG

BULBS

○ Paul Christian, Rare Plants, PO Box 468, Wrexham, Clwyd LL13 9XR

○ P de Jager and Sons Ltd, The Nurseries, Marden, Kent TN12 9BF

○ Van Tubergen UK Ltd, Bressingham, Diss, Norfolk IP22 2AB

○ Avon Bulbs, Burnt House Farm, Mid Lambrook, South Petherton, Somerset TA13 5HE

○ For bulbs in larger quantities at wholesale prices: Peter Nyssen Ltd, Railway Road, Urmston, Manchester M31 1XW

TREES, SHRUBS AND PERENNIALS: GENERAL

○ The Beth Chatto Gardens, Elmstead Market, Colchester, Essex CO7 7DB

○ Blooms of Bressingham, Diss, Norfolk IP22 2AB

○ Bridgemere Nurseries, Near Nantwich, Cheshire CW5 7QB

○ Cally Gardens, Gatehouse of Fleet, Castle Douglas, Scotland DG7 2DJ

○ Plants From The Past, The Old House, Bellhaven, Dunbar EH42 1NU, Scotland

TREES, SHRUBS AND PERENNIALS: SPECIALIST

○ **Aquilegia:** John Drake, Hardwicke House, Fen Ditton, Cambridge CB5 8TF

○ **Asters:** Misses I Allen & J Huish, Quarry Farm, Wraxall, Bristol, Avon BS19 1LE

○ **Bellis:** Shrewley Gardens, Crossways, Shrewley, Nr Warwick, Warwickshire CV35 7AU

○ **Campanula:** Padlock Croft, 19 Padlock Road,

West Wratting, Cambridge CB1 5LS
○ **Clematis:** Treasures of Tenbury Ltd, Burford House, Tenbury Wells, Worcestershire WR15 8HQ
○ **Fruit Trees:** Scott's Nurseries, (Merriott) Ltd, Merriott, Somerset TA16 5PL
○ **Hardy Geraniums:** Coombland Gardens, Coneyhurst, Billingshurst, West Sussex RH14 9DG
The Margery Fish Plant Nursery, East Lambrook Manor, South Petherton, Somerset TA13 5HL
○ **Hellebores:** Helen Ballard, Old Country, Mathon, Malvern, Worcestershire WR13 5PS
Phedar Nursery, Bunkers Hill, Romily, Stockport, Cheshire SK6 3DS
○ **Herbs:** Iden Croft Herbs, Frittenden Road, Staplehurst, Kent TN12 0DH
Cheshire Herbs, Fourfields, Forest Road, Nr Tarporley, Cheshire CW6 9ES
○ **Lavender:** Norfolk Lavender Ltd, Caley Hill, Heacham, Kings Lynn, Norfolk PE31 7JE
○ **Pulmonarias:** Stillingfleet Lodge Nursery, Stillingfleet, Yorkshire YO4 6HW
○ **Pinks:** Kingstone Cottage Plants, Weston-under-Penyard, Ross-on-Wye, Herefordshire HR9 7NXL
○ **Roses:** Acton Beauchamp Roses, Acton Beauchamp, Worcester, Hereford and Worcester WR6 5AE
David Austin Roses, Bowling Green Lane, Albrighton, Wolverhampton, West Midlands WV7 3HB
Peter Beale's Roses, London Road, Attleborough, Norfolk NR17 1AY
○ **Snowdrops:** John Morley, North Green Only, Stoven, Beccles, Suffolk NR34 8DG
Foxgrove Plants, Foxgrove, Enborne, Near Newbury, Berkshire RG14 6RE
○ **Violas:** C.W. Groves & Son, West Bay Road, Bridport, Dorset DT6 4BA
Elizabeth MacGregor, Ellenbank, Tongland Road, Kirkcudbright, Dumfries and Galloway DG6 4UU
○ **Wild Flowers:** John Chambers' Wild Flower Seeds, 15 Westleigh Road, Barton, Seagrave, Kettering, Northants NN15 5AJ

AUSTRALIA
○ Norgates' Plant Farm, Trentham, Victoria 3458
○ Mount View Nursery, Summertown, South Australia 5141

CANADA
○ Alpenflora Gardens, 17985 40th Avenue, Surrey, BC V3S 4
○ Hortico, Inc, Robson Road, RR 1, Waterdown, ON LOR 2

NEW ZEALAND
○ Peter B. Dow and Co, South Pacific Seeds, Gisborne
○ Duncan and Davies, Christchurch
○ Harrison and Co Ltd, PO Box 1, Palmerston North
○ D. J. Liddle Ltd, Ngarara Road, Waikanae
○ F. M. Winstone Ltd, Remuera 5, Auckland

UNITED STATES
○ Andre Viette Farm and Nursery, Route 1 Box 16, Fisherville, VA 22939
○ Bluestone Perennials, 7211 Middle Ridge Road, Madison, OH 44057
○ Burpee Ornamental Gardens 300 Park Avenue, Warminster, PA 18991
○ Busse Gardens, Route 2, Box 238, Cokato, MN 55321
○ Caprilands Herb Farm, 534 Silver Street, Coventry, CN 06238
○ Canyon Creek Nursery, 3527 Dry Creek Road, Oroville, CA 95965
○ Carroll Gardens, PO Box 310, Westminster, MD 21157
○ Clifford's Perennial and Vine, Route 2, Box 320, East Roy, WI 53120
○ Donorama's Nursery, Upper Main Street, Box 2189, Edgartown, MA 02539
○ Lamb Nurseries, E. 101 Sharp Avenue, Spokane, WA 99202
○ Montrose Nursery, PO Box 957, Hillsborough, NC 27278
○ Siskiyuo Rare Plant Nursery, 2825 Cummings Road, Medford, OR 97501
○ Wayside Gardens, Garden Lane, Hodges, SC 29653
○ Whayes End Nursery, PO Box 310, Burgess, VA 22432
○ White Flower Farm, Route 63, Litchfield, CT 06759
○ Wrenwood of Berkeley Springs, PO Box 361, Berkeley Springs, WV 25411

SOCIETIES

THE COTTAGE GARDEN SOCIETY
The Cottage Garden Society, founded in 1982, is an informal and friendly society which welcomes British and overseas members. Its aims are to keep alive an interest in worthwhile old-fashioned flowers and their cultivars, and to encourage the plant-centred style of gardening which is at the heart of the cottage garden. It offers its members a quarterly newsletter, a seed exchange, a list of cottage gardens to visit, local groups in many areas of the UK, plant sales, a plant bank of rarer plants, and a summer programme of national visits.
○ *Membership Secretary*: Mrs C Tordoff, 5 Nixon Close, Thornhill, Dewsbury, West Yorks. WF12 0JA

NATIONAL COUNCIL FOR THE PRESERVATION OF PLANTS AND GARDENS
The Pines, c/o Wisley Garden, Woking, Surrey GU23 6QB

THE HARDY PLANT SOCIETY
Administrator, Mrs Pam Adams, Little Orchard, Great Comberton, Nr Pershore, Worcs WR10 3DP

THE WAKEFIELD AND NORTH OF ENGLAND TULIP SOCIETY
Secretary: Wendy Akers, 70 Renthorpe Lane, Renthorpe, Wakefield WE2 0PT

ACKNOWLEDGEMENTS

The editor is grateful to the University of Liverpool Botanic Gardens, Ness, for permission to copy the black and white drawings by Edward Hulme, and to the director and staff for allowing her to use their library facilities.

She would also like to thank the librarians of the Royal Horticultural Society, the Cheshire Library Services – in particular, Pat Underwood – and also Elizabeth L. Pettitt, the Assistant Archivist of Clwyd, for their help.

Thanks are also due to Anne Hamblin and the other members of the Cottage Garden Society, who have given their help and encouragement. Also to Nada Jennett, Alex Pankhurst, Jacquie Moon and Elisabeth Frood.

The following people supplied photographs for the book: Trevor Bath: p152; Marilyn Buekett: p92; Pat Collison; pp 4, 8, 32, 37, 40, 44, 45, 100, 108, 116, 121, 141, 145; Tom Deanes: 157; Elisabeth Frood: pp 64, 85, 149; Dave Hampton: pp 41, 120, 124; Ron and Lyn Hill: pp 24, 52, 57, 61, 69, 73, 76, 132; National Federation of Women's Institutes: p65; Sarah Orr: p97; Alex Pankhurst: pp 5, 13, 17, 20, 25, 29, 36, 44, 49, 68, 81, 92, 105, 113, 117, 125, 128, 129, 137, 140, 153; Sally Pasmore: pp 1, 60; Pat Taylor: pp 72, 77, 88, 140, 148

The sweetly-scented **Iris unguicularis**, *one of the joys of the winter garden*

NDEX

Illustrations are shown in **bold** type